A SMILE IN THE MIND

A SMILE IN THE MIND

Witty thinking in graphic design

Beryl McAlhone & David Stuart

Greg Quinton & Nick Asbury

PREFACE

Greg Quinton & Nick Asbury

When the first edition of this book was published in 1996, it had the feeling of a generational event.

In a time before blogs, social media and a proliferation of design publishing, it represented a treasure trove of work gathered from previous decades – essential reading for a generation of design students, and a fixture on every agency shelf.

This revised and updated edition – the first in twenty years – enters a different world, in which creative projects can be shared more readily than ever before. Yet there is still something special about a physical book, with its ability to concentrate a considered selection of work between two covers, revealing new discoveries and connections every time you flick through the pages.

Such was the influence of the original book that it has achieved totemic status, standing for a certain way of thinking about design – ideas-led, problem-solving, penny-dropping, smile-raising. However, as the work it featured recedes in time, there is a risk that the perception of wit recedes with it, so that it becomes associated with a single era and the forms of media that prevailed.

The purpose of this new edition is to show that the opposite is the case. The story of wit in the last twenty years is in fact one of scaling up. As designers have enjoyed access to new technologies and greater freedom to move across disciplinary boundaries, so the realm of wit has become larger, not smaller.

Wit is big business, integral to the success of giants such as Google, Apple and Coca-Cola. Yet it is also more democratic than ever – as is evident in the wave of sophisticated homage and pastiche that greets every brand identity launch. Wit makes memes – the currency of the sharing age.

Still central to branding and marketing, wit is equally formative in the products being marketed and the environments in which we encounter them. Wit is the alchemy that turns suitcases into adventure vehicles, vacuum cleaners into household friends. Wit is light bulbs, clocks, cars, apps, gadgets, bridges and gravestones.

At its best, wit is a force for good, transforming literacy centres into fantastical worlds (see p.91), intravenous drips into superpower supplies for children (see p.190) and park benches into celebrations of life (see p.196).

In updating the book for a new generation, we have kept three aims in mind.

Firstly, to honour the spirit and structure of the original, which was not only a diverse compendium of work but also an entertaining and enlightening analysis of what makes wit effective.

Secondly, to let the work tell the story. Every design and editorial decision has been taken with a view to creating maximum space for new work and mixing it with the most enduring of the old.

Thirdly, to celebrate the diversity of wit at work today – not only in the classic graphic applications, but also in areas such as digital, writing, politics and environmental. This diversity is further reflected in the cast of contributors to the final section of interviews, where an international and interdisciplinary mix of voices sets current practitioners alongside past masters.

In selecting new work, we have sifted through an overwhelming range of contenders, added to daily by the accumulation of projects on blogs and feeds around the world. The sheer scope presented an editorial challenge, but also a continual reassurance that wit is alive and well.

The work is its own best argument. Here you will find a joyful mix of ideas bouncing across disciplines and decades, working wonders for their clients and creators, and offering a new reason to smile with each turn of the page.

We thank the original authors of this book and hope this update pays their inspiration forward.

A big brand with a little
secret. Between the E
and the X lies the most
famous negative space
in logo design. Landor
Associates, USA, 1994.

INTRODUCTION

Beryl McAlhone & David Stuart

Alan Fletcher once said that the reason he wrote his own book on graphic design was that, when he read other people's, he often couldn't recognize the business he was in or what he did. He was probably not alone in thinking that 'the graphics of the critics' is not quite graphics as designers know it.

In this dichotomy, we are for graphics as designers know it. This is no scholarly, theory-driven, academic book on wit. Humour is notoriously difficult to analyse. When pundits try to discuss humour, the smiles tend to disappear. Here analysis is implicit not explicit, expressed in clarity of structure not weightiness of text.

For wit is not a subject to be treated with a heavy hand. When we wrote the book we had in mind Benjamin Britten's comment on a special quarterly devoted to the analysis of his music in 1952. As reported by Imogen Holst: 'He said it made him feel like a small and harmless rabbit being cut up by a lot of grubby schoolboys, when he'd much rather be frisking about in the fields.'

Wit is also of the frisky tendency, in that it makes its impact through sudden jumps, skips, somersaults and reversals in the mind. We are fans of wit, and this is a book of practical advocacy. We have set out to say what wit is and does, and to make the case for humour in graphic design. In these pages you will find material from many sectors and parts of the world to demonstrate the witty routes designers take, and to illustrate how and where wit can aid communication.

The book can be used for work or play: the content is entertaining, but the structure is educational. In the section on 'Types of wit' we group examples to clarify the options designers have in using wit. All rely on the collision of two ideas – what Arthur Koestler, in his influential book *The Act of Creation*, called 'bisociation'. Designers can create that collision in different ways – using juxtaposition, conjunction, incongruity, interpolation, discontinuity, distortion, substitution and all kinds of manipulation. By grouping examples, we show the simple techniques behind those abstract words, and identify twenty-one ways of triggering the humour mechanism in the brain.

We have also organized the book by design application and sector. The section on 'Wit in practice' runs through the main categories of item that designers design, from posters and packaging to annual reports and environmental graphics, recording examples of the use of wit. The section on 'Wit in the world' shows how organizations in areas from health to travel, retail to politics, have used the higher gear of wit to speed their messages.

We conclude with witty people – designers from all over the world talking about how and why they do what they do. We have written this book in the hope that soon there will be more of them.

Michelin man in the early years. Monsieur Bib still has the same bounce today, showing the power of graphic wit to last a hundred years. O'Galop, France, 1898.

THE CASE FOR WIT

TYPES OF WIT

WIT IN PRACTICE

WIT IN THE WORLD

HOW I GOT THE IDEA

INDEX & CREDITS

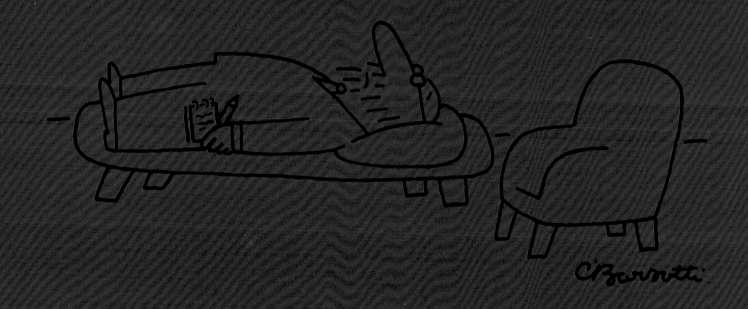

A therapist lies on
his own couch –
cartoon from *The
New Yorker*. Charles
Barsotti, USA, 2003.

THE CASE FOR WIT

WHAT WIT IS

Graphic wit is not really very different from verbal wit. The medium changes, but the underlying technique is the same.

Anyone familiar with quotes from the American critic and humorist Dorothy Parker can spot the parallels between her sallies and witty graphics:

Brevity is the soul of lingerie.

One more drink and I'd have been under the host.

If all the girls attending [the Yale Prom] were laid end to end, I wouldn't be surprised.

What Parker is doing is purloining an existing phrase to say what she wants to say. Her message resides in the unexpected twist. This book is about the Dorothy Parkers of the visual world. What she does with words, they do with images. They take something familiar, and play off it.

Witty thinking is always structural. It is not witty for a designer to decide to use Garamond as the typeface for a particular job – unless he or she uses Garamond to set the word 'Helvetica' on a

T-shirt (as Jack Summerford did for Southwestern Typographics). Here the familiar idea is that, in terms of typefaces, Helvetica is (or was) the holy of holies for designers. The play is to portray the standard-bearer of Modernism using good old-fashioned Garamond. If you want to recognize wit in graphics, look for 'the familiar' and 'the play'.

'The familiar' may be a standard visual cliché, a graphic icon, a genre, a well-known phrase or a proverb. Surprisingly, designers play off verbal concepts almost as often as they play off visual ones. 'The play' involves an agile or acrobatic type of thinking – a leap, a somersault, a reversal, a sideways jump – where the outcome is unexpected. The result is not arrived at through logic, but reaches an undeniable truth.

We talk about 'witty thinking' because wit is both conceived and recognized within the mind. The raw materials are ideas and concepts, and devising a witty solution, or cracking it, means holding more than one concept in the mind at once. This is good exercise for the mental faculties as ideas are juggled.

Once again, there is a parallel within language. The influential educational theorist Basil Bernstein, who studied the language experiences of children, used simple examples to show how parents influence mental development. When they use the word 'whereas' in a sentence, they require children to hold two ideas in the mind at once, and this exercises a child's conceptual muscles. In the same way, witty thinking can be like a workout for the intelligence.

The view we take of wit goes right back to the original sense of the word, which is 'intelligence' and 'understanding'. This meaning survives in the plural form 'wits', as in 'keep your wits about you', 'out of your wits', 'live by your wits' and 'at your wits' end'. The wittiest work is that which contributes the highest insight, and any really witty work manipulates ideas in a way that redefines what is apt.

The two elements – 'the familiar' and 'the play' – are responsible for the two main emotions experienced by someone 'getting' a witty idea: recognition and surprise. These two characteristics of wit provide a kind of matrix of success. If a witty solution involves

a great deal of recognition but little surprise, the solution will be obvious and weak. If, on the other hand, the solution involves a great deal of surprise but little recognition, it will be baffling, enigmatic and impenetrable to most people, prompting anxiety and a feeling of failure. If the solution is low on both recognition and surprise – total failure. If it is high on both – if it combines great familiarity with a big surprise – the solution will be a success, a hit.

As we talked to designers while working on this book, people constantly asked us about two aspects of defining wit: Is witty graphics the same as 'ideas' graphics? And is wit synonymous with humour? The first question has a few terminological traps. People use the word 'idea' in so many different ways. 'My idea is to make it a square brochure.' That isn't a witty idea, unless the brochure is, say, a foot square and deals with how companies can maximize their land assets or use of space.

Overall we have made a distinction between 'controlling ideas' and 'witty ideas'. Controlling ideas are judgements that influence the whole range of decisions taken on a piece of graphics. For example, the controlling idea behind a university prospectus might be to focus on what students want to know, not on what the university wants to tell them, and this judgement would influence the structuring of the prospectus, the content, the style of language, everything.

A 'controlling idea' is straightforwardly thoughtful. A witty idea is more playful, more explicitly clever – like a selling brochure for a hundred-acre development that draws attention to the unusual size of the site by putting forward one hundred reasons for considering it. Instead of being a twelve-page A4 brochure, it is a fat paperback. When people talk about 'ideas graphics' they usually mean this kind of witty idea, which is more than just intelligent – it adds frisson.

What about the relationship between 'wit' and 'humour'? We see wit as a subdivision of humour (humour is the folder and wit is the file). Other subdivisions might be farce or slapstick. But although wit is often humorous, it is not invariably so. Some witty ideas provoke a laugh, some a smile, some an inward nod of respect, some a feeling of awe. Hence the title of the book. A smile in the mind more or less covers it.

As we collected examples of witty work, designers sometimes asked for guidance on what they should submit. The most obvious expression of wit is the single image – the poster, the logo, the book cover. This is wit in its purest form, as a total statement. The idea reaches a single point of culmination.

You could say that, here, wit is a chord: at other times it will be a melody, something that stretches over time. A calendar, for example, offers a series of twists. Or a piece of literature takes a core idea and, page by page, plays different tunes. This is sustained wit, which relies, as Koestler says, 'on a series of minor explosions or a continuous state of mild amusement'.

So there are different forms of wit for different forms of communication. Similarly, there are different roles for wit within a design. Sometimes wit carries the whole message. Sometimes wit has only a cameo role. Within technical literature and websites, wit may have a supporting role, but on a poster or a stamp it is more likely to take the lead.

We have given the dates of all the work in the book, because ideas need to be seen in the context of their period. Inevitably, what is considered witty changes over time. A job that was startling when it appeared might not be startling if it were done now. Ideas that broke on an astounded world in the 1960s and 1970s have been pounced on by other designers and subsequently become commonplace.

But that is not always the case. Some of the oldest work in these pages retains its power to delight as much as the most recent. While styles change, individual businesses come and go and whole industries evolve beyond recognition, wit gives longevity to the work. A truly good idea remains as fresh as the day it sparked in the mind of its creator.

WHAT WIT CAN DO

If you ask designers why they like to use wit, they will often talk in terms of delight and pleasure. But behind the warmth of wit is real commercial benefit.

It wins time

Apart from commuters on platforms reading posters until the train comes in, or people idly reading cereal boxes over breakfast, few of us have time to spare for all the messages brands want to communicate. How many do more than skim-read a website or flick through a brochure? The most precious gift a designer can give a client is the gift of someone else's time.

There are many graphic ways of stopping people in their tracks. The whole nature of graphic design is concerned with creating difference – otherwise designers would all use the same typeface and paper. The audience can be arrested by bold imagery, a startling use of colour or elegant photography. But for how long? The best way to win time for the message is to offer something that intrigues. Then the recipient is seduced into making a commitment. Someone who is intrigued will stay with the item until curiosity is satisfied. So the first benefit of witty design is that the recipient becomes willing to hear the message. The audience becomes captive. The communication has the best possible start.

This is a benefit of the most basic kind. As Quentin Newark at Atelier has pointed out, it is easy for designers to worry about the wrong things – about type, grids and colour instead of communication. 'You're always told at college that basically Helvetica has a fatter letter form than Univers, and ultimately this couldn't matter less. Nobody says to you: "What you've got to worry about is whether someone actually reads this."' Wit can be the difference between a communication that is glanced at for ten seconds and one that is pored over for ten minutes.

It invites participation

Witty graphics have always been interactive. The designer sets up an open rather than a closed system. The viewer is invited to participate in the completion of the thought.

For example, most signs are straightforward, like 'Fire Exit' or 'No Parking'. What about a sign that gives the information in a witty way? Suppose it says 'No Parking – don't even think about it'? This is a message with more than one layer. It acknowledges that not all drivers will simply go off and look for another space. Some people see the message, read the message, think about the message – and decide to ignore the message. The 'don't even think about it' wording accompanies that thought process, as it were. As the mind considers the options, the sign makes a second hit. This is one aspect of participation – predicting and entering the dialogue.

Another aspect of participation is making demands on the audience. Imagine a clothes line stretching from the designer sending the communication to the person receiving it. If the communication is merely 'Fire Exit', the designer comes 100% along the clothes line, and the person at the other end doesn't have to move an inch. It is the same with any piece of straight information – it expects a passive recipient.

But when wit is involved, the designer never travels 100% of the way. The idea has to be 'seen' or decoded, and this demands an active recipient. The audience may need to travel only 5% or as much as 40% towards the designer in order to unlock the puzzle and get the idea. Wit invites participation because it asks the reader or viewer to take part in the communication of the idea. It is as if the designer throws a ball which then has to be caught. So the recipient is alert, with an active mind and a brain in gear.

It gives the pleasure of decoding

With a witty design, the recipient makes the necessary act of completion. This response is based on intellectual curiosity. The urge to understand, according to Arthur Koestler, is derived from an urge as basic as hunger or sex. It is the driving power that makes the rat learn to find its way through the experimental maze even though it has not been given any obvious incentive.

The urge to complete something can be witnessed in many ordinary activities. Have you ever sat up late at night watching a thoroughly mediocre film on TV? You don't want to watch it. You know you are wasting your time. You'd much prefer to be in bed. But you just need to know how it turned out – even though you could probably find out easily with a minute or two online. The incomplete asks to be completed.

In an informal discussion it frequently happens that, when someone is making a point, as soon as the meaning is grasped and the final destination is in sight, others jump in and communicate their understanding by completing the point themselves. People like to make a contribution.

The advertising thinker Jeremy Bullmore expressed very cogently the benefits of giving the audience a role: 'Involvement seems to me to be everything in communication.

If I do everything as the sender, the only thing left for the receiver to do is to refute it. Because the only contribution you can make is to disagree with me.'

Bullmore believes that all good storytellers, all good comedians, all good makers of advertisements (and presumably all good designers) 'entice their receivers into willing and constructive collaboration. It's a skilful, delicate and difficult thing to do – particularly in advertising where the pressures of committees and cost tend to favour the "explicit", the "unambiguous", the "message which just can't fail to be understood".'

But of course the explicit and the unambiguous shut out the recipient. Wit always asks for a contribution.

It gives a reward
The rat goes through the maze for the sake of going through the maze. The reward at the end is unexpected. There is the same double pay-off with a witty communication: there

is the pleasure of the process of deciphering the puzzle and the feeling of satisfaction at having deciphered it. First the pleasures of pursuit, then the delight of capture. In fact Koestler identifies a triple pay-off, because he detects two separate feelings in the moment of capture: 'Laughter contains admiration for the cleverness of the joke and also satisfaction with one's own cleverness in seeing the joke. Admiration plus self-congratulation equals intellectual gratification.'

It amuses
As we have said, not all wit is humorous. But most wit prompts an explicit or implicit smile. Smiling and laughing mark the most enjoyed moments of our lives. 'The sound of laughter', said the Czech writer Milan Kundera, 'is like the vaulted dome of a temple of happiness.' The poet W.H. Auden used laughter as the key when he made the ultimate distinction: 'Among those I like or admire, I can find no common denominator, but among those whom I love, I can: all of them can make me laugh.'

Laurence Sterne, the eighteenth-century novelist, thought that nothing was 'so perfectly amusing as a total change of ideas'. It is a delicious shock to the brain cells. In layman's terms it seems entirely probable that a chemical is released when an idea strikes, because the moment is so pleasurable. It is the exact reverse of the mental pain at having to listen to a story heard many times before. Clearly the brain prefers to find new tracks rather than to keep going over the old ones. It's like the difference between being kissed in a new place and having someone press on a bruise.

The creative process. Christoph Niemann, Germany, 2013.

The critic and director Jonathan Miller has described humour as 'vague, runaway stuff that hisses around the fissures and crevices of the mind, like some sort of loose physic gas, more valuable than oil, much harder to get, and we are always prospecting for it'. When we are prospecting, and find humour in a piece of graphics, the delight is such that only 1% of the job may be witty, but the wit makes it 100% better.

Traditionally humour has been linked with selling. In the public mind, the classic salesman is the one who is regaling everyone in the bar. You name a subject, and he's got a story for it. Humour is an essential part of his act of persuasion.

Designers are also salespeople. Even when they are creating identities and brand communications outside the realm of direct selling, they are influencing the commercial outcome – because they create the context in which the sales message will be understood. In that implicit transaction, something looked at with pleasure will be thought of with sympathy.

It gets under the guard

If designers make you smile, they get you on their side, because humour has the capacity to override the normal defences. The designer Paul Rand pointed this out many years ago: 'Humour is a means of establishing good will, good fellowship, confidence and the right frame of mind towards an idea or product.'

This power to defuse opposition and lower the normal barriers has been recognized by people who practise the art of persuasion in many different fields. For example John Mortimer, the barrister and writer who created the British television series 'Rumpole of the Bailey', observed: 'If you can make the jury laugh, you're home and dry.'

The academic and management expert Jean-Louis Barsoux, who wrote on humour, management and business culture in his book *Funny Business*, says: 'Humour puts the audience in a relaxed and warm frame of mind, in which it is more attentive to what is being said.' Barsoux argues that in advertising the conventional frontal assault has been dropped in favour of humour, which he describes as 'a sort of Trojan-horse approach where the well-packaged commercial subtly sheds its brand load to ferment in the consumer's unsuspecting mind'.

What a witty approach does is to focus as much on receptiveness as on what is to be received. It creates a welcome for itself. This is like persuading the goalkeeper to stand aside before you shoot at the goal.

It forms a bond

There is something essentially complicit about humour. It detonates a shared understanding. When the witty idea is 'over and understood', it produces a flash of insight and creates a link. It is a bit like the way two people can be attracted to each other in a large meeting by recognizing a common attitude. It may be just a glance, but it carries a current. Wit is about the pleasure of decoding, which is a moment as complicit as reading a note slipped across the table.

Two comedians have emphasized this link-up. Victor Borge defined humour as the shortest distance between two people, while Sid Caesar observed, 'The best thing about humour is that it shows people that they're not alone.' It's rather as though a joke we get has our initials on it. It feels like a private communication between minds that think alike. Commenting on the reverse situation, the Victorian novelist George Eliot said: 'A difference of tastes in jokes is a great strain on the affections.'

We would argue that the reason people pin up cartoons in the workplace or put stickers in their car is in order to create allegiances. 'This is me: does it tickle you?' The implicit outcome is greater rapport: 'We both enjoy it, so we're alike.'

The British humorist and playwright Alan Bennett doesn't welcome the closer acquaintance that seems to be invited by humour: 'Any third-rate journalist putting together copy feels entitled to be matey simply because one makes jokes.' For the designer, though, drawing people into a friendlier relationship is entirely beneficial.

One reason why wit has become traditionally associated with British graphics and advertising may relate to this phenomenon. Wit implies joining, in the sense of 'if you understand this, you're one of us.' This has particular resonance in a structured, hierarchical society, in which a great deal of negotiation goes on around the core question, 'Are you one of us?' However, as we now live in increasingly multicultural societies around the world, wit has the ability to find underlying connections – using humour not to reinforce old divides, but to break barriers and create new bonds.

It goes deeper

Wit can be both emotional and intellectual. It relies on a truth, and this has a force that touches the feelings and the imagination as well as pleasing the brain. The American architect, designer and writer Richard Saul Wurman

expressed well the difference between a straight communication and one that is witty: 'Consider the doorway as a metaphor for information; humor is a passageway to understanding.'

Humour can also be a passageway to general well-being. Just how strong the effect of a momentary smile can be on the psyche is indicated by the increasing interest in the links between humour and healing. A British psychotherapist, Robert Holden, believes humour can help cause a valuable shift in perception, from pessimism to optimism; while Dr Lee Berk from the Department of Preventive Medicine at Loma Linda University in California argues that a positive mindset and happiness have beneficial effects on physiology. A field of research known as psychoneuroimmunology (or PNI) explores the impact of the mind on the immune system, and the neuroscientist Candace Pert argued that the immune system can be boosted by chemical changes triggered by our feelings. It seems possible that humour

goes much deeper than anyone would have thought.

It is memorable

We end this section as we began – with an utterly basic issue. We go from 'Does the audience read it?' to 'Does the audience remember it?' Why is witty work more memorable? We would argue that an idea that happens in the mind, stays in the mind. Whatever happens when an idea strikes, it leaves a stronger trace. People can remember that flash moment, the click, and re-create the pleasure just by thinking about it.

Reverting to brain chemistry again, it seems as if a kind of explosion takes place when ideas collide. A new pathway is created between the two. An insight is born. Both intelligence and emotion are present at the birth – the first as midwife, the second as sipper of champagne. The event is burned into the brain.

Conclusion

Wit first entices the reader to spend time on the communication, and then helps the message linger in

the memory. Time and memory. These are often problems for the busy people designers usually address. The more bombarded the consumer, the more pronounced the problem. Shortage of time and an overloaded memory co-exist with an information explosion that inundates people with ever more material about a greater number of subjects. In this battle for cognitive attention and mental retention, designers need all the help they can get. As they consider the tools at their disposal, what has more seductiveness and staying power than wit?

Sometimes wit has only a walk-on part, but even a little touch in the corner of the design can lift the spirits. Stamp celebrating the centenary of the American poultry industry, USA, 1948.

WIT AT FIRST HAND

We can make the case for wit in these pages, but it is as nothing compared with the case wit makes for itself in reality.

When you encounter wit in this book, it is in an artificial situation. For one thing, the wit is expected; for another, something three-dimensional has been confined to the page, so the work is represented, reproduced and at one remove. In a natural encounter, wit makes a much greater impact.

In choosing the work for this book, we found most examples from memories, contacts, archives, blogs and other sources. But others came up naturally in the course of daily life, when we were simply part of the audience for a particular piece of communication. In these latter cases, we made an interesting discovery.

As we worked on the book, we found that most of the time our feelings about a piece of work were fairly similar. In a few cases there was some give and take, as our opinions differed. But by and large the consensus has been remarkable.

Except for one type of work.

The 'action research' – where wit was found by accident – provoked a much sharper division of opinion. In every case, the one who found the example was decidedly the more enthusiastic. Sometimes a clear 'yes' faced a definite 'no'. This even happened when what was brought back was not a photograph or link, but an actual example. What was missing for the non-finder, of course, was context. What was lost was surprise – an unlooked-for example in an unexpected location.

We were seeing the difference between encountering wit by chance as a member of its intended audience and searching it out professionally; between seeing a poster on the street and seeing it in a book; between finding something and being shown something. The difference between the reactions of the finder and the non-finder is the X factor – the extra charge a job carries when it is real. The X factor is made up of three components: surprise, context and actuality.

Any delightful experience has an extra frisson when it is not planned but unexpected – like the brilliant film running in the cinema you went into out of the rain. The superb restaurant that came highly recommended never stays as bright in the memory as the superb restaurant you went into unawares. Context heightens pleasure even further. A 'find' restaurant is much more thrilling in the back of beyond than it would be in Paris. This is thanks to 'actuality', by which we mean all the incidentals of time and place that surround an experience. Actuality in this sense is the difference between the bottle of wine you discover on holiday and the one you take back and drink at home.

Graphic wit does travel. But it is easy to underestimate its impact by assuming that seeing it on the page is pretty much like encountering the real thing. The X factor is bigger than we expected. It not only adds excitement, it also multiplies delight.

Wit snapped on the street, in the Place Vendôme in Paris, January 1995.

Three of the great names
of commerce present
themselves with wit: Shell
developed by Raymond
Loewy in 1971; Nipper first
painted by Francis Barraud
in 1898; Apple created
by Rob Janoff in 1977.

THE MOMENT

The exact second when wit strikes can be a moment of magic. What does it feel like for you?

This is a small experiment. We want you to try to capture exactly what it feels like when you 'get' someone's witty idea – the pleasure, the feeling of satisfaction. Notice everything you can about the experience. The idea we are using in this experiment is on the right.

The sort of thing we'd be interested to know is, when you got it did you smile? Did you show your reaction in some other way – by expelling breath perhaps in one of those humphy noises that signal amusement? How long was it before you got it?

We've selected a new piece from a famous designer, to make sure you won't have seen it already. As for the background to the idea, this is a poster for a UK charity called the Smithson Trust that provides funding for cancer research. So look at it now, and remember that we want you to record all the sensations and feelings that hit you.

Have you got the idea? Right. Now, before you forget, scribble down the main things you noticed. You don't have to write much, just enough to help your memory later.

Did the penny drop? If so, we'd be really surprised. Because this is not a witty job at all. It is not even a real job. It is an invented piece of nonsense. There is no idea to get. What this experiment is really about is what it feels like when you can't get the idea. We wanted to remind you of that predicament.

When someone shows you a witty job, it's like a test. You know you've got to crack it. You look at it intently, feeling that the person is waiting for you to react. You're allowed about twenty seconds to take it all in, and then you're expected to come up with the answer. All the while you're being watched, of course. You get a bit panicky. The brain seizes up. Time's running out.

If you don't get it, you seem to fail a test. Do you pretend or own up? No one likes feeling stupid. It undermines you and spoils your

mood. You'd much rather you hadn't been shown the idea in the first place.

These are feelings most people will recognize. Even witty designers aren't necessarily quick at decoding other people's ideas. Often when a witty idea is explained, it seems so obvious you feel like a half-wit for not seeing it straight away. Other times you decide the idea wasn't worth getting anyway, and vent your irritation at the designer.

So the feelings aroused by wit can be negative as well as positive. The attempt to entertain sometimes falls flat on its face. The next subject we tackle is the risk of alienating people by wit that misfires, and how to avoid that danger.

**The Smithson Trust for Cancer Research
117 West Highbury Place, London W1**

Why not take part in a little experiment? Read the text, then look at the image.

THE RISK

A witty idea that baffles people is worse than no idea at all. It alienates the audience rather than enticing them. So what are the traps for the designer, and how can they be avoided?

Some witty design avoids the danger of alienating the audience altogether, because it is witty in an almost secret way. The idea is subtle, and does not involve an enigma that demands to be decoded. So the wit is there for those who want to discover it. And the job merely seems handsome to recipients who have no idea there is any more to it than that.

We think of this as 'bonus' wit. If people miss the hidden joke, there are no penalties. But anyone who spots it gets an extra reward. There are often jobs of this kind on awards shortlists. They look straightforward, but to have got past the jury you know there must be something more. This observation triggers the closer scrutiny that uncovers the idea. Such jobs can also be 'sleepers', known to individuals in the business but not decoded by others until months or even years later.

These are not the projects at issue in this section. Here we are looking at work that is patently enigmatic. The audience realizes there is a padlock to be unlocked, but simply cannot find the key. People's failure to unlock, decode or understand the riddle puts the whole communication at risk. The designer may wilfully or inadvertently outwit the audience.

Big-head design
Wit and ego don't mix.
A designer who is showing off is not communicating. Wit is clever, but as the French writer La Rochefoucauld said in the seventeenth century: 'The desire of appearing clever often prevents our becoming so.' The first danger for the designer, therefore, is self-indulgence. The temptation is to insert the difficulty of the process into the solution, to make the work seem as intellectual as possible. But to put up barriers for the audience is simply wrong-headed. As the American poet Ogden Nash said in his no-nonsense way:

Here's a good rule of thumb,
Too clever is dumb.

But we do not underestimate the temptations of the 'too-clever'

solution. Working on ideas is a thrilling journey, as the mind pushes ever deeper into the interior of the problem, strikes out in weird directions and makes curious finds. The true destination is the heart of the issue, the task is to distil the problem to its essence. But what may happen instead is that the designer enters the abstruse reaches of the far-fetched. The resulting design comes from such a distance that to decode it requires someone in attendance, standing at the viewer's elbow. It's tempting to feel that such a solution is 'deep', when in fact it is merely unfathomable. In communication, unfathomable equals unusable.

Intellect-flaunting or arcane solutions are the main reasons why wit misfires. The designer is strutting or struggling. Some design just seems so desperate, you can almost hear the fingernails scratching down the rock face.

Over-coding
In other cases, the wit mechanism simply doesn't work as it should, because the structure is inefficient. The designer has gone too far in making the idea intriguing, and put up too many veils. Most work of this kind, of course, doesn't see

the light of day, because clients reject it. Aziz Cami at The Partners believes that, for a successful creative consultancy like theirs, any rejections that occur are usually because the designer has overstepped the mark in terms of coding.

A common problem is that designers fail to share with the audience an essential piece of context. The Israeli designer Yarom Vardimon was surprised to find just how much context people require when he visited the UK for an Alliance Graphique Internationale conference on humour and showed the same slides to two audiences – students at Pentagram in London and his AGI peers in Cambridge. He talked the students through his work in detail, and got an enthusiastic reception. He merely showed the work to AGI members, without comment, and there was a lot less laughter.

This issue of context is tackled head on by Milton Glaser in a poster for the School of Visual Arts in New York. The text on the poster is like a running commentary on Glaser's thought process, or a private conversation with himself as he develops the idea (see p.237).

This is to poster design what the Centre Georges Pompidou in Paris is to architecture. In both cases you can see the works. Glaser's commentary, far from detracting from the 'mystery' of the solution and of the designer's art, actually reveals the depth of the idea and the fascination of what a designer does.

The cue
It seems to us that the biggest difference between wit that works and wit that doesn't is 'the cue'. Designers need to make sure a witty idea is strongly cued. The better the cue, the bigger the leap the reader can make. Koestler (referring to verbal wit) said: 'Words are merely stepping stones for thought. Economy means spacing them at intervals just wide enough to require a significant effort from the receiver of the message.' In design, too, the challenge is to space the stepping stones 'just wide enough'.

Cueing is identified as a core issue by both Jeremy Bullmore and Milton Glaser. Bullmore compares the advertising idea to a good joke: 'Has it asked enough, but not too much, of its selected audience?

Has it allowed that audience to see something for itself? Creative skill is needed to ensure that the recipient cannot fail to arrive at the desired conclusion.' Glaser points out that understanding a design (as opposed to a painting) has to occur within prescribed limits: 'How familiar can it be so that it's understood, and yet how unusual can it be so that it is engaging? You can get someone engaged, and you then have to be able to deliver the understanding. Because if people get engaged in something and then don't understand it, they get irritated and angry. That interval is a critical interval in design.'

The arbitrary
One difficulty for the witty designer is that so much design is arbitrary. The New Typography movement, for example, is often an attempt to change the notion of what is obscure. When people are frequently exposed to arbitrary design, it affects their normal response, so that when they see a witty design that initially looks odd, they assume it's meant to be odd. They fail to conclude that oddness signals an underlying rationale, and therefore don't look for it. This is potentially the biggest

hurdle to be overcome. Many ideas can be decoded very quickly, if people only realize that a game is being played. Designers have to signal that they are not being wayward or arbitrary, or following some private trail, but that the design has a real, public meaning. They have to switch on the audience's perception, to reanimate their curiosity.

The journey
It is commonly said that when a witty idea is transferred from a designer to the recipient, the recipient makes the same journey as the designer. For example, Koestler said that someone hearing a joke is 'compelled to repeat to some extent the process of inventing the joke, to re-create it in his imagination'. We believe that there is an important step missing in this observation. The audience may make the same journey as the designer, but does it *in the reverse direction*.

If designers want to say 'witch', they may show a black cat. The audience has to create the association the other way round – see the black cat and immediately think 'witch'. Designers need

to check that the link 'back' is as obvious as the link 'out'. For example, 'witch' suggests 'broomstick', but 'broomstick' may suggest Cinderella, 'sweep clean' or even 'The Sorcerer's Apprentice' (as in Disney's *Fantasia*).

Designers need to have the common touch here. Their associations must be the associations most people make. There have been TV game shows built around this feeling for the obvious, this homing in on the norm. In Britain, 'Family Fortunes' rewards contestants who can supply the right missing word, and 'right' means 'the majority view'. It is curious that witty design, which depends so heavily on individual creativity, should also require this feel for what is common, what is shared.

Making associations backwards, as it were, is only one of the problems of the reverse journey the audience must make. A witty idea is the end point, and the audience has to get back to the starting point – the issue being communicated. It is a bit like saying, 'Here is the answer; what was the question?', as in that other TV game-show

'Jeopardy!' In some ways, it is much easier for the designer travelling out than for the audience travelling back.

Take the designer who needs to send out a change of address card. What must he communicate? The new address. He looks at it. Is there anything he can build on? The new studio will be in Red Lion Mews, Upper Thames Street, London EC4. He looks at those eight words. It is not too hard to find the most interesting ones. Red Lion Mews. A little lateral shift and the idea emerges. The red lion doesn't roar, it mews. A change of address note can now be designed.

But what does the recipient get? More than eight words to be sure. The recipient gets a little concertina-fold leaflet with various animals on it. Each one is making the wrong noise. The last one is the red lion, which duly mews.

It was easy for the designer to get to 'red lion mews', but the recipient is looking at a much more complex package. Those key words are not half so obvious, and the designer does nothing to point them out.

Without this help, the recipient is likely to remain baffled. But with a cue to draw attention to the key words, the recipient will see the wit – and will never forget where the studio is.

Audience

The audience, of course, determines the nature of the cue. The cue can be smaller in a situation where wit is expected, and the audience is receptive and tuned – as with, say, design consultancy Christmas cards or party invitations. The cue needs to be more prominent when the audience has to be 'switched on' to wit, and encouraged to realize that there is something here to find.

The other aspect of audience is shared domain. Wit itself is international. The mechanism underlying wit crosses all kinds of boundaries. It transcends geography and discipline. Putting two ideas together may result in a witty poster, a verbal joke, or a breakthrough in science. Wit crosses all these territories because it is a type of brain event. But what is not international is the content. That is bounded by both time and space. The reference a

witty item relies on may be familiar in one place, but not everywhere; it may have been familiar at one time, but not now. The mechanism of wit can work everywhere, but the ingredients of a specific job may or may not travel.

Safer wit

Wit is safe to use in three situations: when it is properly cued (and this can be tested on other people); when the clichés it relies on are shared with the audience; and when wit is an unobtrusive part of the communication. In this last category, the graphic item makes sense whether or not the wit is 'seen'. To use wit as a bonus removes the risk of alienating the audience, though it also limits the number who get the joke. But there are some situations where an unlooked-for bonus is the perfect climax to a design.

Pentagram in New York was once designing a hamburger restaurant, a contemporary diner with plain food at honest prices in a clean, well-lit space. The diner was furnished with items from the usual catalogues, deliberately chosen to create clashes of colour. The problem was that there was no

budget for pictures on the large bare walls. Pentagram decided to glorify the sort of objects found in these catalogues by using a series of giant, single images, each four feet by eight feet. Then one of the designers said: 'Why don't we make them mean something?' Not only would this add another layer, but it would actually help with the decision as to which four objects to choose. So the images became the four primal elements: a salt shaker for the earth, a tea bag for water, a matchbook for fire and a wire whisk for air.

We don't know how many people spotted the link between the images – quite a lot might, once they realized there was a link to spot. The most powerful assistance for wit is an audience that asks 'Why?'

ANSWERING OBJECTIONS

Wit is a favoured technique of start-ups and challenger brands, but what about larger, global players? As companies 'grow up', does humour become inappropriate?

Humour debunks. It is not respectful. As the British writer George Orwell said: 'Whatever is funny is subversive; every joke is ultimately a custard pie.' In ancient Greece, Aristotle saw it in a darker light: 'Wit is educated insolence.' Wit may suit individualistic enterprises and niche players, but is it off limits for clients of stature? Is it inappropriate for important situations?

Wit is certainly not good news for the pompous. Ralph Emerson recognized that it takes little note of hierarchy: 'Wit makes its own welcome, and levels all distinctions.' An enterprise that takes itself too seriously will not feel comfortable with wit. Ditto any organization that equates 'serious' with 'solemn'.

But in the same way that using wit requires confidence, it also shows confidence. It makes an organization seem above petty worries, untroubled about its place in the world. Wit is actually a better

expression of how companies need to be in today's world – with its requirement for better ideas, quicker reactions and smarter thinking – than any sombre approach. Light beats heavy in the modern marketplace.

One reason companies may fight shy of wit is that it is unknowable. Wit has a power that no one can actually quantify. This can be alarming for people within the world of commerce who operate under quite different criteria. If they are insecure, they can find that the element of magic in wit is unsettling. They would prefer to exclude it, and to reduce design to elements that can be quantified, tracked and worked out in some kind of procedure. In a sense this attitude objects to creativity of any kind, not just to wit, and bars clients from taking advantage of the real contribution that design and only design can make to business.

Comedy is simply a funny way of being serious, as the British performer Peter Ustinov said. In the UK the red nose has become an enduring symbol of the annual campaign to help people in need in Africa. The linking of humour with matters of high moment has

been practised for centuries, not least in Shakespeare's great tragedies. An actor who cannot manage the wit of Hamlet had better stay at home, or the audience will.

While some companies may resist the use of humour, others explicitly or implicitly acknowledge its power. For all its minimalistic cool, Apple has long recognized the power of wit, particularly when confronting its 'straighter' rival Microsoft. In the long-running 'Get a Mac' campaign (2006–9), two actors played the role of Mac and PC to highlight the differences between the products. In a battle between two branding giants with billions at stake, humour was the chosen weapon.

Sometimes it can seem as though a double standard operates, where on one level people are presumed to want serious discussion, but on another we all know they like to laugh and smile. When one of the authors, Beryl McAlhone, was on The Observer, the newspaper prided itself on its leader pages – yet when the paper wanted to boost circulation, the two journalists given the greatest prominence in the advertising campaign were the columnists

Clive James and Katharine Whitehorn, who wrote the funny bits.

Advocates of humour are now to be found in the most unexpected places, whether it is researchers suggesting that putting people in a good mood by telling them jokes makes them think through problems with more ingenuity, or hospitals using laughter therapy for patients with chronic pain. There are advocates galore in this book – clients and designers who know what wit does. Their example today provides an argument for the designer of tomorrow.

HERBERT READ

THE MEANING OF ART

ff

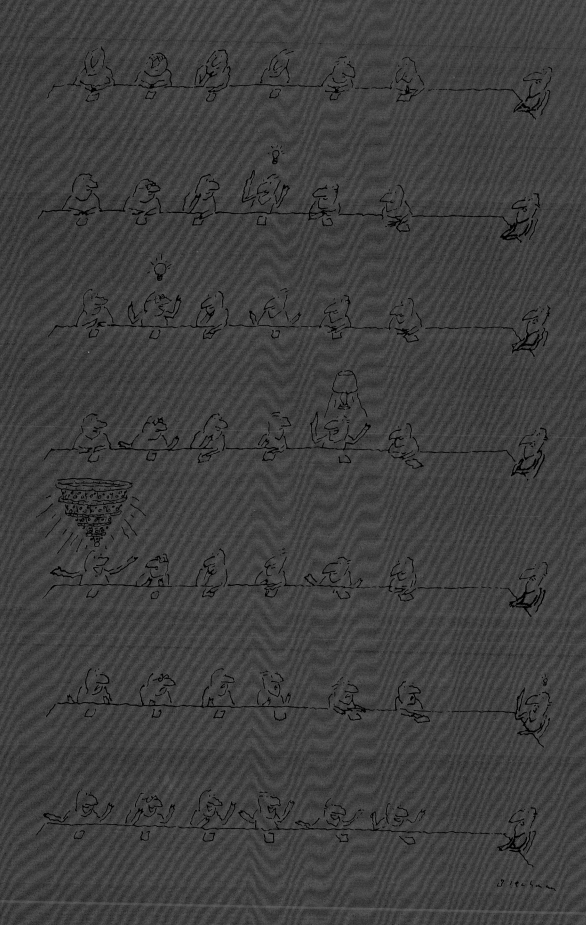

Illustration for *Punch*.
R.O. Blechman,
USA, 1957.

TYPES
OF WIT

TYPES OF WIT

Wit is more like opera than theatre. It is concurrent not consecutive. If two people speak at once in a play, the audience can't hear either of them. But the whole point of a sung quartet is the interlacing of several strands.

Wit is similarly multiple. There are always at least two elements in a witty idea – whether the wit is visual or verbal. The moment when they collide or combine produces the click of pleasure in the brain. However, the types of elements and the way they come together is a matter of almost infinite possibility.

When thinkers define wit, they inevitably tell only part of the story. Early in the nineteenth century Madame de Staël saw it in terms of comparisons: 'Wit lies in recognizing the resemblance between things which differ and the difference between things which are alike.' Later that century the American humorist Mark Twain chose to focus on collision or linkages: 'Wit is the sudden marriage of ideas which before their union were not perceived to have any relation.'

You will find many examples of both juxtaposition and combination in this book – but also other types of smart thinking. We have observed graphic wit in action, and found the main routes designers take. In this section we map possible paths for others to follow.

Where to begin? In starting to think about witty solutions for a job, designers have a choice of entry points. They can root the idea in something about a) the client (which may be the designer), b) the client's business, c) the medium, d) the message or e) the audience – or a combination of any or all of these. Sometimes the right lever or pivot for the idea is obvious. A witty identity usually plays against the client's name or business area. Other assignments have wider possibilities. Designers who are stuck can find that a switch of entry point will free up ideas.

The choices then broaden considerably. All wit involves some kind of 'two-ness' – a two-in-one idea, say, or one idea with two pay-offs. All the different ways of using what we call 'two-ness' and

Arthur Koestler calls 'bisociation' are explored in the following pages, where examples make the differences clear. Broadly, these routes fall into seven groups.

Comparisons

The 'juxtaposition' route reveals unexpected similarities or significant differences (Pairs). The other 'comparison' route involves clashes and jars (Incongruity).

Two-in-one

This is a mainstay of wit, as when designers need to say 'animals and accountancy', or 'cooking and fear' in the same image. They can combine the two, A and B, in several ways. They can, for example, make a hybrid, of which there are three types: B is substituted for a part of A, like a cuckoo in the nest (Substitution); or A takes a particular form that brings B to mind (Modification); or something is added to A to turn it into B (Addition).

Another form of two-in-one draws on famous imagery: A is dressed in a form usually associated with B (Homage).

The final sort of two-in-one doesn't combine A and B in one image, but presents them as alternatives: designers create an image that can be read both ways (Ambiguity). A favourite type of ambiguous design plays with the image that makes us most recognizably human (The face).

Shifts

Wit often defies what is normal, disrupting expectations (Shift: scale, Shift: time and Shift: view). The two-ness here is the usual versus the actual, the normal versus what you're looking at. Real also fights with fake (Trompe l'oeil) and the true with the literal (Taking it literally).

Deduce

Wit can be enigmatic, suggesting A by showing B. The two-ness here is 'See this, think that' (Missing link or Puns & rebuses).

Changes

This is wit with a timescale. It starts as this, but turns into that (Transformations). It makes the audience zig, then zags (Expectations confounded).

It plays the game of theme and variations (Series of twists).

Two pay-offs

This is double-agent wit. One element plays two roles (Economy).

Chance

This is two-ness in the lap of the gods. The designer exploits the 'something in common' between two utterly different things (Coincidence).

These routes are not unique to design and can also be found in verbal wit, because they relate to structure not technique. We have included a section on verbal thinking (Power of words) to show how words, often a powerful ally in design, can also play the lead role.

Such distinctions and subdivisions provide useful entry points for creative thinking, but wit is not ultimately susceptible to conventional analysis of the 'take-it-apart' kind. What is instinctively understood can be arduous to explain. Koestler gave a perfect example of the economy of wit, of the subtle and reverberant messages it carries, when he commented on a story about Picasso.

A dealer who often visited the artist bought a canvas signed 'Picasso'. He travelled to Cannes and asked Picasso to authenticate it. Picasso said it was a fake. The dealer protested that he previously saw the artist working on it. Picasso countered: 'I often paint fakes.'

Koestler explained: 'Picasso does not say: "Sometimes, like other painters, I do something second-rate, repetitive, an uninspired variation on a theme, which after a while looks to me as if somebody had imitated my technique. It is true that this somebody happened to be myself, but that makes no difference to the quality of the picture, which is no better than if it were a fake; in fact you could call it that – an uninspired Picasso apeing the style of the true Picasso." None of this was said; all of it was implied.'

Wit is the shortcut to profundity.

Double invitation to two events at the International Design Center in New York – a reception for the Progressive Architecture International Furniture Awards and a lecture by NASA designers on spacecraft interiors. From bloom to boom. Pentagram, USA, 1984.

ADDITION

Two elements become more than the sum of their parts. In some cases, an element may be added to something that already exists, using a technique familiar to the graffiti artist or defacer of posters. In others, the design creates its own set-up and pay-off.

Above Poster for a Dracula Party at the London Hospital. Where vampires and medicine meet. CS&S, UK, 1983.

Above Cover for the January issue of *Architectural & Engineering News*. A graphic ad lib. Robert Brownjohn & Tony Palladino, USA, 1961.

Left Peace poster. The transformation is startling, from the black and heavy ace of spades signalling death to the hesitant innocence of the marks which spell a different message. Robert Brownjohn, USA, 1970.

Right Environmental protest demanding removal of Matilija Dam. Anonymous, USA, 2011.

Below 'Tis the season. From the *Abstract Sunday* sketches repurposing everyday objects. Christoph Niemann, Germany, 2014.

Left Software piracy: cover from the quarterly *Newsnotes* sent out by solicitors Lewis Silkin. Remember floppy disks? The Partners, UK, 1993.

Above Cover for Penguin paperback on the trade unions. A graphic infiltrator. Derek Birdsall, UK, 1974.

Opposite & overleaf 'I almost have it!' Two-part cover describing the process of creativity. Christoph Niemann, Germany, 2012.

ZEIT MAGAZIN

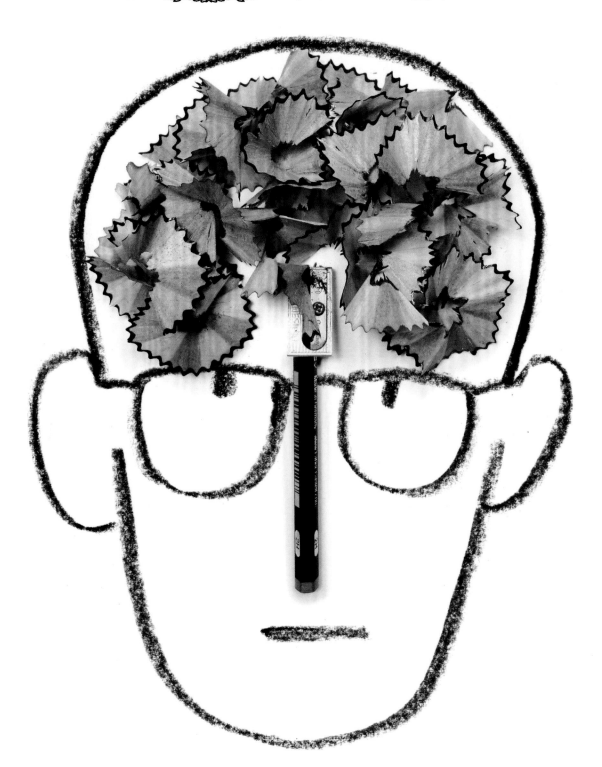

Nicolas Berggruen im Gespräch, Seite 28

Ich hab's gleich!

Nr. 16 12. 4. 2012

Wie kommt man auf gute Ideen?
Antworten von dem Künstler und Illustrator Christoph Niemann

Left Branding for hearing-loss charity, eliminating the negative and accentuating the positive. Hat-trick, UK, 2011.

Right Innocent Targets: a series of posters highlighting the everyday victims of gun violence. Anthony Burrill, UK, 2014.

Left & below Interactive fruit and vegetable stamp set with extra stickers to create fun faces. Johnson Banks, UK, 2003.

+

=

Above Logo for Security Shopper. An example of artful synchronicity. Designframe Incorporated, USA, 1982.

Left Logo for United Nations luncheon. Bob Gill redefines the problem: logo for an institution that has boring lunches, but which, this time, might be different. Bob Gill, USA, 1974.

Left Internal sign for a design office. Marcello Minale finds an Italian solution, and a way of putting his name on one of Michael Peters's doors. Minale Tattersfield, UK, 1975.

Right Self-censoring book cover for George Orwell's *Nineteen Eighty-Four*. David Pearson / Type as Image / Penguin Books, UK, 2013.

AMBIGUITY

A form of two-in-one design that works like an optical illusion. The image is not half one idea, half another. Both ideas are complete and autonomous, and the mind flip-flops between the two. The artistry is in the synchronicity, as each detail in the design fits both readings.

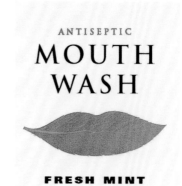

Above Own-brand packaging for Makro's Body Benefits mouthwash. Many ambiguous images rely on tiny little bendings done with the pen, but this mint leaf is photographed. Horseman Cooke, UK, 1994.

Above From the series Rock Legends by Mini, each execution celebrating a well-known band. DLV BBDO Milan, Italy, 2004.

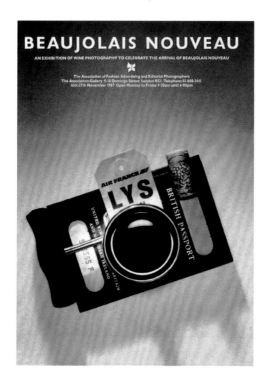

Above Image from an invitation to a christening. Church first, then the knees-up. Jim Sutherland, UK, 1994.

Above Symbol for Quality Foodcare, which supplies food to hospitals. Atelier Works, UK, 1992.

Above Poster for the Ministry of Housing. No carrot, no stick, just the good manners of wit. Abram Games, UK, 1963.

Below Visual twist on the *Economist* campaign: the magazine that makes you smarter. Ogilvy & Mather Singapore, 2004.

Right Poster for AFAEP's wine photography show, when the race to bring the first Beaujolais Nouveau into Britain was fashionable. A snappy way to convey wine, travel and France. The Partners, UK, 1988.

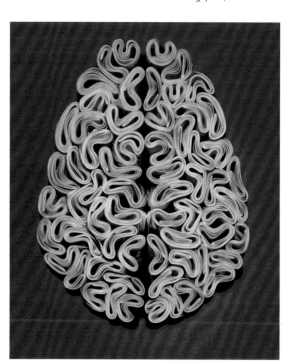

Above A mint-leaf moustache for a gentle-man's chewing gum. B&B Studio, UK, 2009.

Above Surprisingly friendly logo for a yacht company named Brigand. Hope they had a flag too. David Pelham, UK, 1981.

Right Poster for the University of California, Los Angeles. Books make the reverse journey. Pentagram, USA, 1989.

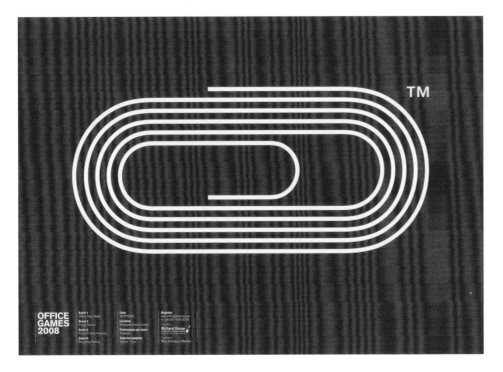

OFFICE GAMES 2008

Left Workmanlike identity for the restoration fund of St Mary's Church in London. Rose, UK, 2009.

Left Identity for an athletics fundraising event in the City of London, for Richard House Children's Hospice. The Partners, UK, 2008.

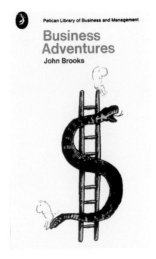

Above Cover for a Pelican paperback. A minimalist solution: one snake and ladder is enough. Mel Calman and Philip Thompson, UK, 1971.

HEDGEHOG BOOKS

Above Logo for a book packaging company. The designer finds a hedgehog in the leaves. David Pelham, UK, 1993.

NEW **GUINNESS** EXTRA COLD

Left & above Pret A Manger playing with food: sea-salt crisps, coconut water, sea-salt & cider vinegar crisps. Pret A Manger, Balloon Dog, UK, 2011.

Right An ice-cold pint. Abbott Mead Vickers BBDO, UK, 2000.

SUBSTITUTION

One element playfully swapped with another. Success depends on introducing a rogue element that is visually similar but remote in meaning and relevant in message. This fusion of two normally incompatible components produces the characteristic response to wit – recognition and surprise.

Above Logo for the music and arts organization Melodious Accord. Is there a bit of extra quaver in Blechman's line? R.O. Blechman, USA, 1992.

Left Safe sex poster produced by the Terrence Higgins Trust. Verbal and visual punning embrace. Simons Palmer Denton Clemmow & Johnson, UK, 1992.

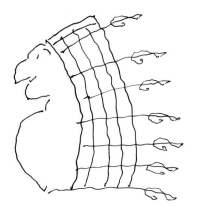

Left Logo for Mohawk Trail Concerts. Drawn in Blechman's minimal wobbly style, an American Indian headdress turns out to be the blood brother of the musical stave. R.O. Blechman, USA, 1969.

Above Logo for handyman Jack Etter. Pennebaker Design, USA, 1990.

Left Logo for an Adventure 16 leisure venue. The botanical characteristics of palm trees support a double wordplay. Mires Design, USA, 1992.

SASSOON

Left Logo for the 50th anniversary exhibition of the Vidal Sassoon organization. The logo not only combines name and number, but also translates into seven giant-letter exhibition stands. The Partners and The Association of Ideas, UK, 1992.

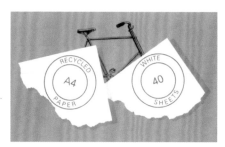

Left Personal stationery pads (recycled), for WHSmith. Trickett & Webb, UK, 1992.

Left Illustration for a travel feature on the front page of the Review section of *The Sunday Times* newspaper. The brief was to represent France and everything French. Peter Brookes, UK, 1980.

Right Image from a greetings card for film production company BFCS. Season's recyclings. R.O. Blechman, USA, 1992.

Lest We Forget: Royal Mail
stamp commemorating
the 90th anniversary of the
Battle of Passchendaele.
Hat-trick, UK, 2007.

Creativity in Industry
P.R. Whitfield

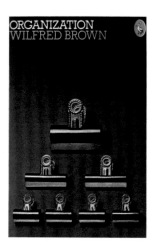

ORGANIZATION
WILFRED BROWN

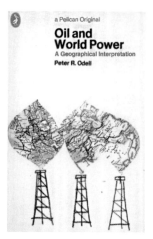

a Pelican Original
Oil and World Power
A Geographical Interpretation
Peter R. Odell

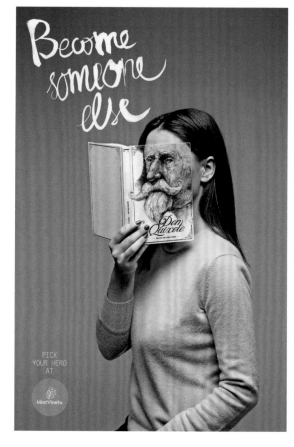

Above Cover for a Pelican paperback – pencil power. David Pelham, UK, 1975.

Above Cover for a Pelican paperback. Organization as understood in the boardroom and at the office desk. Pentagram, UK, 1975.

Above Cover for a Pelican paperback. The shape peculiarities of Bartholomew's re-centred sinusoidal projection entirely suit the designer's purpose. Mel Calman and Philip Thompson, UK, 1972.

Below Posters with a twist to the Hollywood script to promote the Gay & Lesbian Film Festival: Pink Film Days. Lernert & Sander, The Netherlands, 2010.

Right The transformative effect of reading: print advertising campaign for Mint Vinetu Bookstore. Love Agency, Lithuania, 2011.

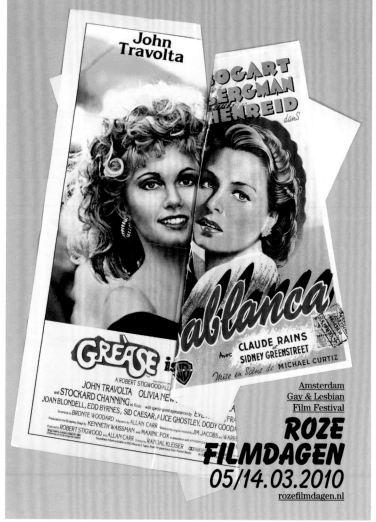

Right Detail from an image in David Gentleman's book *A Special Relationship*, prompted by the USA strike on Libya from UK bases. The designer comments without words on the UK/USA relationship. David Gentleman, UK, 1987.

Right Protest poster. In this double-barrelled switch the USA flag gets minimal changes for maximum effect. Unknown designer, USA, 1970.

Right Protest poster. Flagging the figures. Unknown designer, USA, 1960s.

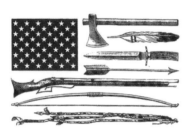

U.S.A. SURPASSES ALL THE GENOCIDE RECORDS
KUBLAI KHAN MASSACRES 10% IN NEAR EAST
SPAIN MASSACRES 10% OF AMERICAN INDIAN
JOSEPH STALIN MASSACRES 5% OF RUSSIAN
NAZIS MASSACRE 5% OF OCCUPIED EUROPEANS AND 75% OF EUROPEAN JEW
U.S.A. MASSACRES 6.5% OF SOUTH VIETNAMESE & 75% OF AMERICAN INDIAN
FOR CALCULATIONS & REFERENCES WRITE TO: P.O. BOX 180. NEW YORK.N.Y.1001

Right Image from a National Film and Television School brochure. The designer gives a visual rundown of the film *The Last of the Mohicans* – an example of high-profile work by NFTS graduates. Atelier Works, UK, 1994.

Left Self-portrait. The artist takes a bird's-eye view. André François, France.

Right Drawing for *The Times* on the day the news broke on the consequences of the Chernobyl disaster. The artist recalls the nuclear symbol and gives it a twist. Peter Brookes, UK, 1986.

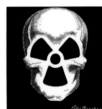

Below Tribute to the maker: Waitrose Honey Bee. Turner Duckworth, UK, 2007.

Right Cuban Missile Crisis: illustration for *The New York Times Sunday Book Review*. Office of Paul Sahre, USA, 2008.

PAIRS

A juxtaposition of ideas, usually enjoying 50:50 billing. Pairing may unite incompatibles or highlight differences. In the first case, unexpected similarities reveal hidden links between incongruous elements. In the second, a small change produces a somersault in meaning.

 TREASURES

Above Identity for Imagination Incorporated. The name seems contradictory: it is vindicated by the design. May & Co., USA, 1986.

Right Unnatural juxtapositions: poster for the Natural History Museum's 'Treasures' exhibition. Krow Communications, UK, 2012.

4.5 billion years of nature. 70 million specimens. 22 objects. One very special gallery.

Discover the highlights of our world-famous collections in a new gallery.

South Kensington

Above & right Fold-out Christmas card for a design firm based in London and San Francisco. Turner Duckworth, UK/USA, 2012.

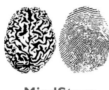

MindStore
Developing the individual

Left Identity for MindStore. The problem, how to say 'development' and 'individual': the solution, brainy and unique. The Partners, UK, 1994.

BIKE EXPO NEW YORK

N.Y.C.

MAY 2–3 2014

BASKETBALL CITY PIER 36, NYC FREE & OPEN TO THE PUBLIC

bikeexponewyork.org

For the Two Fred's Cricket Match

Please give generously

CASSONS

Above Poster for a cricket match benefit. Now they play: now you pay. John Gorham, UK, 1966.

Above My other half: wedding invitation for contrasting couple. Purpose, UK, 2009.

Above Perfect circle for Bike Expo New York poster. Emily Oberman / Pentagram, USA, 2013.

Left Invitation to a wedding reception. The bride is American, the groom is Welsh. Williams & Phoa, UK, 1994.

CHICAGO BORN LONDON BASED
CME Europe

Left Hybrid taxi for CME Europe, a London financial firm with Chicago roots. London Taxi Advertising, UK, 2013.

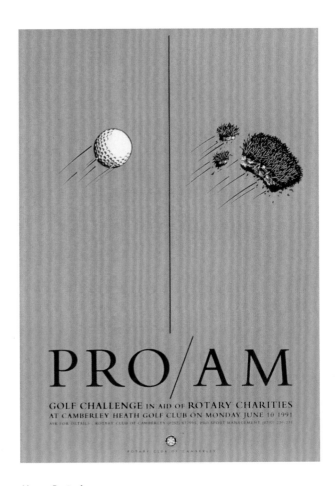

Above Poster for a charity golf match. A juxtapositional event prompts an appositional design. Turner Duckworth, UK, 1991.

Right Image for the film *Oranges are Not the Only Fruit* from a brochure for the National Film and Television School. The story of a religious mother: the revolt of a lesbian daughter. Atelier Works, UK, 1994.

Above Poster for a Mucho exhibition of graphic interpretations of San Francisco, city of the San Andreas Fault. Purpose, UK, 2014.

Above Signs for men's and women's restrooms in the Main Street Grill. Wee difference, big implications. The Martin Agency, USA, 1992.

Right Identity for September: a husband-and-wife team running separate businesses – a brasserie and hair studio – from one address. The Chase, UK, 1995.

MODIFICATION

A two-in-one approach, but with degrees of intervention. A primary image contains a subtle but meaningful variation. The technique is often used with familiar icons that set up an expectation to be subverted. The resulting image acts out of character, but within the limits of the believable.

Above Magazine illustration to represent improvisational jazz. Bob Gill, USA, 1962.

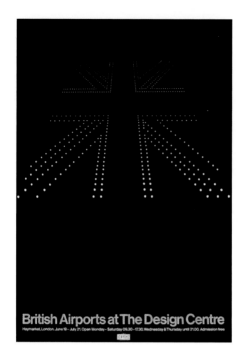

Above Poster for a Design Council exhibition on British airports. Entirely recognizable and almost probable. Minale Tattersfield, UK, 1981.

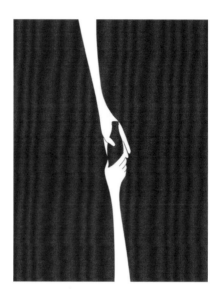

Above The white ribbon transformed into a symbol of sharing for Coca-Cola by design student Jonathan Mak Long. Ogilvy & Mather Shanghai, China, 2012.

Above Catalogue cover for the Italian knitwear exhibition at the Italian Institute for Foreign Trade. A silky-smooth convergence of the two messages. Minale Tattersfield, UK, 1976.

Left Cover of the Galt Toys catalogue. A commission demanding a playful solution. Ken Garland, UK, 1969.

Above Trademark for F. W. Purser, builder. Created when the joiner putting up shelves in their first studio didn't understand what the Pentagram partners did. Fletcher Forbes Gill, UK, 1962.

Above Poster for the Investors Overseas Service. When were two clichéd symbols better suited? Minale Tattersfield, UK, 1962.

Right Illustrations in the *Radio Times* promoting a 'World Around Us' programme on cats. Not less of a cat for being more than a mouse. Peter Brookes, UK, 1979.

Clockwise from top left S.M.L. / Erotic writing / Where there's darkness / Pensions and property. Illustrations by Noma Bar, UK, 2006–9.

MISSING LINK

The best wit doesn't explain itself,
but invites the viewer to fill in the gap.
The answer may come in a reward
that reveals itself over time, or a rationale
that is evident only to the thoughtful
viewer. The punchline often lies in a
verbal cliché expressed visually. The idea
completes itself in the mind of the viewer.

Above The universal
language of slapstick.
Hsieh Chen-Yuan and
Associates, Taiwan, 2012.

Right Poster for the film
Advise & Consent. The
White House dome is not
only instantly recognizable,
but also becomes a fairly
convincing lid. Saul Bass,
USA, 1962.

Above Identity for a charity
that finds life-saving bone
marrow matches. Johnson
Banks, UK, 2010.

Below Down Below hair by
Gee Beauty: a surprisingly
elegant clue to where the
depilatory is applied. GJP
Advertising, Canada, 2008.

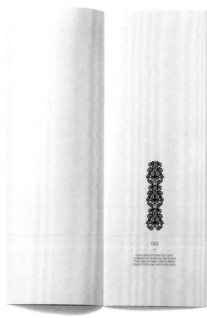
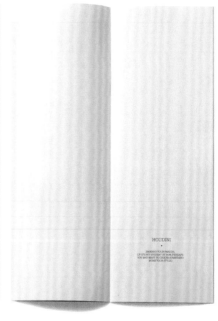

Left Visual prompts
for accidents
waiting to happen.
Turner Duckworth,
UK/USA, 2004.

WOMEN   MEN

GEFFRYE MUSEUM

Left Keyhole identity for
the Geffrye Museum, which
presents rooms through
the centuries. Offering
visitors a peep into the
past. Lewis Moberly,
UK, 1992 (signage 1994).

Heraldic designs for
British coins: and an extra
reward when you put them
together. Matt Dent for
Royal Mint, UK, 2008.

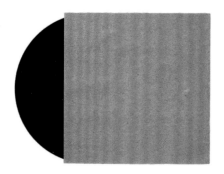

The Silk Purse Company

Left Identity for software providers The Silk Purse Company. Serendipity in the solution: the snout can also be seen as a high-tech symbol. The Partners, UK, 1986.

Left Sandpaper sleeve for the Durutti Column, designed to damage every other record in your collection. Peter Saville / Factory Records, UK, 1979.

Above 'Spend a Penny' calendar – a daily reminder of Thrislington Cubicles' core business. The Partners, UK, 1993.

Below Poster for an exhibition of D&AD Black Pencil winners: rare ideas with extraordinary power. Dentsu, Japan, 2013.

Above Christmas card for advertising agency Abbott Mead Vickers. Showing the camels riderless nudges the viewer towards the missing phrase. Abbott Mead Vickers BBDO, UK, 1982.

Nicholas Jenkins will be on holiday from July 23 till August 19

Left Announcement for The Jenkins Group. The image makes a kind of surreal sense even without the point about the hands. The Jenkins Group, UK, 1975.

美しき、ブラックリスト展

2013.10.19（SAT.）−2014.1.19（SUN.）
アド・ミュージアム東京（入場無料）

ADMT

D&AD Awards 1963–2013

HOMAGE

In one sense, this is design about design, using visual iconography as raw material. But it usually contains a bigger message, running the spectrum from respectful tribute to pointed critique. As many have discovered, it's difficult to launch any major identity now without a wave of instant 'homage'.

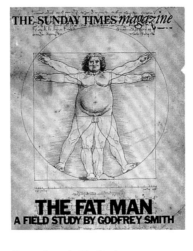

Above Cover for *The Sunday Times Magazine*. This is a fully committed spoof, down to the last Renaissance squiggle. Peter Brookes, UK, 1981.

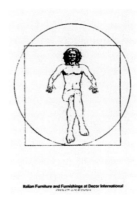

Above Poster for an exhibition of Italian furniture at the Italian Institute for Foreign Trade. See the chair when you go. Minale Tattersfield, UK, 1973.

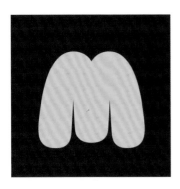

Above XXXL: a satirical nod to the effect of too many Big Macs. Maentis, France, 2013.

Above A merging of two identities for the super-powered Volkswagen Golf R32. DDB, New Zealand, 2004.

Above From the FoolsDoArt website, re-creating classic paintings using only office props and phone editing. Chris Limbrick & Francesco Fragomeni, USA, 2014.

Above Anti-racism T-shirt for Fashion Action, which borrows the homely anti-litter symbol of the 1950s. Low-key approach to an issue of high emotion. Judy Blame, UK, 1992.

Right Logo for a design firm. The first Mike to spot the possibility. Michael Stanard Inc, USA, 1989.

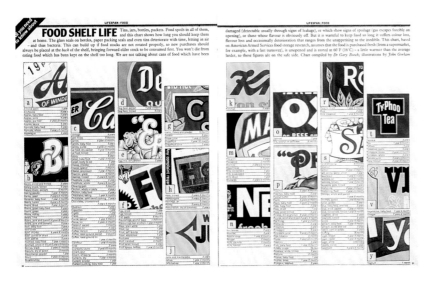

Above Illustration for a food feature in *The Sunday Times Magazine*. An alphabet of big-brand lettering, entirely repainted by the designer. John Gorham, UK, 1976.

Above May the froth be with you: tribute t-shirt. Anonymous.

Above Design for the twenty-first D&AD dinner. Celebrating the organization that gave designers more muscle. Pentagram, UK, 1983.

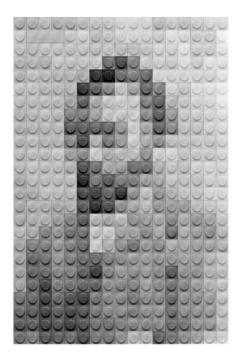

Left Tiffany & Co. trompe-l'oeil window display: surrealism on the high street. USA, 2011.

Right Cover depicting Muhammad Ali as Saint Sebastian, following his refusal to fight in the Vietnam war. George Lois / *Esquire*, USA, 1968.

Right Cover image from *New Songs for Children* for Wise Publications. One of the songs is 'The Candy Man'. John Gorham, UK, 1982.

Above Lego Masters: Van Gogh. Print ads celebrating the art of Lego. Geometry Global, Hong Kong, 2014.

Below Pixelated Eustace Tilley: updating the cover from the first edition of *The New Yorker* in 1925. Christoph Niemann / Francois Mouly, USA, 2002.

Below Some parodies of the London Olympics identity (Wolff Olins, UK, 2007) became as well known as the identity, Donovan Graphics, UK, 2007.

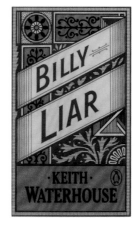

Above Logo for the tenth anniversary of The Paul Martin Design Company. It coincided with the Tour de France going past the door, so the studio entertained clients and friends for the day. The Paul Martin Design Company, UK, 1994.

Left Cover for a Penguin paperback. Taking advantage of the cultural reverberations of the legendary Woodbine cigarette pack. Tony Meeuwissen, UK, 1972.

Left Manetone: Manet re-created with thousands of Pantone chips. The Partners, UK, 2008.

Thanks, Steve. Graphic
tribute to Apple
founder Steve Jobs.
Jonathan Mak Long,
Hong Kong, 2011.

TROMPE L'OEIL

The collision here is between the real and the fake. Designers either mix illusion with reality, or use skilful artifice to allow one thing to pretend to be another. As the mind is forced to spend longer processing what it is seeing, so the message becomes more memorable.

Above Ballet classes. Tear off for details. Grupo Gallegos, USA, 2006.

Left Cover for *Do You Sincerely Want To Be Rich?* for Penguin. During the launch period the book was actually wrapped with the band, but subsequent editions made do with simulation. John McConnell, UK, 1971.

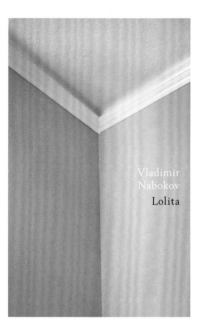

Above A claustrophobic room morphing into the book's title character. Jamie Keenan, UK, 2012.

Left Cover and inside pages for *The Connoisseur's Book of the Cigar*, complete with wood-grain printed paper, authentic border and Victorian chromolith centrepiece. The Pushpin Group, USA, 1967.

Above FedEx: Always first. Miami Ad School, Germany, 2011.

Left Record label for a trio with an unorthodox style. A little fakery with the black vinyl and sleight of hand with the 'O's produces a truly eccentric result. Bob Gill, USA, 1970.

Left Bandeck: skateboard design for those inevitable scrapes. Thinkmo, USA, 2006.

Above Packaging for Safeway. A plug does what it does best. Pocknell & Company, UK, 1989.

  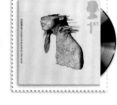  

Left Royal Mail stamps celebrating classic British album covers, with a glimpse of vinyl. Studio Dempsey, UK, 2007.

Book jacket for *Notes of a Dirty Old Man* published by Melzer. More than just a spine. Mendell & Oberer, Germany, 1979.

Above Illustration for *Wallpaper** magazine: a 3D room set featuring products from the issue. Noma Bar, UK, 2012.

Above Animal Farm: limited-edition tent design. FieldCandy, UK, 2012.

Left Ticket validator: street art on ticket machine. Mentalgassi, Germany, 2008.

Above Cover for the Pelican paperback *The Parent's Schoolbook*. This is now an old design, but it was born aged. John Gorham, UK, 1976.

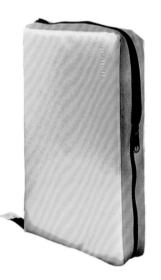

Above D&AD Annual cover. A case for the famous pencils. Michael Johnson, UK, 1995.

Above The 'Have a break' slogan brought invitingly to life. JWT London, UK, 2009.

Above Packaging for Boots first-aid plasters. Embossed examples identify product types, and bring a little stature to a humble product. The Partners, UK, 1986.

Above Packaging for Woolworths swing bin liners. A mundane purchase delivering a little pleasure. Coley Porter Bell, UK, 1987.

Below A global brand with a sense of fun. Turner Duckworth, UK/USA, 2006.

Proof bags for printer
Gavin Martin Colournet
turn every delivery into
something unexpected.
Magpie Studio, UK, 2010.

PUNS & REBUSES

Puns exploit the different meanings of two words of similar sound. Koestler defined the mechanism with great wit: 'two strings of thought tied together by an acoustic knot'. Just make sure both halves of the pun are relevant. The rebus plays a similar game – a puzzle combining letters and images that invite decoding.

Right Poster for the Association of Photographers show 'Ten Ate: an exhibition of food photography'. No doubt the designer contributed the title as well. The Partners, UK, 1990.

TEN ATE: AN EXHIBITION OF FOOD PHOTOGRAPHY

BEAR WITH ME

Above Puns with bears are the best. Illustration by Matt Blease, UK, 2014.

Above High-street punning reaches its apex with this Plymouth hairdresser: the co-founder had German connections. Anthony Braddon, UK, 1982.

Right Slogan for New York. Probably the most famous, and copied, piece of graphic wit in the world. Milton Glaser, USA, 1975.

Left Cover of the special Money Issue of *Designer* magazine. The bank manager, of course, is somewhat under-represented. Peter Brookes, UK, 1981.

Designer

Money Issue

September 1981

BANK MANAGER

PB

"You're ridiculously overdrawn"

Right Identity for The Breakfast Club, a meeting place for businesswomen in New York. The pun spans the Atlantic, linking the Americans' small crisp batter cake with the aimless chitchat of the Brits. Pentagram, USA, 1986.

Van Rouge

Above Logo for the launch range of Citroën small delivery vans. An unobtrusive application on the vehicle allows the idea to be inadvertently discovered. Smith & Milton, UK, 1986.

PORTUGAL

Above Playing with words and images, from the sketchbook of illustrator Luiz Stockler, UK, 2014.

Left Title of brochure promoting Trickett & Webb. This rebus has perfect balance, and a second layer of satisfaction in the emphasis on the key senses. Trickett & Webb, UK, 1991.

Q8

Left Name and identity for Kuwait Petroleum's European petrol-station chain. A letter-number combination is memorable, even if the penny doesn't drop. Wolff Olins, UK, 1986.

Detail from a poster for
IBM. A classic identity
smiles at itself. The
designer spotted that
nature was on his side,
putting bees in stripes.
Paul Rand, USA, 1981.

TAKING IT LITERALLY

A useful shortcut to an interesting idea,
usually involving a transition from the abstract
to the concrete. Design here is self-evident
rather than enigmatic, providing an instant
click as the mind makes the same leap.
The effect is like short-circuiting the brief:
if you want to create a sausage brand,
why not brand a sausage?

Left Poster for Pirelli. Pre-computer, the lettering was laboriously drawn by hand over several days. Fletcher Forbes Gill, UK, 1961.

The British Land Company PLC Annual Report and Accounts 1991

Above Cover of an annual report for British Land. For inside illustrations the designers used British landscape paintings with entertaining quotes such as 'I am not the type who wants to go back to the land; I am the type who wants to go back to the hotel.' CDT Design, UK, 1992.

Above Packaging company website literally under construction. B&W Studio, UK, 2007.

Above Duracell batteries: a powerful energy source. Grey Singapore, 2014.

Above Unambiguous exhibition graphics for D&AD New Blood show. The Oldham Goddard Experience, UK, 2014.

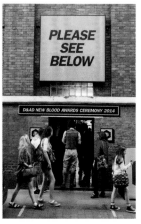

Right Cleaning company gives your screen a spray and wipe. The Partners, UK, 2009.

Helvetica
Neue Bold

Courier
Regular

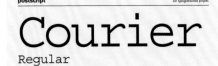

Eurostile
Bold Extended Two

Künstler
Script Medium

TIMES
TEN BOLD ITALIC

Verdana
regular

Fraktur
Fette

UNIVERS
CONDENSED BOLD

Bodoni
Book

If fonts were dogs. Prints by Grafisches Büro, Austria, 2002.

Above Page on the history of letter forms from the magazine *U&lc*. The designer emphasizes the structure of the letter R with its component column, bowl and tail. WBMG Inc, USA, 1992.

Above Suitably patriotic identity for a British food game show. Optomen / BBC, UK, 2006.

Left & below Words come to life and express themselves typographically. Brownjohn, Chermayeff & Geismar, USA, 1962.

Above Image from a booklet promoting Conways' photographic equipment for distorting images. Fletcher Forbes Gill, UK, 1965.

Above Logo for Octopus Productions, contractors specializing in conferences, promotions and conventions. Many hands make for a light touch. Minale Tattersfield, UK, 1970.

Above Moving card for photographer Laurie Evans. A device built around the client's calling. Lewis Moberly, UK, 1993.

Left Packaging for Boots rubber gloves. Finding magic in a mundane product. Lewis Moberly, UK, 1994.

Left Meloncholy. From the Tutti Frutti series finding new meanings in foods. Sarah Illenberger, Germany, 2011.

Mr Singh's Bangras: Indian sausages with henna-inspired branding. And not just on the packaging. The Partners, UK, 2009.

EXPECTATIONS CONFOUNDED

This is graphic wit with a punchline. The design sets up expectations only to explode them. This technique exploits the brain's wish to find a pattern. The recognition comes first, as we interpret the cues and see what we expect to see. The surprise comes later.

Left Season's greetings from advertising agency Mavity Gilmore. For once there's something at the end of the false trail... possibly. Mavity Gilmore, UK, 1985.

Above A brochure of contrasting pairs for James McNaughton Paper. Radley Yeldar, UK, 2000.

Below Promotion for photographer Marshall Harrington. This one really lulls the unsuspecting mind. Vitro Robertson, USA, 1988.

Right Promotional package for photographer Doug Bradshaw. The disarming power of self-deprecation. Henderson & Company, USA, 1992.

Right A book cover of book spines, the rationale in the title. David Pearson / Type as Image, UK, 2008.

Above Announcement for Rod Kilpatrick. A-below-the-belt deception. Fallon McElligott, USA, 1988.

WORDS LOOK MUCH NICER WHEN THEY'RE HAND LETTERED

ALISON CARMICHAEL   Lettering Artist   phone/fax +44 (0)20 8789 3509   mobile +44 (0)775 398 6699   www.alisoncarmichael.com

INCONGRUITY

This is the juxtaposition that jars –
the builder and the hummingbird, the
human and the animal, the Christmas gift
and the barbed wire. As two apparently
conflicting elements are combined in
one image, we are invited to question our
preconceptions – of work and play, the city
and wildlife, or the holiness of Helvetica.

Above Cover for *Esquire*
magazine, introducing the
'Instant Vin Rouge' sachet.
Marvellous cover, but luckily
it never happened. Henry
Wolf, USA, 1958.

Above Mafia cookbook.
Recipes as enjoyed by
the godfathers in a book
that has been physically
shot with a rifle. vLSP,
The Netherlands, 1975.

Above City textures
appropriated to advertise
Bronx zoo. Y&R New York,
USA, 2006.

Above Identity for building
contractor Bovis – the famous
hummingbird. The identity
consultant Wally Olins said
of the original presentation to
the board: 'I've had some bad
receptions in my time, but I've
never had anything like this.'

Keith Joseph, subsequently
a cabinet minister, said:
'I don't understand it. Explain it
again.' Of course it was a great
success, so much so that even
after being bought by P&O, the
company refused to give it up.
Wolff Olins, UK, 1971.

Left Illustration announcing
the show 'Communicating
with Children' at the American
Institute of Graphic Arts.
The shock of little horrors.
R.O. Blechman, USA, 1979.

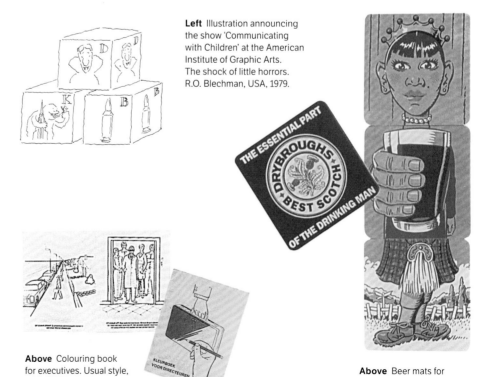

Above Colouring book
for executives. Usual style,
new subject matter. vLSP,
The Netherlands, 1972.

Above Beer mats for
Drybroughs. Mix and mismatch.
The Partners, UK, 1986.

WWF *Give a hand to wildlife*

Above Body painter Guido Daniele brings WWF's fundraising message to life. Saatchi & Saatchi Simko, Switzerland, 2008.

Above Detail from a Helvetica alphabet with snow, created as a Christmas greetings card for Typeshop. An idea borrowed from children's books, which dares to defile a revered typeface. John Gorham, UK, 1969.

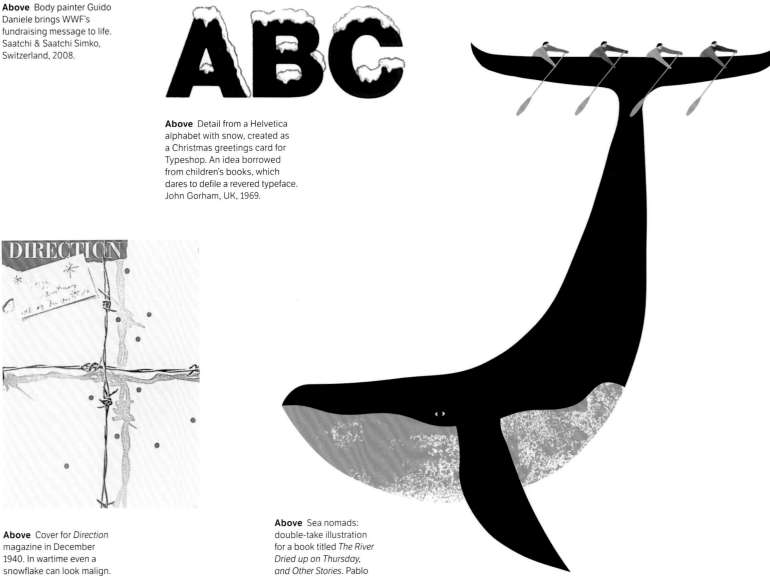

Above Cover for *Direction* magazine in December 1940. In wartime even a snowflake can look malign. Paul Rand, USA, 1940.

Above Sea nomads: double-take illustration for a book titled *The River Dried up on Thursday, and Other Stories*. Pablo Amargo, Spain, 2006.

ECONOMY

Wit at its most satisfying – finding the answer within a requirement of the brief. If the product has to appear, transform it. If the stamp needs perforations, maybe that's all it needs. Some ideas present themselves like miracles of nature, waiting to be discovered. What if 'Friends' had aired on a Thursday?

Above Packaging for Boots own-label hosiery. Normally a window is just a window. Lewis Moberly, UK, 1991.

Below Marinated sprat fillets never looked so tasty. Stockholm Design Lab, Sweden, 2011.

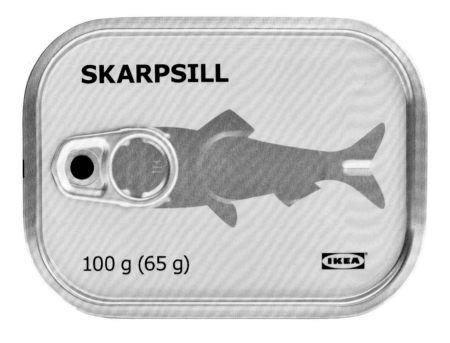

Above Packaging for Toblerone. The standard brand packaging is artfully dressed up for special occasions. KSDP Pentagraph, South Africa, 1992.

Below Pack for Clinomyn Smokers' Toothpaste, making a virtue of necessity. The Chase, UK, 1992.

Left Poster for Bic pens. For the pen, by the pen, of the pen. Ruedi Külling, Switzerland, 1968.

Left Milking cow: concept illustration. Pablo Amargo, Spain, 2008.

Below Logo for design consultancy Carter Wong. A little typographic sleight of hand gets double value from the G in the firm's name. Carter Wong, UK, 1994.

CARTER WONG PARTNERS

Above Teaser for the final episode of 'Friends', airing Friday. 4Creative, UK, 2005.

Right Poster for a sailing regatta. The designer discovers the wonderful marine qualities of a torn edge. Mendell & Oberer, Germany, 1985.

Left Self-promotion poster for design consultancy Anspach Grossman Portugal. Showing who they are by what they do. Anspach Grossman Portugal, USA, 1990.

Kieler
Woche
1986
21.–
29.
Juni

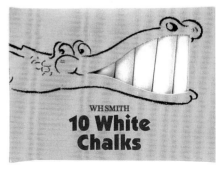

WH SMITH
10 White Chalks

Left Chalks pack from a range of children's paints and drawing materials for WHSmith. The parent can see the product, and the child can see the funny side. The Ian Logan Design Company, UK, 1990.

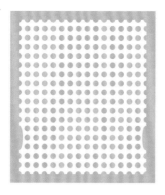

Above Proposal for a perforated Royal Mail stamp. Daniel Eatock, UK, 2014.

Above Film-strip minimalism for post-production house The Mill. North, UK, 1998.

Right Identity for film production company Brooks Baker Fulford. The idea was conceived in a haze of wine in the days of white shirts and white laminate conference tables. Crosby Fletcher Forbes, UK, 1969.

Below Letterhead for opticians: take a close look at their initials. True North, UK, 2006.

Below Egg preserving its modesty for Pret A Manger. Pret A Manger, Balloon Dog, UK, 2011.

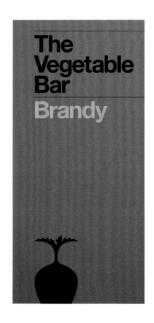

Below A pop-up evening bar on the site of a vegetable market. Magpie Studio, UK, 2007.

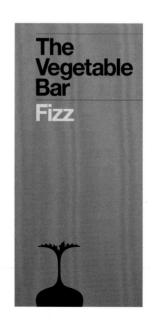

A product shot
with a poetic twist.
TBWA\NEBOKO, The
Netherlands, 2005.

COINCIDENCE

The greatest friend of the witty designer. Where economy draws on a 'given' that is standard or straightforward, coincidence exploits a fortuitous circumstance or connection. The wit is not so much crafted as spotted: the skill is in staying alert.

Left Christmas card from LA film-maker Arnold Schwartzman. The Hollywood sign is so recognizable that its constituent meaning can no longer be seen. Arnold Schwartzman, US, 1979.

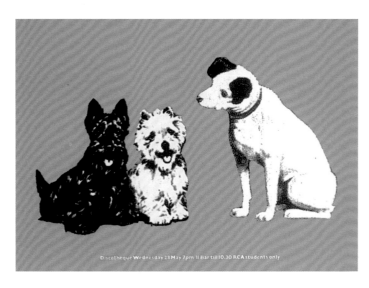

Above Poster for a night of drinking and dancing at the Royal College of Art – a nod to Black & White whisky and HMV. Laurence Bradbury, UK, 1974.

Above Promotion for finished artist Cliff Smithson. An idea that unites the man and his materials. Jim Sutherland, UK, 1993.

Above Identity for advertising agency Leagas Delaney. The agency's Egyptian Revival building prompts a luck-driven solution, where the three 'A's in the name are not only turned into pyramids, but together form another pyramid. The Partners, UK, 1986.

Above left Poster for a Milton Glaser lecture. The great man speaks at eight. Robert Burns, Canada, 1977.

Left Cover for *Designer* magazine. The magazine rule was, whoever designs the cover also designs the masthead. The result was never more integrated than when Mrs Thatcher held the first tentative, exploratory, uncertain Government seminar on design. Springett Associates, UK, 1982.

Right Poster for AFAEP exhibition of twenty-two contemporary women photographers. The number becomes the focal point of the idea. The Partners, UK, 1987.

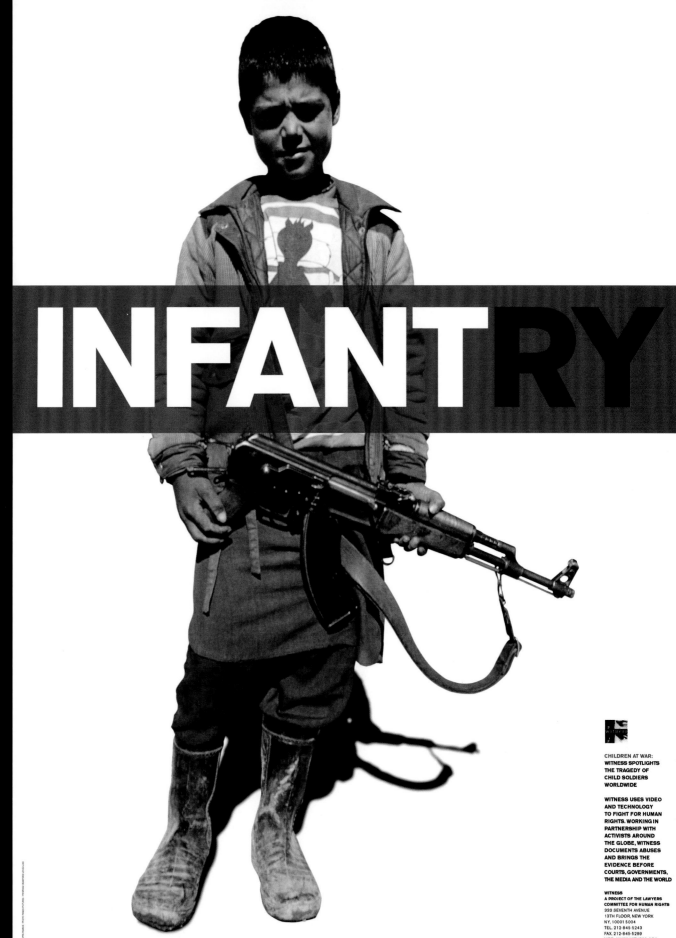

INFANTRY

CHILDREN AT WAR:
WITNESS SPOTLIGHTS
THE TRAGEDY OF
CHILD SOLDIERS
WORLDWIDE

WITNESS USES VIDEO
AND TECHNOLOGY
TO FIGHT FOR HUMAN
RIGHTS. WORKING IN
PARTNERSHIP WITH
ACTIVISTS AROUND
THE GLOBE, WITNESS
DOCUMENTS ABUSES
AND BRINGS THE
EVIDENCE BEFORE
COURTS, GOVERNMENTS,
THE MEDIA AND THE WORLD

WITNESS
A PROJECT OF THE LAWYERS
COMMITTEE FOR HUMAN RIGHTS
333 SEVENTH AVENUE
13TH FLOOR, NEW YORK
NY, 10001 5004
TEL. 212-845-5243
FAX. 212-845-5299
WEB: WWW.WITNESS.ORG
E-MAIL:WITNESS@LCHR.ORG

Children At War:
poster for human-
rights charity
Witness. Harry
Pearce, Pentagram,
UK, 2007

F[knife+fork]ASTING

A medically-approved
no-gimmick guide to the ultimate diet
SHIRLEY ROSS

Above Cover for a Pan
paperback on the ultimate
diet. The designer was given
Fasting as the title, but
saw greater possibilities.
Paul Martin, UK, 1978.

Right Poster for
an Association of
Photographers exhibition
of nude images.
The Partners, UK, 1999.

Left Logos for the Earth
Art Institute. One powerful
word is hidden within another.
Top, Kiyoshi Kanai Inc, and
below, Michael Stanard Inc.
USA, 1992.

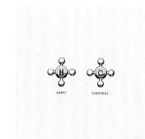

Left & below Identity and
Christmas card for a heating
engineer. Adapting the
identity for a Christmas card
provides the twist in the tail.
The Partners, UK, 1986.

CENTRAL   HEATING

Naked

Left A sporting
event for wounded
soldiers: the solution
in the name. Lambie-
Nairn, UK, 2014.

INVICTUS
GAMES
LONDON 2014

SHIFT: TIME

Graphic wit with the added dimension of time. The audience is invited to consider what happened first or guess what will come next. It is a storyteller's technique, which invites the audience to complete the narrative. Sometimes it is also a trick – suggesting a history where none exists.

Right Poster for a spoof anti-dog campaign. A Royal College of Art student thinks the worst and wins his first award of many. Nick Wurr, UK, 1977.

Left Neglected works: aged brickwork and concrete reimagined as art. Basile Cuvelier / Seth Armstrong-Twigg, UK, 2014.

Above Christmas gift promotion for Topic Typesetting. Just occasionally it helps to say things twice. Minale Tattersfield, UK, 1978.

Right Coaster with etched grooves to suggest rivers being carved by condensation. Part of the Slow airport lounge concept for the busy traveller. Grid Worldwide Branding and Tonic Design, South Africa, 2010.

Right Christmas card for the Quintons. Mrs Quinton, as all their friends would know, was pregnant at the time. Greg Quinton, UK, 1993.

Above Title page of a self-promotional booklet. A how-I-got-there idea, which gently mocks designerly subtlety. Bob Gill, USA, 1968.

Above Personal greetings card. How Christmas got its tree. Lucy Walker, UK, 1984.

Above Talking about his generation: promo for an exhibition on youth culture. Coy! Communications, UK, 2011.

Left & right Book for photographer Jason Orton documenting the effects of coastal erosion, the pages crumbling with the landscape. The Chase, UK, 2003.

Left Stamps celebrating the two hundredth anniversary of Ordnance Survey. Showing Hamstreet (the village in Kent where the first mapmaking surveys were undertaken) in 1816, 1906, 1959 and 1991. Howard Brown, UK, 1991.

Left & below Poster for Black Sabbath's comeback album, appearing to emerge from layers of old flyposters. McCann Copenhagen, Denmark, 2013.

Below Stomach postcard for Restaurant Florent in New York. An apparently unassuming little bistro in the meat district advertises itself as interesting. M&Co, USA, 1991.

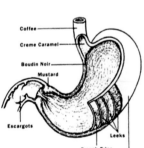
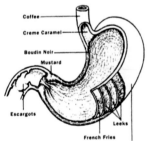

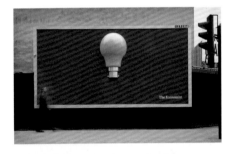

Left Motion-sensor poster for the thinking person's magazine. Abbott Mead Vickers BBDO, UK, 2004.

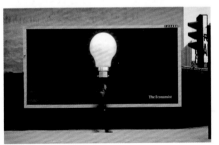

Right Pages from the cookbook *Eerlijke Gerechten*. It comes ready stained, with clippings, bay leaves and scribbled notes inside, starting out where most end up. vLSP, The Netherlands, 1972.

Opposite Timeless Beauty. From the Mag + Art series mixing magazines and classical art to create portraits with a third dimension of time. Eisen Bernard Bernardo, The Philippines, 2014.

SHIFT: SCALE

Nothing disrupts expectation quite like a shift in scale. As a technique, it directly links recognition with surprise. For a moment, we rediscover a childlike sense of wonder. We are Gulliver in a land too minuscule or gigantic to make sense.

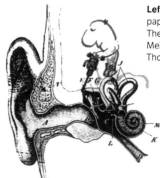

Left Cover for a Pelican paperback on *Noise*. The ear under attack. Mel Calman and Philip Thompson, UK, 1972.

Below Promotional mailer for Westerham Press. The eyeglass allows inspection of the smallest brochure ever, set in one point type, to demonstrate just how fine print can be. The Partners, UK, 1994.

Right Moving announcement for Bobby & Bob Gill. Displacing attention from 'where' to 'what'. Bob Gill, USA, 1968.

Above Booklet for a car rental firm. Four words on the cover make both an ethical and a literal point. Bob Gill, USA, 1970.

Above Promotional hoarding for Land Securities, owner of Piccadilly Lights in London. Hat-trick, UK, 2008.

Left Image from a calendar for Face Ronchetti. O is for October and for Harry Obese, a letter with a great big personality. John Gorham and Howard Brown, UK, 1982.

Right Small is beautiful: pencil wood and graphite sculptures. Dalton Ghetti, USA, 2007.

Right The Binoculars Building in Los Angeles, built for advertising agency Chiat/Day. Frank Gehry with Claes Oldenburg and Coosje van Bruggen, USA, 1991.

Above Giant envelope mailing for Bass Developments. The enormous letter inside announced the availability of an unusually large site. The Partners, UK, 1992.

Below Window display to advertise retail space to let for S C Properties. A giant surveyor's tape runs the whole length of a corner site. The Partners, UK, 1992.

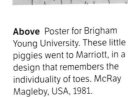

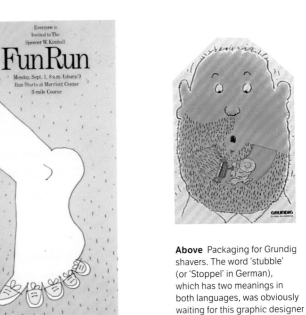

Above Packaging for Grundig shavers. The word 'stubble' (or 'Stoppel' in German), which has two meanings in both languages, was obviously waiting for this graphic designer to come along. Heye & Partner, Germany, 1988.

Above Poster for Brigham Young University. These little piggies went to Marriott, in a design that remembers the individuality of toes. McRay Magleby, USA, 1981.

Below Big excuses: mailer for Boss Print parading the most common excuses from printers. Hat-trick, UK, 2006.

Above Office development branding, featuring Bob, an oversized white plastic figure from architects' models. Radford Wallis, UK, 2006.

Above The Guitar Store in Southampton: making creative use of security grilles. Ed (the manager), UK, 2008.

Above Creative sectioning of a giant floorspace to show prospective tenants where divider walls could go. Radford Wallis, UK, 2011.

Right Advertising the Smart Car's ability to park anywhere, much like a bicycle. BBDO Toronto, Canada, 2010.

Below Volkswagen advertising campaign encouraging people to use the stairs – with a giant, functioning keyboard. DDB Stockholm, Sweden, 2009.

Right Packaging for Waitrose soft drinks. More apple or melon than before. Miller Sutherland/ Blackburn's, UK, 1992.

Left Good-humoured naming for a modestly sized IT store in Macclesfield. Tim Swift, UK, 1985.

Left Exhibition of postage stamp design in locations around London: a trail of mini masterpieces. Hat-trick, UK, 2012.

Opposite Giant rubber duck touring the world, by artist Florentijn Hofman, The Netherlands, 2007.

Above Hoarding system for the Post Office. Business as usual during building works: a solution in which envelopes and parcels figure large. Minale Tattersfield, UK, 1984.

Right Paper Dreams: installation for Art Basel, Miami Beach, celebrating the wonder of the waterfront. Luis Pons, USA, 2013.

Above Marking five years of the Levi's Ambiance Mix collection with a lamp post, a paint pot and some red foil. King George, Belgium, 2010.

Right Big nudes: poster for an exhibition in the School of Visual Arts gallery in New York. Milton Glaser, USA, 1969

Below & right Concentrated designer monograph: 800 pages, 50 x 38 mm. Irma Boom, The Netherlands, 2010.

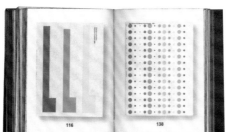

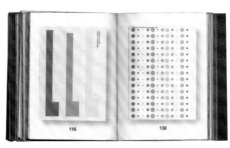

Above What's up, doc? Handpainted hoarding for Warner Bros' NYC flagship store. The Partners / Warner Bros, USA, 1996.

Packaging for Harvey
Nichols' Christmas pudding,
the traditional hidden
sixpence now much harder
to miss. Michael Nash
Associates, UK, 1993.

SHIFT: VIEW

A technique that includes but is not restricted to trompe l'oeil. The viewer is invited to look at the world differently: up becomes down, front becomes back, life becomes art. Viewers actively enter the conundrum, as they realign themselves to unlock the puzzle.

Above Packaging for Cricketer's Gin. Followers of the game will notice the shape of the bottle. Michael Peters & Partners, UK, 1985.

Above Notch Showroom for the BEST Products Company. From the Peeling Project, examining buildings as art. SITE, USA, 1977.

Right Disconcerting fuzzy wallclock for M&Co Labs. M&Co, USA, 1989.

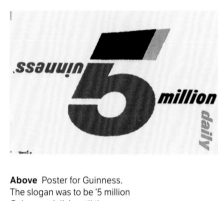

Above Poster for Guinness. The slogan was to be '5 million Guinness daily', until the designer gave it a twist. Abram Games, UK, 1958.

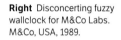

Left *New York Times Book Review* illustration for a book on asymmetry. Christoph Niemann, Germany, 2000.

Below Illustration from *The Penguin André François*. 2D is translated into reality. André François, France, 1955.

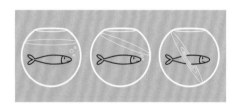

Left Detail from Aspen International Design Conference poster. It was the eleventh attempt to solve the problem by Michael Bierut, who says 'a lot of the best solutions emerge from exhaustion or frustration.' Pentagram, USA, 1987.

Left Image from the poster for a Fukuda exhibition at Keio in Tokyo. Positives play against negatives. Shigeo Fukuda, Japan, 1975.

Left Christmas card for F Bender. Elevated greetings from a manufacturer of disposable tableware. The Partners, UK, 1992.

Opposite The Upside Down House. Art installation using a false façade. Alex Chinneck, UK, 2013.

Above Either a chair and a camera case, or a sheep. From the personal sketchbook of Dominic Wilcox, UK, 2011.

Above Invitation for a client's private party. The viewer moves the horizon back to the right angle, and enjoys a drink. Pentagram, UK, 1985.

Above Mail-order brochure for the Ladybird collection at Woolworths. A gymnastic spectacular, shot in a studio with a very high ceiling. The Partners, UK, 1991.

Left Logo for New Man. A perfect inversion. Raymond Loewy International, UK, 1966.

Right Image from poster 'Adopt an Animal at Whipsnade Park Zoo'. The baby returns the favour to the stork. Minale Tattersfield, UK, 1987.

Above Logo, or possibly two logos, for Truce vodka. Turner Duckworth, UK / USA, 2003.

Above Ceramic egg boxes, from a personal project exploring the three-dimensional illustration of graphic ideas. Malcolm Kennard Associates, UK, 1976.

The Gargoyle presents

PETER BJORN & JOHN

w/ El Perro Del Mar

Friday, Nov. 13th

doors – 7:30 | show – 8

$15/public | free w/ WashU ID

Left Perspective-challenging gig poster. Logan Alexander, USA, 2009.

Left Poster for The Association of Photographers Blu-Tack Exhibition. The Partners, UK, 1989.

Left Letterhead for Theo Crosby. For an architect in a tower, the designer thinks vertically, and takes steps to use both sides of the paper. Pentagram, UK, 1977.

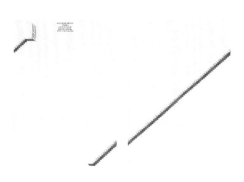

Above Eurostar First Class catering: trompe-l'oeil graphics set a playfully upmarket tone. GBH, UK, 2005.

Above Ambient campaign for online gallery britart.com, breaking down barriers between art and life. Mother, UK, 2000.

Above Poster for an exhibition at the Royal College of Art. An idea beyond reality. Ray Gregory, UK, 1971.

Above Wrong film, right poster. Kevos Van Der Meiren, USA, 2012.

TRANSFORMATIONS

A gentle way of colliding two ideas is to turn the first into the second. The transition may reveal itself slowly to the viewer, or we may see the result of a preceding journey that is implied. Either way, the process becomes part of the idea.

Above Poster for the Royal College of Art Film and Television Degree Show. As wit goes, quite sharp. Paul Martin, UK, 1977.

Above Identity for building firm Property Specialists. One man's brick is a designer's house. David Stuart, UK, 1981.

Above Invitation to the Dallas Symphony Orchestra League Ball. The invitation specifically mentions cocktails. RBMM, USA, 1983.

Right Christmas flick-book from a design consultancy. How Santa got to be red. Robinson Lambie-Nairn, UK, 1982.

Above Cover for *Designer* magazine. The main article was about design as an invisible export, and the brief was for an invisible cover. John Gorham, UK, 1978.

Left Illustration for *Radio Times*. A tribute to Alfred Hitchcock, the maestro of horror, on his eightieth birthday. Peter Brookes, UK, 1979.

Below Annual report for solar energy company Austria Solar, printed in light-sensitive ink that reveals itself only in sunlight. Serviceplan, Germany, 2011.

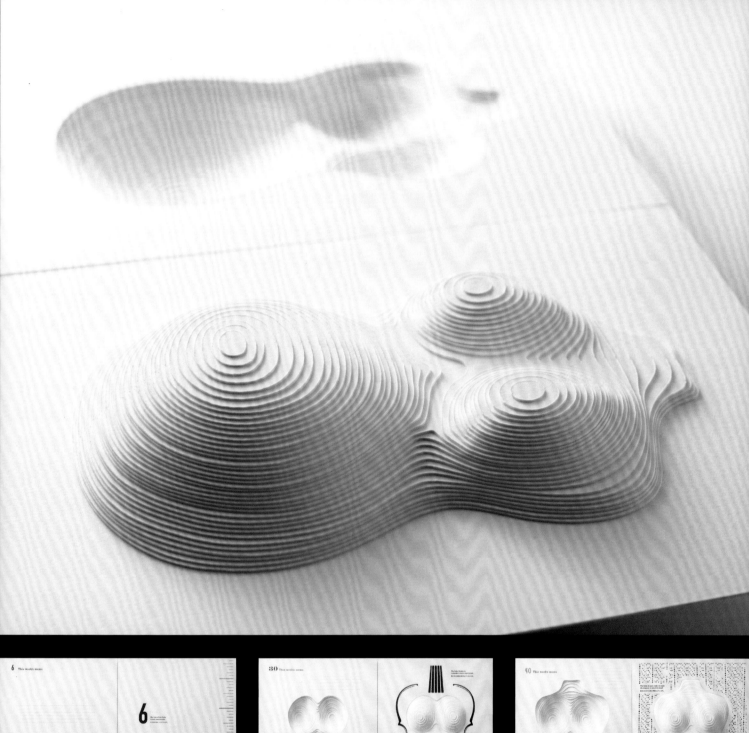

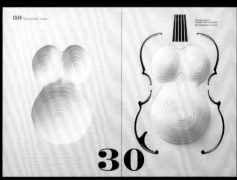

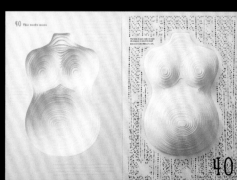

Kishokai *Mother Book:*
a pregnancy diary with
embossed pages that
grow as the weeks pass.
Dentsu, Japan, 2013.

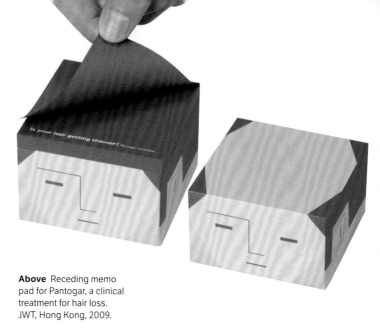

Above Receding memo pad for Pantogar, a clinical treatment for hair loss. JWT, Hong Kong, 2009.

Above Illustration for *Swiat* weekly magazine. An artist protesting against power politics reinterprets loss of face. Jan Lenica, Poland, 1956.

Above & left Posters for Dubonnet. The series ran for about twenty years and became one of the most famous examples of graphic wit in the world. Cassandre, France, 1932.

Right Poster for the War Office. You eat what you sow. Abram Games, UK, 1942.

Below Invitation to a high-school reunion. Over ten years, memories fade. RBMM, USA, 1983.

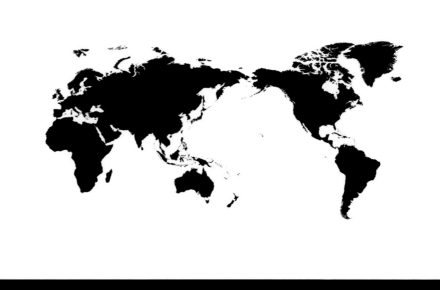

Piece Together For
Peace: the world map
rearranged into the
twelve animals of
the Chinese zodiac.
Kentaro Nagai /
Graflex Directions,
Japan, 2007–12.

SERIES OF TWISTS

Some ideas lead to others. A theme is
established, which is then extended and
reinterpreted, either within a single piece,
or in a series that unfolds over time.
The effect is game-like: the rules are
established, then the playing begins.

Below Seventh anniversary
booklet for a design consultancy.
The material for a seventh
anniversary is wool: the
theme is the seven deadly
sins. The Partners, UK, 1990.

Above A series of posters
for Art & Architecture, an
independent pressure group.
Pentagram, UK, 1972.

Left Packaging for
Cleeves. This is where
sweet thoughts lead.
Blackburn's, UK, 1993.

Above Poster for the
celebration to mark thirty-
five years of music at the
Royal Festival Hall.
Musical notation as
a design playground.
The Partners, UK, 1987.

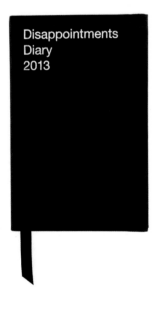
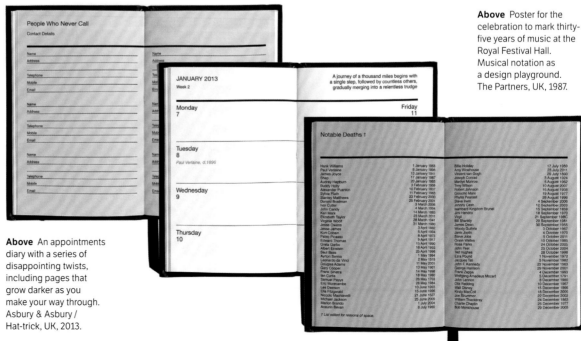

Above An appointments
diary with a series of
disappointing twists,
including pages that
grow darker as you
make your way through.
Asbury & Asbury /
Hat-trick, UK, 2013.

Right Direct mail for paper company Wiggins Teape. Business cards for anyone who wants to make ripples, be they upholsterers, financiers, vets or computer programmers. Silk Pearce, UK, 1992.

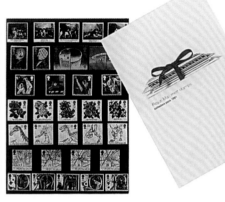

Below Poster series for Interior Design International. Ten posters show the ten types of content to be seen at the Earls Court exhibition. Pentagram, UK, 1992.

Above Collectors' pack for Royal Mail stamps. The eight special issues set the themes (here dogs, scientific achievements, Europe in space, sport 91, roses and dinosaurs) and the designers do envelopes to match. Williams & Phoa, UK, 1991.

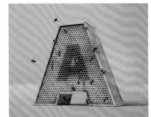

Above A continually evolving AA identity for the Advertising Association. The Partners, UK, 2014.

POWER OF WORDS

Writing plays its part everywhere in design, but sometimes it takes the lead role. While much is made of 'tone of voice', these examples draw their energy from an idea, which motivates the tone. Design plays a key part, either clearing the stage for the words, or skilfully setting an expectation that the writing subverts.

Right Moving card for Baxter and Bailey, relocating to 54B. Baxter and Bailey / Reed Words, UK, 2014.

Below Life turns in a sentence: poetic insurance company marketing. Leo Burnett Schweiz AG, Zurich, Switzerland, 2011.

Right Limited edition release of Marmite to mark the Queen's Diamond Jubilee. Hornall Anderson, UK, 2012.

She's my everything went wrong.

For all life's twists and turns:
Flexible financial plans.

SwissLife

I never want children are great.

For all life's twists and turns:
Flexible financial plans.

SwissLife

We've got everything we need a loan.

For all life's twists and turns:
Flexible financial plans.

SwissLife

Listen, I don't wanna be a whiner but nobody here really appreciates me or has the slightest idea how creative I could be if they'd just keep their blundering meathooks to themselves and stop trashing my stuff and now I've got this *1991 Addy Call for Entries* in front of me and all I can think is how good it would feel to win but let's face it, 1991 was a sorry year and frankly a big dud for me since I don't have any decent work to show, even though the cleaning lady seemed to like that piece I did a while back and maybe I should stop being so modest and seriously think about entering it and maybe a few more pieces, too, I mean they might be better than I'm giving myself credit for, they might actually win and jeez, if I won, it would be complete vindication, nirvana, it would be just like in my dreams, people would leap up to give me a standing ovation and crowd around me to they'd fight to woo me away, everybody would be smarmy and coveting, and all that would be just fine, it would be terrific, if I won all my clients would personally thank me for working on their accounts, all my co-workers would throw me a gala victory party, all my ex-lovers would rue the day they left me and it's a sure bet if I won I would get more respect, more recognition, more yeah maybe a bonus, and maybe even a bonus on top of a salary raise, maybe even a huge Christmas bonus on top of that because nobody's more talented than me me me

Left Call for entries for the Phoenix Advertising Club. The subtext of competition entry. PS Studios, USA, 1991.

Below Happily counter-intuitive signage for National Trust properties. The Click, UK, 2013.

One bright and
blustery September morning,
bit
by
bit,
box
by
box,
Baxter and
Bailey
bagged their
belongings and
bade farewell to 6 Hoxton Square.
Bravely
biting
back the emotion, they stepped
boldly out into a
brave new world. Feeling
blue, of course. A little
bittersweet.
Because the
business
began here, after all.
Brainstorms
blew through here.
Battles were won.
Breakthroughs were made.
Brands were
born (and reborn). And
bottles were downed (now and then).
But now it's time to go.
Bye-
bye,
baby studio.
Bonjour,
brand new chapter. New
bookshelves. New
buddies. New
briefs. New
biscuits.
Break out the
balloons and
bunting and
booze!
Because
bright days lie
before us.
Blank pages wait to be filled.
Broad horizons to be explored.
Beginnings are
brilliant. Why not
beetle round soon and
behold our lovely new home at
54B.

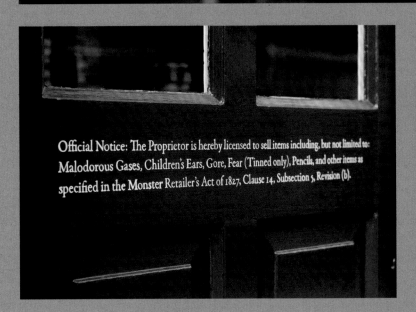

Hoxton Street Monster Supplies

ESTᴰ 1818

~ Bespoke and Everyday Items for the Living, Dead and Undead ~

Official Notice: The Proprietor is hereby licensed to sell items including, but not limited to: Malodorous Gases, Children's Ears, Gore, Fear (Tinned only), Pencils, and other items as specified in the Monster Retailer's Act of 1827, Clause 14, Subsection 5, Revision (b).

ONLY ONE GIANT IN THE SHOP AT A TIME

·

CUSTOMERS ARE POLITELY REQUESTED TO REFRAIN FROM EATING THE STAFF

·

NOCTURNAL OPENING (BY APPOINTMENT) FOR VAMPIRE CUSTOMERS ONLY

BEANS (MAGIC OR OTHERWISE) ARE NOT ACCEPTED AS PAYMENT

·

HUMANS WELCOME, BUT ENTIRELY AT THEIR OWN RISK

·

ANGRY MOBS PLEASE DOUSE YOUR TORCHES BEFORE ENTERING THE SHOP

Hoxton Street Monster Supplies: London branch of the 826 Valencia network of inner-city literacy centres hidden behind fantastical shopfronts, originally an ingenious way round planning laws. We Made This, UK, 2010.

Above RNLI Homewares: the language of the shipping forecast relocated to the kitchen. The Workshop / Roger Horberry, UK, 2013.

Below Wine bottle persuading people to buy beer instead. Bring it to the counter for a discount. Colenso BBDO Auckland, New Zealand, 2012.

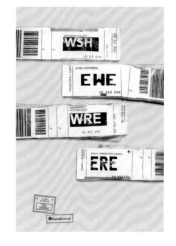

Above Three-letter airport luggage tags turned into playful messages about travel. Ogilvy & Mather, UK, 2013.

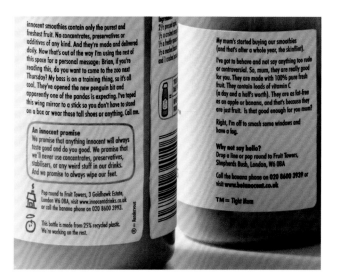

nature made brussel sprouts. we all make mistakes. but at least she* made strawberries too. innocent by nature

Above Innocent Drinks: the archetypal brand built on witty words, from packaging to posters. Innocent / Dan Germain. UK, 2007.

Above & right Puccino's coffee shop: every item branded by the same designer–writer. Jim Smith / Waldo Pancake, UK, 2001.

Opposite A Picture Speaks a Thousand Words: mailer for photographer describing one of his pictures and inviting you to his website to see it. The Chase / Nick Asbury, UK, 2011.

This picture is what you see when you find yourself walking through BBC Television Centre during the recording of 'Strictly Come Dancing' and you push open a door marked 'Not for broadcast' and walk inside. This picture is what I drew in the team-building workshop when they asked me how I saw the future of our company. This picture is 64 per cent sky, 33 per cent sand and 3 per cent built environment. This picture is what it was like when you told that joke the other night. This picture details the measures that will be taken to ensure a banking crisis on this scale can never happen again. This picture is why I love you. To walk from the front of this picture to the back of this picture would take about 25 minutes. This picture is what I heard when you said you were sorry for any distress caused and that naturally you take full responsibility. This picture is a difficult spot-the-ball competition. This picture is of Simon Cowell's life flashing in front of his eyes. Key words in an image library search for this picture might include landscape, barren, sand, empty, sign, cloud, dry, tracks, sky, existential. Key words least likely to result in this picture include Christmas, bouncy, loose, mélange, cosy, beef, nonchalant, cornflakes, splash, companionship. This picture was most likely taken on a Tuesday, possibly a Saturday. This picture reverberates. This picture is concerned more with the spaces between things than it is with the things themselves. This picture is very beautiful. If you took down every billboard advertisement in the world and replaced it with this picture it would take a while for people to notice. This picture is what I think of your customer service helpline. This picture is worth whatever someone is willing to pay for it. Frequently Asked Questions about this picture include: "What made you be a picture of that thing?"; "Where did you first get the idea to be a picture of that thing?"; and "Do you have any plans to be a picture of other things in the future?" The answers to the Frequently Asked Questions about this picture are not as frequent as the questions. I think I once went out with this picture. Someone somewhere thinks I am like this picture, which is a disturbing thought. This picture is what you see when you find yourself walking down a long carpeted corridor in Whitehall towards a door marked 'Big Society' and you push it open and walk inside. This picture would serve a useful function in the Oval Office, or on the walls of the staircase at 10 Downing Street. The place that this picture is a picture of is a real place that exists right now and probably looks very similar to the way it does in this picture. We could both go and stand in this picture if we wanted to. Which is to say, we could both go and stand in the place that this picture is a picture of. If we had been standing there at the time this picture was taken, it would be a different picture. Or possibly just the same picture with us in it. I spy with my little eye something in this picture beginning with 's'. This picture is what I'm thinking about whenever you ask me what I'm thinking about. This picture is what my careers development officer saw in me. This picture is a machine for remembering itself. Two X-Factor judges were discussing this picture – I forget which ones – and the first one said, "Wow! This is one of the best pictures I have ever seen!" & started to cry. The second one said, "I like this picture but I don't like its choice of material. I would like to see more from this picture in next week's Beatles night!" This picture is art. This picture doesn't know much about you but it knows what it likes and it doesn't like you. This picture is of a woman in a red dress with a white umbrella running laughing across the sand and into a flock of startled seagulls, but without the startled seagulls, the white umbrella, the red dress and the laughing, running woman. This picture is of the centre ground in American politics. This picture confused me when it came out of the passport photo machine. This picture is of a characterful property in a beach location with plenty of off-street parking. Just beside the person who took this picture is a wooden sign with a camera symbol on it and text reading "Non-intrusive backdrop to overlaying type." This picture is of the losing entry in the RHS Chelsea Flower Show. This picture contains a fencing arrangement which may be marking out a track of some sort. This picture wants to be your friend on Facebook. This picture is what you see when you fall asleep on the Piccadilly Line on the way home and wake up at the last stop and walk up the stairs and outside. This picture could not have been taken any other way. Somewhere to the right of this picture is where I think I dropped my watch. Who knows what's going on either side of this picture. I would guess it's around 11AM in this picture. This picture contains a sign that is too far away to read. The small building in this picture is where they keep the on/off switch for the Internet. None of us remember where we were when this picture was taken. This picture is your retirement gift after 40 years in service. This picture was taken during a rollover week. Do you have any wallpaper that matches this picture? I would like my hair cut in the style of this picture. The thing beginning with 's' in this picture was 'sand'. This picture was taken a split second after the spaceship disappeared into the clouds. You really have to see this picture.

1,000 words by NICK ASBURY about a picture by PAUL THOMPSON
To see the picture go to www.paulthompsonstudio.com

THE FACE

The face is such a frequent source of inspiration that it can be considered a technique in its own right. Some designers use it to humanize a design. Others use it as a recurring theme and inspiration. The simple combination of eyes, nose and mouth contains endless possibilities.

CROSS

Above Self-portrait drawn for the AGI Congress in California. Like Saul Bass (once his partner), Cross makes his name his image. James Cross, USA, 1985.

Left One of a family of design consultancy logos. The mouth changes: here is the 'this is me' version for the letterhead: there is also a 'nice to meet you' for the business card and a 'dear me' for the invoice. Peter Grundy, UK, 1979.

Right Poster for an Alumni Exhibition at Cooper Union. An animated face from a lively designer. Milton Glaser, USA, 1984.

Above Cover for *Esquire*. The ogling playboy was *Esquire*'s symbol for nearly thirty years. Henry Wolf, USA, 1955.

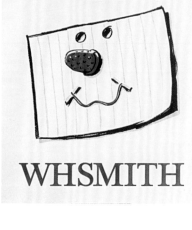
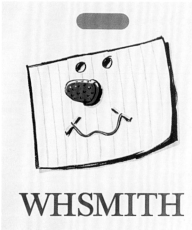

Above U symbol done as personal project. U is for unaffected, understated, unforced. Paul Rand, USA, 1970.

Left One of a range of carrier bags for WHSmith. There are faces from each department, with office stationery providing the 'claret-y' nose. The Partners, UK, 1989.

Above Cover for *How* magazine. The name of the magazine suggests what, and the title of the special issue suggests how. Chermayeff & Geismar, USA, 1993.

Above Al U Minium, a die-cut and hinged metal postcard for Purgatory Pie Press. Putting a face to the name. Steve Guarnaccia, USA, 1992.

DELIVERING GOODNESS

Annual Report 2012

Above Image from a calendar on the 'birthday' theme for the printer Applied Graphics. John McConnell celebrates the change of name from New Amsterdam to New York. Pentagram, UK, 1991.

Above Logo for Face Photosetting. A solution with teeth. John Gorham, UK, 1979.

Left Annual report cover for OzHarvest, a charity that redistributes excess food. Frost*collective, Australia, 2012.

Above Poster for the Icograda Student Seminars in London. In this innocent-seeming arrangement, the Kodak flash hints at the concealed art. Pentagram, UK, 1991.

Below House full of anthropomorphic details, inside and out. OPEN! Design, Russia, 2005.

SOS Sumatran Orangutan Society

Above Identity for a conservation charity with a useful acronym. Hat-trick, UK, 2008.

Below Faces in Places: a blog devoted to a popular form of pareidolia – the tendency to see faces in things. Jody Smith, UK, 2007.

Above *The Typefaces*: a book for discovering the designer in every child and the child in every designer. Scott Lambert, Singapore, 2015.

Above Image from Pentagram Papers 4, *Face to Face*. These found faces were assembled over two years. Pentagram, UK, 1977.

Above Poster for the Royal Shakespeare Theatre centenary appeal. You see the man in all his plays. Abram Games, UK, 1975.

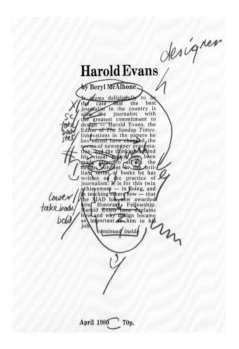

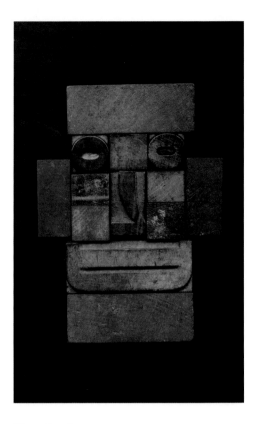

Above Identity for Silo Theatre, referencing the key tool of the actor's trade. Alt Group, New Zealand, 2012.

Above Identity for a film-maker, portraying the man, projecting his business and reflecting his name. Arnold Schwartzman, USA, 1978.

Above Cover for *Designer* magazine. The man from his marks. Bob Norrington, UK, 1980.

Left Poster for Stravinsky ballet programme. The movement of dance inspires a flowing portrait. Karl Domenig Geissbühler, Switzerland, 1986.

Right Christmas greetings sent from Moscow by an American design consultant. Kuo Design Group, USA, 1987.

Above From the Emoticon series: type making faces. Tomato, UK, 2000.

Above Logo for Solo Editions in New York, publisher of promotional books for photographers and illustrators. The Pushpin Group, USA, 1989.

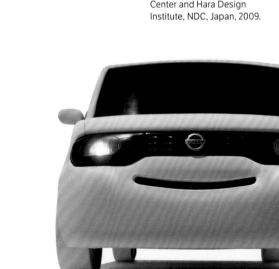

Left Google self-driving car: driverless technology with a reassuringly human face. Google, USA, 2014.

Below The Smiling Vehicle concept, able to change its facial expression. Nissan Motor Co., Ltd., Design Center and Hara Design Institute, NDC, Japan, 2009.

Themes and Variations:
a collection of over
350 porcelain plates
reinterpreting a
single found portrait.
Piero Fornasetti,
Italy, c. 1946–88.

Wit gets to work.
Matt Blease /
Breed, UK, 2014.

WIT IN PRACTICE

WIT IN PRACTICE

Your father's garage. Your eyes scan the shelves. Row upon row of dusty tools and rusting paint pots. Then something catches your eye.

First it's the elegant graphics – the attractive colours and playful outline of a bird's body. Then the name: Oily Bird. A nicely punning name for a household lubricant and preserver. You take it down from the shelf and open the precision spout – a neat piece of functional design. Then you notice the spout has become the beak.

Oily Bird (p.142) is wit in practice. The cue for the wit comes from thinking about the medium to which it is applied. The fun lies in the functional requirement. Created in 1963, it remains as delightful as any display of wit created today.

In the pages that follow, we look at how witty thinking is applied to every item that designers design. We have organized the section broadly by scale – from the ultimate graphic concentration of the logo to the expansive wit of three-dimensional objects and large-scale applications such as signage and environmental designs.

In between lie the heartlands of graphic wit. From the logo, we scale upwards through typography to the classic print applications – stationery, invitations and cards, self-promotional items, direct mail, reports and technical literature. All have assumed a different role in a digital era, often for the better: the printed item has taken on an almost fetishistic value, while the physical arrival of an object through the letterbox carries more intrigue than the ping of an incoming email.

Other fields have come to the fore in recent years. Data visualization is now a lively discipline of its own, with designers finding ever more playful and inventive ways to convey apparently dry information. When everyone has access to PowerPoint and the tools to generate pie charts and bar graphs, there is even more power in presenting information in a surprisingly human way. Designers of calendars work on the same principle – the information is the same every year, but the ways of framing it are endless.

Next comes the poster, which is to graphic design what the sonnet is to poetry – a classic form that every practitioner aims to master at some point. Or, to use a sporting metaphor, the poster is to design what the football pitch is to football – a flat surface with four corners, never changing, but containing infinite possibilities for play. The posters we have chosen include many golden goals from over the years.

It is worth saying that the poster still matters. While it remains possible to encounter great posters in the physical world, many are now just as likely to be shared as online images. Their ability to condense a message into a single 'hit' stands out in a never-ending flow of information.

For some, packaging might conjure up images of Buy-One-Get-One-Free flashes and shouting contests on supermarket shelves. You might also assume packaging has diminished in importance in an age of online shopping. But the opposite seems to be the case. Innocent Drinks in the UK built an entire brand not on advertising but by using the free real estate of its packaging, right down to the 'Enjoy by' instruction that replaces the usual 'Use by' date.

The hordes of Innocent imitators have inevitably missed the point, but the smartest brands have gone a different way. Rather than relying on words, Coca-Cola has tapped into the power of its rich visual iconography. Other brands make playful use of new packaging technologies, or put the packaging itself to a new purpose. But even decades after they were created it is hard to beat the all-round wit of Oily Bird, or the sheer economy of Jif Lemon (p.145).

The section ends with three-dimensional and environmental graphics, where wit takes on added heft and physicality. While we may be primed for a persuasive message when we look at a poster, mailer or piece of packaging, there is an extra element of surprise when we encounter something in the physical world – a bridge becoming a toy, or a table floating mysteriously on balloons. The surprise is like that of a child encountering snow for the first time: for a moment, the world is new again.

If there is a conclusion to this section, it is that wit is media-agnostic. There is nothing intrinsic to a letterhead or logo that makes it more wit-friendly than a calendar or poster. There is no application,

however unpromising, that can't be enlivened by wit – even the humble cardboard box. The simple addition of a smile works wonders for Amazon, mimicking the pleasure many feel when their latest order arrives.

The most important circumstance is a client who likes wit, stands by it and gets it produced. Witty work, like anything that breaks creative ground, needs a champion. The work in this section is testament to many champions – designers and clients – prepared to rewrite the definition of what is appropriate.

Right Amazon packaging: delivered with a smile. Turner Duckworth, USA, 1999.

LOGOS

Rumours of the death of the logo have been greatly exaggerated. In an age of apps and avatars, there is more power than ever in a single mark that communicates the essence of a brand. Wit can tie a graphic knot between 'who we are' and 'what we do', often with a hidden twist that becomes a form of word-of-mouth marketing.

1.

2. **PILOT MODELS**

3.

THE ROYAL PARKS

4.

5.

6.

7.

8.

9.

Lila (everything you've always wanted to know about London and didn't know who to ask) **Burkeman**

10.

11.

12.

13. FINE CELL WORK

14.

15.

16.

---

1. National Museum of Science and Industry. Peter Leonard Associates, UK, 1988.

2. Pilot model-makers. The Partners, UK, 1994.

3. Open House, a day when the public has access to over 200 buildings as a celebration of London's architecture. Newell & Sorrell, UK, 1994.

4. The Royal Parks. Nature and artifice shake hands. Moon Communications, UK, 1994.

5. Helbros watch company. A solution that is as much about form as it is about an idea. Paul Rand, USA, 1944.

6. Endura Nail Corporation. The hidden elegance of nails is revealed. Alancheril Design, USA, 1993.

7. Association of Ideas – architectural and exhibition designers. The Partners, UK, 1993.

8. Tony Muranka, Independent Creative Director. Tony Muranka / Colin Moody, UK, 1990.

9. Nina Triggs, masseuse. The flesh-coloured letterhead is slightly crumpled where the logo appears. Bull Rodger, UK, 1990.

10. Needle & Thread clothes designers. Adam Mitchinson, UK, 2013.

11. Identity for a travel consultant. A simple verbal substitution. Pentagram, UK, 1972.

12. Alvin Ailey Dance Company in New York. Human body solutions can be mechanical, but this includes an ingenious twist. Chermayeff & Geismar, USA, 1988.

13. Fine Cell Work: a charity teaching prisoners needlework skills. The Partners, UK, 2011.

14. Thatcher and Thompson architects. Sue Crolick, USA, 1984.

15. Hipwell Bookbinders. The idea was found in a party game – the 'charades' mime makes 'book' using hands. Silk Pearce, UK, 1991.

16. Letterhead for a designer and his family. It works for all four, or for each one individually. Pentagram, UK, 1980.

QUINTET

17.

ᴴᴴsit⁴⁴

18.

 yoga australia

19.

 **KABUTO NOODLES**

20.

 M◯RNINGSTAR

21.

child support agency

22.

 MITCHELL PHOENIX

23.

 **NOTTINGHAM JAZZ™**

24.

amazon.

25.

 *the* **BENCH**

26.

 **FALKLANDS FINEST**

27.

 *Spratt's*

28.

uƃısǝpıʌol

29.

freedoᴟ

30.

MyFonts

31.

Re

32.

Destination

33.

Shelter

34.

LSO

35.

f◯t◯

36.

---

17. Quintet ad agency. Pierre Vermeir / HGV, UK, 2004.

18. "Sit": an exhibition of chair design. Trickett & Webb, UK, 1983.

19. Yoga Australia. Roy Smith Design, UK, 2008.

20. Kabuto Noodles. B&B Studio, UK, 2010.

21. Morningstar. An idea expressed through letter shape and alignment. Paul Rand, USA. 1990.

22. Child Support Agency. Halpin Grey Vermeir, UK, 1991.

23. Mitchell Phoenix consultancy firm. Alter egos. Halpin Grey Vermeir, UK, 1989.

24. Nottingham Jazz. David Burdon, Glad Creative, UK, 2011.

25. Amazon. From A to Z. Turner Duckworth, UK / USA, 1999.

26. Crafts-inspired identity for a new café at The Goldsmiths' Centre. Neon Creative, UK, 2012.

27. Falklands Finest, homegrown quality mark. The Partners, UK, 2002.

28. Spratts dogfood. Max Field-Bush, UK, 1936.

29. Pivot by name... Pivot Design Inc, USA, 1992.

30. Freedom Travel Group. The Chase, UK, 2009.

31. MyFonts. Nick Sherman / Underware, The Netherlands, 2009.

32. The perfect rebus for an organization refitting buses for educational use. Per Mollerup Designlab, Denmark, 1992.

33. Destination: an in-flight magazine. Eisenberg and Associates, USA, 1986.

34. Shelter: charity for the homeless. Johnson Banks, UK, 2004.

35. London Symphony Orchestra. The Partners, UK, 2003.

36. Foto Graphics. An upside-down inside-out reversal. George Tscherny, USA, 1968.

37.

38.

39.

40.

41.

42.

43.

44.

45.

46.

47.

48.

49.

50.

51.

52.

53.

54.

55.

56.

---

37. Layezee Beds.
The Chase, UK, 2004.

38. Guild of Food Writers.
300million, UK, 2005.

39. Identity for film production company BSB. Arnold Schwartzman, UK, 1977.

40. English National Opera.
CDT Design, UK, 1991.

41. Chairish: furniture store for design lovers.
Mucho, USA, 2013.

42. Surrey Institute of Art & Design. For colleges in a leafy situation, the designers nod in the direction of the tree of knowledge and combine the brushwork of art with the typography of design.
The Partners, UK, 1994.

43. The Sign Design Society, advancing standards in the use of signs. Atelier Works, UK, 1994.

44. Knoll Christmas Collection.
NB Studio, UK, 1999.

45. Mr & Mrs Hair.
Pentagram, USA, 1976.

46. Routledge, a publisher specializing in the humanities and science.
Newell & Sorrell, UK, 1989.

47. National Lottery UK. Saatchi & Saatchi, UK, 1994. Updated by Landor Associates, 2002

48. Rebel, sports retailer.
Hulbosch, Australia, 2012.

49. Goal, football news site.
Elmwood, UK, 2013.

50. Wedgwood bone china.
The Partners, UK, 1997.

51. Nexcite energy drink. Amore, Sweden, 2005.

52. For an exhibition celebrating a hundred years of the automobile. Alan Fletcher / Pentagram, UK, 1985.

53. Fabric Library. The Partners, UK, 2015.

54. Hostage Films. The Chase, UK, 2006.

55. Emergency Telecommunications Systems: a back-up phone network for city traders.
The Partners, UK, 1986.

56. Mouse digital advertising awards. Johnson Banks, UK, 2008.

57.

58.

59.

60.

61.

62.

63.

64.

65.

66.

67.

68.

69.

70.

71.

72.

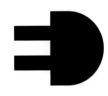

73.

74.

75.

76.

---

57. Ok Textil: clothing company. Sublima Comunicación, Spain, 2009.

58. Igloo, a pay TV service with a playful character. Interbrand, Australia, 2012.

59. Freud Jahr 2006: anniversary identity. Abbott Miller / Pentagram, UK, 2006.

60. Conception Marketing. The Chase, UK, 2002.

61. The Confidante executive coaching service. Re: Sydney, Australia, 2015.

62. Tipton Lakes Corporation. A solution that uses humour to make the name memorable. Paul Rand, USA, 1980.

63. Formula 1 World Championship. Carter Wong, UK, 1994.

64. Hall & Rose handcrafted soft furnishings. Elmwood, UK, 2011.

65. Saint, bespoke men's tailor. Osborn Ross, UK, 2001.

66. Soho's Secret Tea Room. The Partners, UK, 2012.

67. Manchester Literature Festival. MARK Studio, UK, 2008.

68. Adams Trucking. Almanac Advertising, USA, 1981.

69. The Fashion Center. Michael Bierut / Pentagram, USA, 1996.

70. For the web and publishing division of paper company Wiggins Teape. Atelier Works, UK, 1993.

71. Lone Star Donuts in Texas. The hole is the star. Sibley/Peteet Design, USA, 1986.

72. H Electrics. Dave Burdon, UK, 2009.

73. Knapp Shoes. Chermayeff & Geismar, USA, 1968.

74. Fitness First gym clubs. The Clearing, UK, 2014.

75. Martin Newcombe, property maintenance. Buddy Creative, UK, 2008.

76. ED Elettro Domestici (Home Appliances). Gianni Bortolotti, Italy, Year unknown.

TYPOGRAPHY

More than most, designers are aware of language as a physical object. Typographic ideas delight in the visual appearance of the written word, finding endless ways to reinterpret the simple characters of the Roman alphabet. In these ideas, things become letters and letters become things. World and word collide.

Right Gates for a private house and design studio. Alan Fletcher, Pentagram, UK, 1990.

Below Poster for Pirelli tyres. A little licence does the trademark no harm at all. André François, France, 1961.

Left Type the Sky. Lisa Rienermann, Germany, 2007.

Right Fire in the Hole: alphabet of burned and disfigured toy soldiers. Oliver Munday, USA, 2007.

Above Identity for the Tusk Conservation Awards, the logo hidden in a custom pattern. The Partners, UK, 2014.

Above Letters in things: poster for Preston Polytechnic. Pentagram, UK, 1978.

Above Identity for Sibler in Zurich, which sells items for the kitchen and table. Erika Schmid Wiesendanger, Switzerland, 1991.

Right Logo for an exhibition on dinosaur skeletons – the kind of design that gets children into graphics. Samenwerkende Ontwerpers, The Netherlands, 1991.

Above Commissioned print for the London Transport Museum's 'Mind the Map' exhibition. Tim Fishlock, UK, 2012.

Right Typewatch designed at the Type Workshop. Alphanumeric. Janice Davidson and Jim Sutherland, UK, 1994.

London's Kerning:
an A–Z map with
the lines removed,
revealing a city of
words. NB Studio,
UK, 2007

STATIONERY

The business card is a surprisingly enduring form. Nothing has quite replaced its ability to formalize the contact at the end of a conversation and lodge it memorably in the mind. Letterheads have also taken on a rarity value: in an age of emails and status updates, their physicality carries cultural weight.

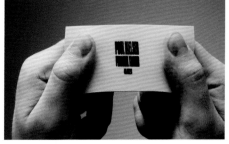

Above Business card and mini-workout. Publicis Toronto, Canada, 2006.

Left & below Appropriately playful stationery for Preston North End Football Club. The Chase, UK, 1990.

Above Mount Fuji Envelope. Tomohiro Ikegaya / goodbymarket, Japan, 2011.

Below Stationery range for a retail writer. Retailers know all about the lure of the sale. Sue Crolick, USA, 1992.

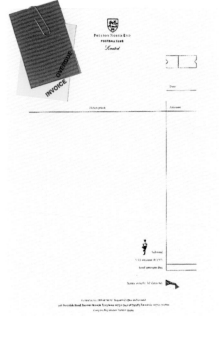

Below A unique maker's mark for a craftsman and carpenter: even his age is coded in the rings. The Partners, UK, 2014.

Below Sandpaper business cards – place carefully in pocket. Rethink, Canada, 2003.

Opposite Used cards: found business cards stamped and reused – for a second-hand car business. Creativeland Asia, India, 2009.

Left Clients donate their business cards, which are then punched with the details: a physical word-of-mouth endorsement. Jason Little, Australia, 2012.

Right Economical letterhead for designer Nick Wurr – the design is printed on the reverse, so that the appropriate corner can be folded for each message. Nick Wurr, UK, 1977.

Left Letterhead for a textile designer. Paper mimics fabric. John Marsh Design, UK, 1974.

Above Glow-in-the-dark for a good reason. The Chase, UK, 2008.

Above Hole-punched stationery making a virtue of the functional holes. The Workroom, UK, 1990.

REVOLUTION

Above Letterhead for a nightclub. The printed stack of letterheads, with a logotype derived from an anarchist broadsheet, was blowtorched to char the top edge. Crosby Fletcher Forbes, UK, 1967.

Below Stellar Productions letterhead reveals a child's face when held to the light – a beautiful production experience in its own right. Neon Creative, UK, 2006.

Below Found graffiti supplies an appropriate identity for Joe Kerr, architectural historian. Studio Myerscough, UK, 1998.

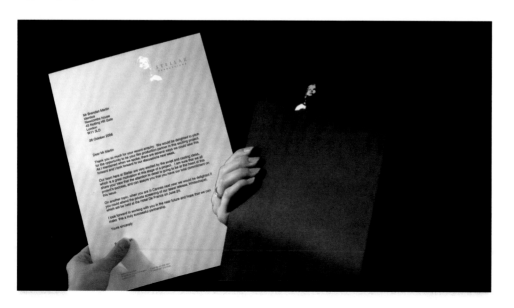

INVITATIONS & CARDS

Moving house, getting married, giving birth – the big occasions in life can be a useful premise for wit. Each presents a unique set of circumstances where the twist may occur: date, names, venue, occasion. There is no recorded instance of a designer getting married purely for the invitation idea, but some must have considered it.

Above Birth announcement playfully revealing the baby's weight. Jim Sutherland, UK, 1994.

Left A no-nonsense birth announcement. Williams & Phoa, UK, 1992.

Left Invitation to a Christmas party with an Alpine theme. The message was burned into slices of wood from storm-damaged trees using a specially made embossing tool heated by a blowtorch. Giant, UK, 1989.

Above Moving announcement for a design consultancy. They moved only a street or two, across about an inch of the London A–Z. Trickett & Webb, UK, 1979.

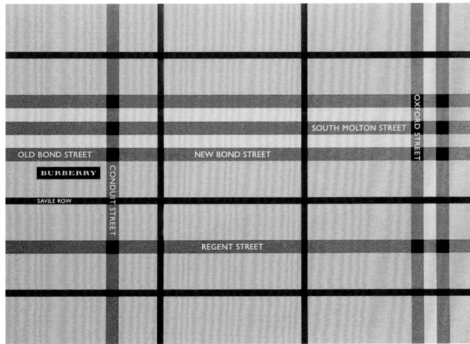

Above Invitation to the launch of a new Burberry store in London. Four IV, UK, 2001.

A LEAN YEAR

Right Design company Christmas mailer in the year following the financial crash. Alt Group, New Zealand, 2009.

HEART & SOLD

Above Identity and exhibition invitation for Heart & Sold: a platform for artists with Down's Syndrome. Matt Maurer, UK, 2012.

Above Pull-tab moving card. From W11 to W2. Carter Wong, UK, 1990.

Above Another pull-tab moving card for a designer moving to London N13, echoing Bruner and Mintum's 1955 study based on an ambiguous shape: people who had previously been shown letters saw a B, those shown a number saw it as 13. Derek Dalton, UK, 1977.

Above Invitation for Wilton Royal Carpets to an evening of Tudor delights, with a tear-off slip. The Chase, UK, 1989.

Left Parcel tape doing the talking. Radford Wallis, UK, 2008.

Above Moving card for a design consultancy. They moved 240 feet down the street. The Paul Martin Design Company, UK, 1989.

Above Invitation to a studio-warming party. The designers use an architectural-style stamp and left-over chunks of drywall to underline who they are and what they do. Hornall Anderson Design Works, USA, 1984.

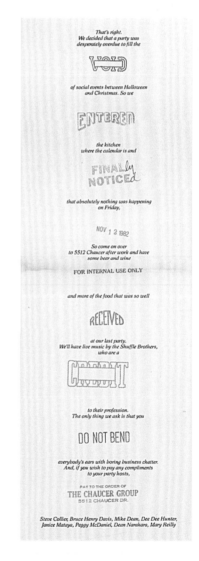

Above Party invitation. Once again the graphic idea is driven by the words. The Chaucer Group, USA, 1982.

SHOW
AND
TELL

DISPLAY AND DISCUSS
YOUR LATEST WORK OVER
A FEW DRINKS WITH THE
LAND SECURITIES ROSTER

THURSDAY FEB.16TH
5:30PM – LATE

PURPOSE
FIRST FLOOR STUDIO
14A SHOULDHAM STREET
LONDON, W1H 5FG

T: +44 (0)20 7724 5890
WWW.PURPOSE.CO.UK

Fun and functional
invitation to a creative
show and tell.
Purpose, UK, 2004.

It is estimated that up to 20 animal species become extinct every day

Left & above Direct mail piece for the Natural History Museum, promoting a series of talks on extinction. Hat-trick, UK, 2006.

POLLY ALEXANDER·LYNN & TERRY TRICKETT HAVE MOVED TO 9 HAMILTON TERRACE · LONDON NW8 · TELEPHONE 01-286 5209

Right Moving announcement for a family. The birds have flown. Trickett & Webb, UK, 1981.

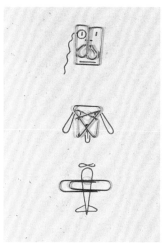

Above Card for a couple moving home, playing on the classic Monopoly graphics. Timberbush Advertising, UK, 1992.

Above Invitation to 'Ironwork', a show of objects and drawings by the designer. Steve Guarnaccia, USA, 1991.

MOVING CARD

Right Wedding invitation for Claire and Dave, separated only by the dot of an i. The Chase, UK, 2005.

claire

dave

I've seen a few bits of work lying around and it looks like it could be quite a good show this year.

KEITH WOOD CLEANER

Above Moving card for a design consultancy. Once they have unpacked the boxes, they will spring into action. The Cade Partnership, UK, 1988.

Left Corporate hospitality invitation for the tennis at Wimbledon. No backhanders either. Radley Yeldar, UK, 1994.

Above Invitation to the final degree show at Kingston Polytechnic. Unexpected and endearing. Peter Hale, UK, 1991.

Mr and Mrs Mercer *JUST ASK* the pleasure of

at the *MARRY ME* of Valerie Anne *DREAM GIRL* to

Stephen John *NICE BOY* Gibbons

at St Mary the Virgin Church Speldhurst Kent on

Saturday September *SWEET 16* 1989 at 3.30 pm

and *EVER AFTER* at Barn House *OUR TREAT*

RSVP to Mrs Mercer Barn House Speldhurst Kent

Above Wedding invitation, usefully planned for the 16th. Val Mercer & Steve Gibbons, UK, 1989.

Right Party invitation. Don't request guests to bring a bottle: blackmail guests into bringing a bottle. Bob Gill, USA, 1968.

Dear friends:

John Cole invites you to a party on Sat. Sept. 9 at 8.30pm at 122 Regents Park Rd. NW1 Flat D. RSVP Gro 2291 Please bring a bottle.

Free loaders:

John Cole invites you to a party on Sat. Sept. 9 at 8.30pm at 122 Regents Park Rd. NW1 Flat D. RSVP Gro 2291

Right Party invitation, for the morning after the night before. Mike Newton, UK, 1965.

Take two in water on the morning after Mike Newton's party

76 Portland Road W11 on December 17 about 9pm RSVP Bay 9444

Left Wind-up toy moving announcement. You turn the handle and the message appears. Sterling Plenert Design, USA, 1993.

Left Screen-printed bubble wrap to celebrate an office move. Hat-trick, UK, 2008.

Left Moving card for a caterer. The existing 'bite' identity drove this idea. Wit on wit. Pentagram, UK, 1991.

Right Self-developing invitation to a Christmas party. Graham Ford, John Horton and Jerry Oke, UK, 1982.

...PS

Peyton Skipwith's

75th Birthday

Peyton Skipwith requests the pleasure of your company to celebrate his

On Saturday 28th June at a dinner at the Art Workers Guild 6 Queen Square London WC1N 3AT

7.30 for 8.00pm

Above & right Postscript becomes the main item. Webb & Webb, UK, Year unknown.

SEASONAL

Set-piece occasions like Christmas can feel like the Olympics of wit. For a short time, everyone's attention is focused on a shared brief and set of cultural references – the challenge being to take it somewhere new. Increasingly, the answer is a film, product or event, but occasionally the card retains its power to surprise.

Right Greetings card employing the design company's trademark scribble. Minale Tattersfield, UK, 1993.

Left Design consultancy Christmas card. Thinking in terms of decoration is a good idea for once. CDT Design, UK, 1994.

Right Design consultancy Christmas card based on rejected ideas. A solution out of the jaws of defeat. Bull Rodger, UK, 1994.

'Christmas Thoughts'

Above Happy sacks. A mundane object given a festive spin for the season of excess. Wieden+Kennedy, London, 2006.

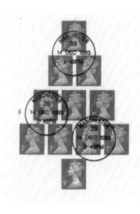

Above Christmas card for a design company, enlisting the inadvertent support of Royal Mail. The Chase, UK, 1993.

Above Metal-ball puzzle centrepiece from a Christmas card for Character Photosetting. John Gorham, UK, 1978.

Above Self-promotional Christmas card. A particularly elegant piece of ambiguity. Darrell Ireland, UK, 1991.

Above Christmas card for photographer Andy Seymour. Three elements say it all. CDT Design, UK, 1990.

Right Typeflakes: designer decorations. The Partners, UK, 2013.

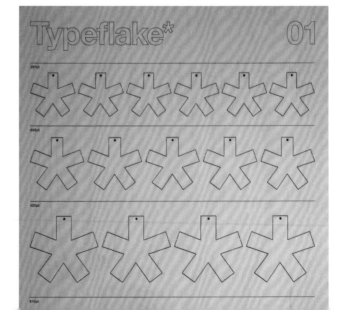

Left Two from a set of four Christmas cards for internal use and sale by the Design Museum in London. Recontextualizing chairs designed by Hans Coray and Mies van der Rohe. Carter Wong, UK, 1989.

Above Recycled cards fashioned from old magazines and brochures. Johnson Banks, UK, 2007.

Above A card for all occasions. NB Studio, UK, 2012.

Above Image from a Christmas card with a transforming pull-down overlay for Character Photosetting. Winter becomes Christmas. John Gorham, UK, 1981.

Below Christmas card for solicitors Lewis Silkin. This being the season of goodwill, the judge changes his robes. The Partners, UK, 1990.

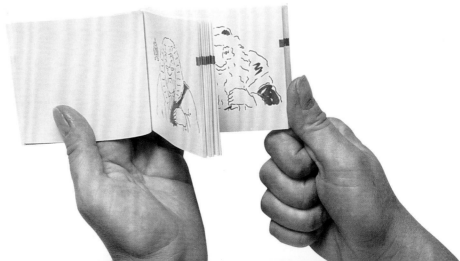

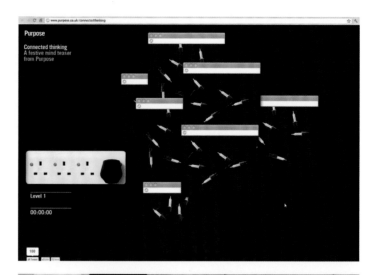

Above Christmas card with an enamel badge from T&W. Trickett & Webb, UK, 1994.

Above Sonny Liston challenging cultural preconceptions on the Christmas cover of *Esquire*. George Lois / *Esquire*, USA, 1963.

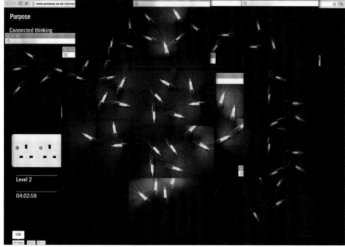

Left Greetings card from a Battersea design company, using a landmark recognizable to Londoners and fans of Pink Floyd. Smith & Milton, UK, 1980.

Above Connected thinking: untangle the fairy lights by moving the browser windows. Philip Skinner/Purpose, UK, 2009.

Above Eco packaging concept for Christmas lights. Audrey Wells, Canada, 2011.

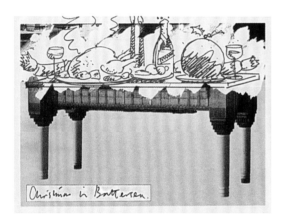

Left Work becomes pleasure in an edible Christmas mailer. Alt Group, New Zealand, 2010.

Left Christmas card for Thrislington Cubicles, whose crayon line identity makes play with the standard symbols. The Partners, UK, 1990.

Fountains have captivated and enchanted human senses since at least the third millenium BC, when man first acquired the principles of hydraulics, and so could artificially reproduce the delightful sound and sight of falling water. Since then the joyful interplay of air and water has exercised the ingenuity of engineers down the ages, and today forms a prominent architectural feature of The Fountains, a prestigious new office development of some 80,000 sq ft in Edmund Street, one of the last substantial locations available in Birmingham's heavily subscribed financial core.

a new development The Fountains

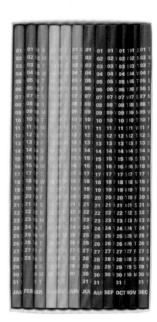

Left Festive mailer for shoe designer Tim Little, inspired by Monopoly pieces – with the shoe taking centre stage. The Partners, UK, 1999.

Right Twelve seasonally colour-coded pencils with days printed along the side for each date to be sharpened off. Mytton Williams, UK, 2008.

Above Mother Miniatures: miniature model kit of non-model citizens. Mother, UK, 1999.

Below Catalogue and bidding kit for Brooklyn Academy of Music. Auction paddles gain a little humanity. Alexander Isley Design, USA, 1990.

Right Direct mail from a different age of design, when keylining was an essential service. Sue Crolick, USA, 1985.

Left Promotional balloons for the mind-expanding magazine. BBDO NYC, USA, 2007.

Above See-through invitation to the launch of a 'Spell cheque' calendar exploring the limitations of automated spell check. Trickett & Webb, UK, 1995.

REPORTS

It takes courage to use wit in documents that are fundamentally about compliance and impressing stakeholders. But in a conservative sector, the annual report with wit is disproportionately visible. It signals an organization that wants to communicate, not just comply, as humour shortens the distance between brand and audience.

Left Annual report for Domino's Pizza. Good news grabs the headlines. Group 243 Incorporated, USA, 1986.

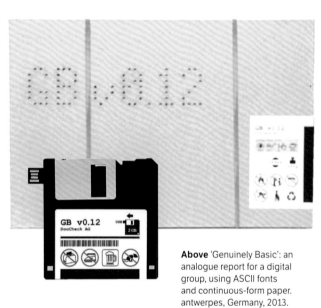

Above 'Genuinely Basic': an analogue report for a digital group, using ASCII fonts and continuous-form paper. antwerpes, Germany, 2013.

Right Illustrations from the Assuranceforeningen Gard annual report. Marine insurers show their fondness for ships. Tatham Pearce, UK, 1989.

Below Annual report for the Burton Group. How *Vogue* might have presented the year's results from the group's fashion chains. Michael Peters Literature, UK, 1986.

Left Annual report for Computer Cab. For a people business, the famous London taxi illuminated sign gets a switch. Trickett & Webb, UK, 1989.

Right City in the Community: CSR report for Manchester City FC turned into an accessible broadsheet newspaper. Music, UK, 2009.

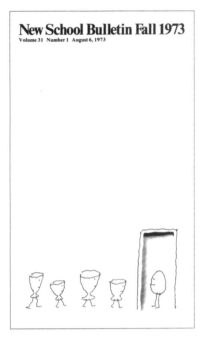

New School Bulletin Fall 1973
Volume 31 Number 1 August 6, 1973

New School Bulletin Fall 1973
Volume 31 Number 1 August 6, 1973

Published monthly by the New School for Social Research
Second class postage paid at New York, N.Y.
66 West 12th Street, New York, N Y 10011

Left & above Images from the cover and title page of the New School Bulletin. Two drawings are as good as a thesis. R.O. Blechman, USA, 1973.

THIS ANNUAL REPORT IS TRASH

Des Moines Metropolitan Area
Solid Waste Agency 1991

Above Inside front cover from the annual report of the Des Moines Metropolitan Area Solid Waste Agency. Trash becomes the opposite of rubbish. Pattee Design, USA, 1992.

Right Employee report for the Asda supermarket group. Giving everyone a picture of what happens in the business. Tatham Pearce, UK, 1989.

Right Annual report for computer systems company BSO/Origin. To avoid corporate speak, this is written as though for children: the financial pages are sealed with a sticker that reads 'Not nice for children, beware'. vLSP, The Netherlands, 1989.

Far right Another annual report for systems consultant BSO/Origin. The tea bag is real. The Partners in association with vLSP, UK / The Netherlands, 1993.

6,796 dogs

were admitted to Manchester Dogs' Home last year. So where do they all come from?

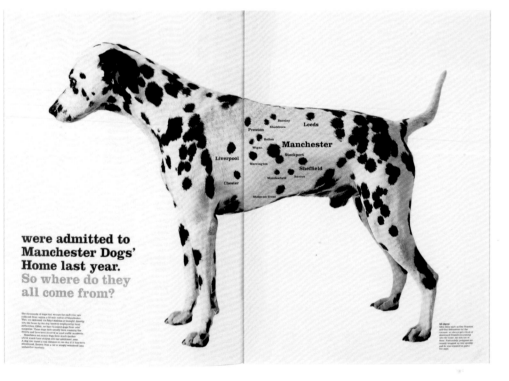

Above Manchester Dogs' Home Annual Review: appealing to the head and heart. The Chase, UK, 2002.

Calgary Society for Persons with Disabilities / Annual Report 2013

Annual report for Calgary Society for Persons with Disabilities. A single staple binds the pages, creating a reading experience that mimics the challenges of disability. Wax Partnership, Canada, 2013.

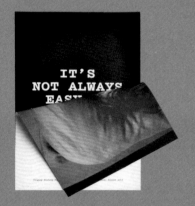

TECHNICAL LITERATURE

Comedy needs a straight man, and the conventions of technical literature provide a useful foil for wit. Sometimes wit can be an aid to digestion, sugaring the pill of the serious content. On other occasions, the apparently serious framework can be a deadpan container for humorous content.

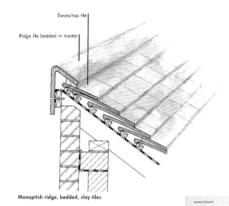

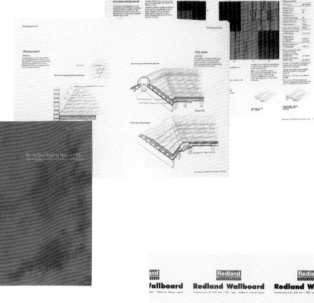

Left & below The Redland Roofing Manual. Tiles are drawn in section in black and white, with their roof position projected off in colour: uniting the sophistication of coded information with the simplicity of how the eye actually sees the world. The Partners, UK, 1987.

Left & below Personal identity guidelines. For one awards scheme, the designer included himself as support material. Christopher Doyle, Australia, 2008.

Right Technical literature for Redland Plasterboard. The nature of plasterboard, a white core within board covers, is mimicked in the form and style of the brochure. The Partners, UK, 1989.

Above Pirelli: a rubber cover announces the contents. Michael Peters Limited, UK, 1992.

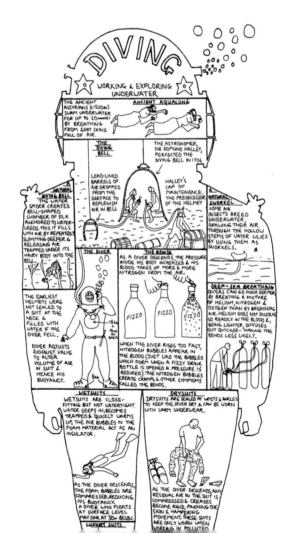

Right A guide to print processes for Gilbert Paper. Technical data is translated into simple terms, as for a children's primer. The Valentine Group, USA, 1993.

Above Out of the Box: manual with die-cut pages to guide you through your new phone. Special Projects, UK, 2010.

Left Embroidered brand guidelines for Fine Cell Work: a charity teaching prisoners needlecraft. The Partners, UK, 2012.

Below Handbook on fire protection for Cape Boards, where the designers exploit new technical possibilities with a heat-sensitive cover. The Partners, UK, 1993.

Left Extract from identity manual for Rowntree. Use the logo big, or small, or as an all-over pattern. Smith & Milton, UK, 1989.

Right Information panel for the series 'The Rudiments of Wisdom' in *The Observer* colour magazine. Knowledge and cartoons meet. Tim Hunkin, UK, 1980.

DATA VISUALIZATION

The alchemy of wit is at its purest when it comes to infographics – translating dry information into entertaining and beautiful images. Some ideas turn the stuff of real life into unexpected informational aids. Others work in the opposite direction, adapting the language of data visualization for playful purposes.

Right Chart for *Time* magazine. The dollar takes a cut. Nigel Holmes, USA, 1979.

Above The best kind of pie chart. Mary & Matt, USA, 2008.

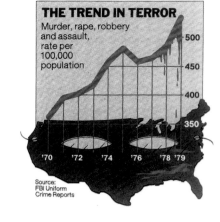

Above Honest chocolate packaging, with calorie intake marked. Ruiz+Company, Spain, 2009.

Right Chart for *The Sunday Times*. Not your usual bar or bar chart. Gordon Beckett, UK, 1982.

Below Fever chart for *The New York Times*. Six charts showing a bravura approach and only a little sleight of hand. Nigel Holmes, USA, 1979.

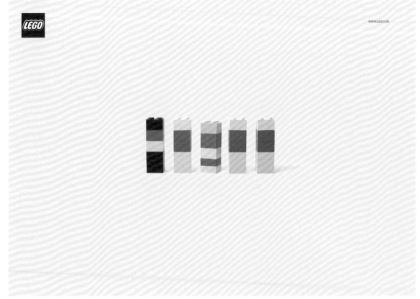

Above Chart for *Time* magazine based on FBI Uniform Crime Reports. America becomes a gruesome mask. Nigel Holmes, USA, 1980.

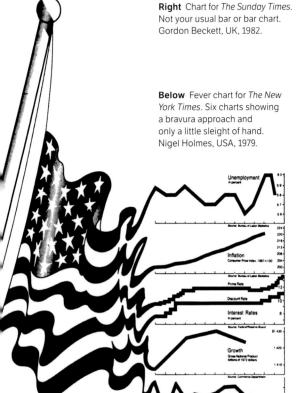

Right Cartoon characters distilled to their essence. Jung von Matt, Germany, 2012.

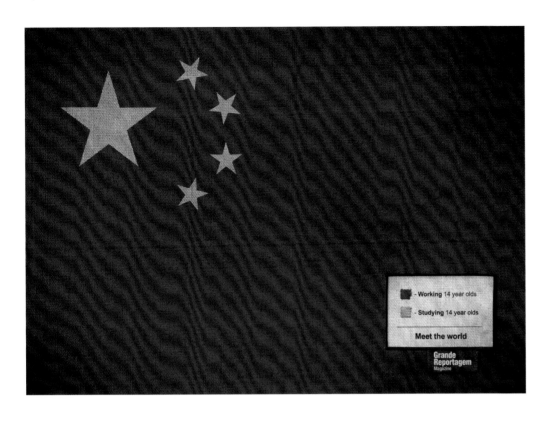

1984	1985	1986	1987	1988
£293.1m	£333.6m	£356.8m	£428.4m	£490.2m

Left In a campaign for *Grande Reportagem* magazine, national flags become infographics to convey disturbing information about each country. FCB Lisbon, Portugal, 2005.

Above Graph from Hewlett-Packard annual report. No retouching or digital manipulation, just patient location shooting. The Partners, UK, 1989.

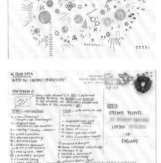

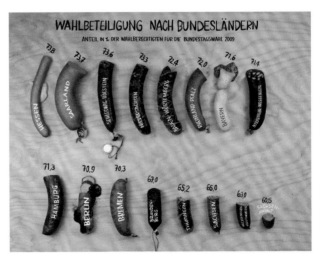

Above Dear Data: two designers visualize the mundanities of daily life in a year-long exchange of postcards across the Atlantic. Giorgia Lupi / Stefanie Posavec, USA / UK, 2014.

Left Visualizing voter turnout in different states of Germany. Anna Lena Schiller / Sylke Gruhnwald / Lisa Rienermann / Zeit Online, Germany, 2013.

Left A deep dive into the lives of the world's wealthiest people. Rich data in every sense. Bloomberg Visual Data, USA, 2013.

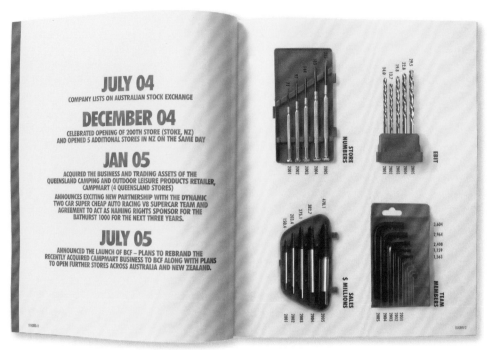

Above Super Cheap
Auto Annual Report:
cheap has never looked
smarter. Frost*collective,
Australia, 2005.

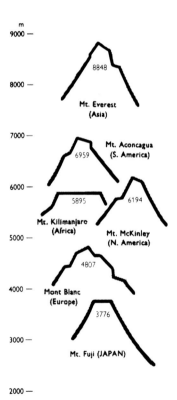

Famous Mountains

Left Charts about
employment in Kansas City
for the *Kansas City Times*.
Information townscape.
Randy Wyrick, USA, 1982.

Above Chart showing the
height of the world's most
famous mountains. Bringing
the visual comparison
to life. Japan Statistical
Association, Japan, 1979.

Below From a brochure
for security group RMC,
showing the increase in
UK burglaries. Tor Pettersen
& Partners, UK, 1988.

Above Chart on college
fees for *Newsweek*.
Christopher Blumrich,
USA, 1982.

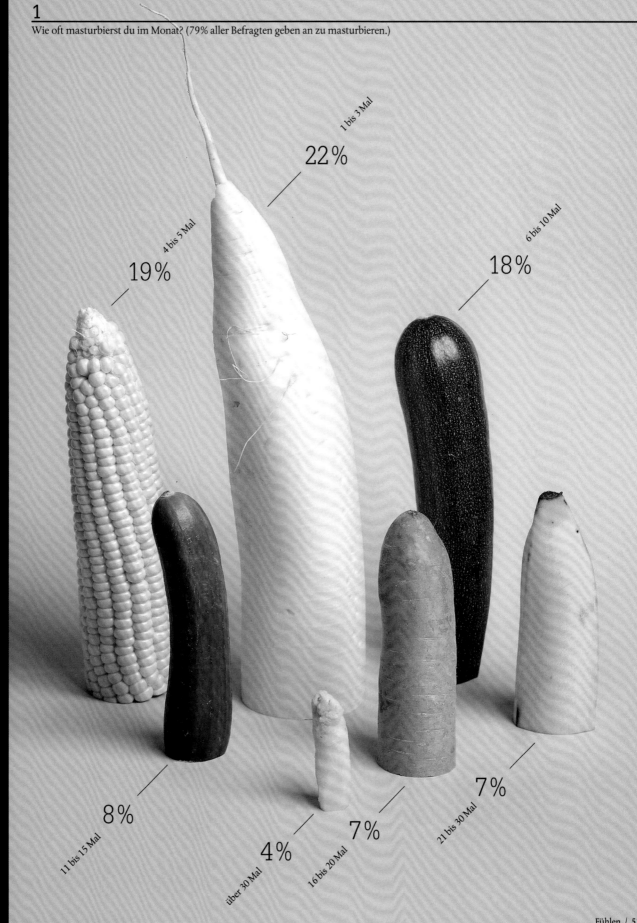

Wie oft masturbierst du im Monat? (79% aller Befragten geben an zu masturbieren.)

1 bis 3 Mal

22%

4 bis 5 Mal

19%

6 bis 10 Mal

18%

11 bis 15 Mal

8%

über 30 Mal

4%

16 bis 20 Mal

7%

21 bis 30 Mal

7%

How often do you masturbate a month? Illustration for *Neon*'s 'Truth About Sex' feature. Sarah Illenberger, Germany, 2008.

CALENDARS

One of the oldest forms of infographic, and a tempting challenge for any designer – the prize being space on someone's wall or desktop for a whole year. As well as playing with the physical format, there is the added intrigue of playing with time, using ideas that tell a story as the year unfolds.

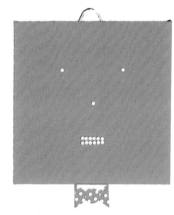

Above Hälssen & Lyon tea calendar: dates made from tea leaves for a daily brew. Kolle Rebbe, Germany, 2013.

Below Chrono-Shredder II: a calendar that shreds each passing day. Susanna Hertrich, Germany, 2010.

Right Pinboard Calendar for Face Type. Use the drawing pins to draw something. John Gorham and Howard Brown, UK, 1981.

Above Celebrating the off-road spirit of the Land Rover, each contour representing a different month. TBWA Istanbul, Turkey, 2014.

Left & below BBC Wildlife Fund calendar, each cross marking another day and another species threatened with extinction. The Chase, UK, 2011.

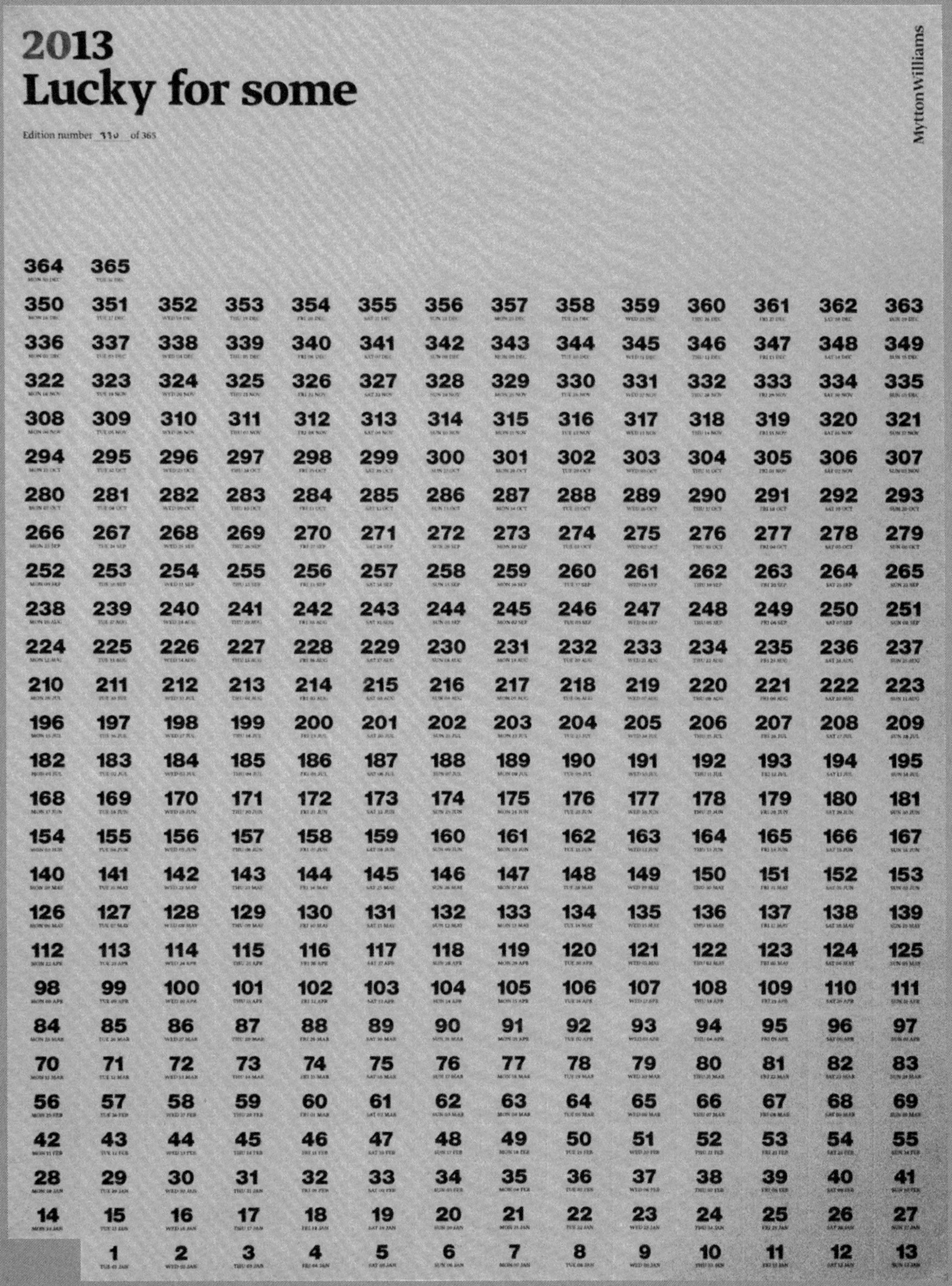
2013
Lucky for some
Edition number ____ of 365
Mytton Williams
364 365
350 351 352 353 354 355 356 357 358 359 360 361 362 363
336 337 338 339 340 341 342 343 344 345 346 347 348 349
322 323 324 325 326 327 328 329 330 331 332 333 334 335
308 309 310 311 312 313 314 315 316 317 318 319 320 321
294 295 296 297 298 299 300 301 302 303 304 305 306 307
280 281 282 283 284 285 286 287 288 289 290 291 292 293
266 267 268 269 270 271 272 273 274 275 276 277 278 279
252 253 254 255 256 257 258 259 260 261 262 263 264 265
238 239 240 241 242 243 244 245 246 247 248 249 250 251
224 225 226 227 228 229 230 231 232 233 234 235 236 237
210 211 212 213 214 215 216 217 218 219 220 221 222 223
196 197 198 199 200 201 202 203 204 205 206 207 208 209
182 183 184 185 186 187 188 189 190 191 192 193 194 195
168 169 170 171 172 173 174 175 176 177 178 179 180 181
154 155 156 157 158 159 160 161 162 163 164 165 166 167
140 141 142 143 144 145 146 147 148 149 150 151 152 153
126 127 128 129 130 131 132 133 134 135 136 137 138 139
112 113 114 115 116 117 118 119 120 121 122 123 124 125
98 99 100 101 102 103 104 105 106 107 108 109 110 111
84 85 86 87 88 89 90 91 92 93 94 95 96 97
70 71 72 73 74 75 76 77 78 79 80 81 82 83
56 57 58 59 60 61 62 63 64 65 66 67 68 69
42 43 44 45 46 47 48 49 50 51 52 53 54 55
28 29 30 31 32 33 34 35 36 37 38 39 40 41
14 15 16 17 18 19 20 21 22 23 24 25 26 27
1 2 3 4 5 6 7 8 9 10 11 12 13

Upbeat calendar
for an unlucky year,
with 365 raffle-style
tickets to tear off.
Mytton Williams,
UK, 2013.

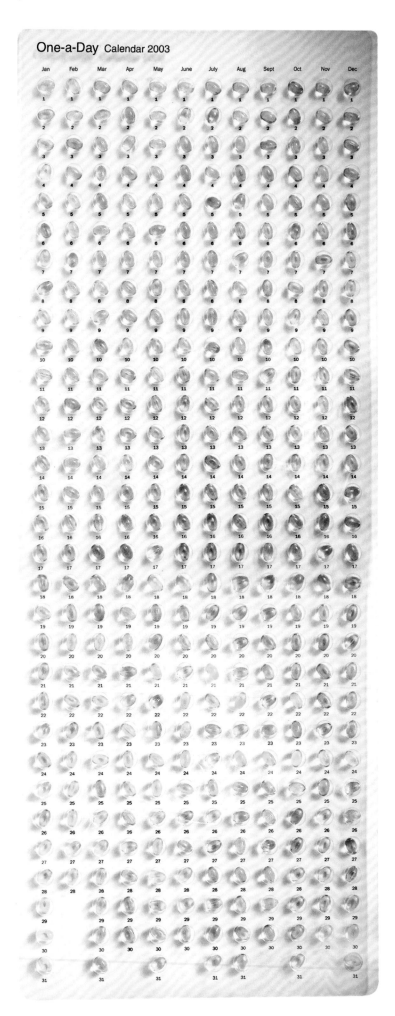

One-a-Day Calendar 2003

Left 365 cod liver oil capsules for a healthy year. Dominic Wilcox, UK, 2003.

Right Calendar for Face Ronchetti. A bi-monthly approach, with twelve faces in six images: a simple reversal achieves a startling change. John Gorham, UK, 1987.

Right Sporting calendar for the Edman Communications Group. Later cited by Steven Fuller as the influence for the 'Mad Men' title sequence. Roundel Design Group, UK, 1985.

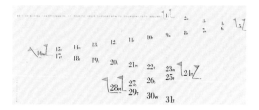

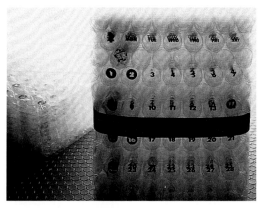

Left Puchi-Puchi Calendar for Packaging Create – everyone likes to play with bubble wrap. Akio Okumura, Japan, 1989.

Left Chain reaction calendar for Trickett & Webb and Augustus Martin. Shapes die-cut from the covers were collected and made into a model of a tree, completing the cycle. Trickett & Webb, UK, 1989.

POSTERS

Still one of the classic canvases for graphic wit. There's nothing quite like the challenge of conveying a message in a single hit, with an artful combination of words and pictures. Some ideas challenge the conventions of the medium, others work brilliantly within them.

Above For an exhibition on car design, starting with the basics. Mendell & Oberer, Germany, 1986.

Above Philishave rotary electric shaver. F.H.K. Henrion, UK, 1955.

Above An elegant solution for Eminence underwear. Herbert Leupin, Switzerland, 1967.

Left Digital subway ads for Apolosophy. Haircare models get flustered as trains arrive. Åkestam Holst / Stopp Family, Sweden, 2014.

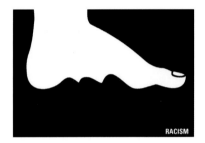

Above A concise anti-racism message. Lex Drewinski, Poland, 1993.

NAPOLI

A poster commissioned by NAPOLI 99 Foundation as a contribution towards the cultural image of the city

Above Commissioned by the Napoli 99 Foundation to promote a city known for its Roman ruins. Pentagram, UK, 1985.

Right Poster for the Ministry of Information during the war. The designer places the idea in the smallest possible area of the poster – one of a series of images that has become part of the folk memory of the war. Fougasse (Kenneth Bird), UK, 1940.

CARELESS TALK COSTS LIVES

Left Satisfying self-initiated project. Eivind Molvær, Norway, 2007.

Above Mini-billboard promoting Channel 4's upcoming series 'Seven Dwarves'. 4Creative, UK, 2011.

Right For a talk revealing the speaker's top ten picks of his company's projects. With twenty-three years of work, it's tough to narrow it down. The Partners, UK, 2007.

Below Street poster for homeless charity Raising the Roof. Leo Burnett, Canada, 2012.

Right For an exhibition of photos taken with disposable cameras. The Partners, UK, 1994.

Below The Paper Prison, for the Mandela95 Poster Project – the poster folds out to the size of his prison cell. Interbrand, UK, 2014.

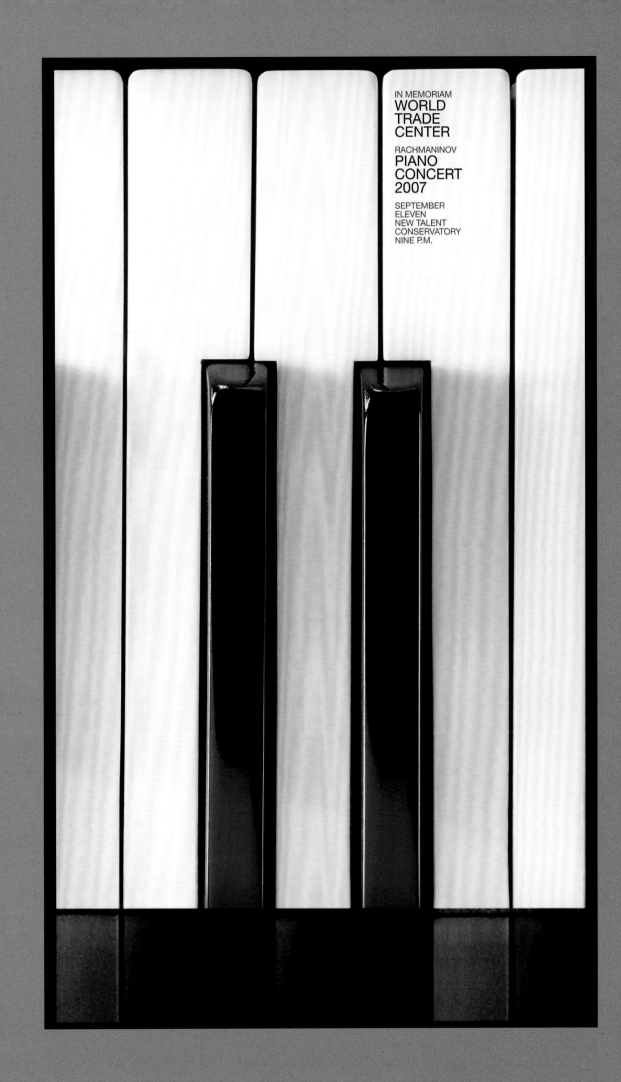

IN MEMORIAM
**WORLD
TRADE
CENTER**

RACHMANINOV
**PIANO
CONCERT
2007**

SEPTEMBER
ELEVEN
NEW TALENT
CONSERVATORY
NINE P.M.

Piano concert,
in memoriam: World
Trade Center. Ziad
Al-Kadri, Canada, 2007.

1.

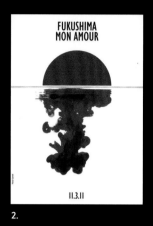

2.

3.

4.

FORGET ABOUT LOVE

LARS VON TRIER
NYMPHOMANIAC

5.

6.

7.

8.

The Modern Poster

9.

10.

FIVE-A-SIDE

11.

BREATHE

12.

FESTIVALI I FILMIT
JAPONEZ

13.

Mobil Showcase presents

BETWEEN

THE WARS

American Diplomatic History from Versailles to Pearl Harbor
A unique 16-week television series. Host: Eric Sevareid
Wednesday evenings beginning April 3 at 7:30. Channel 5

Mobil

14.

15.

1. Charlie 'Bird' Parker, from the JazzTypes series. Mytton Williams, UK, 2013–14.

2. Created in the wake of the nuclear disaster at Fukushima, Japan. Yossi Lemel, Israel, 2012.

3. The Postal Service – Europe Tour. Jason Munn, USA, 2013.

4. Wave of Peace to mark the fortieth anniversary of the bombing of Hiroshima for the Images for Survival project. McRay Magleby, USA, 1985.

5. Lars von Trier: *Nymphomaniac*. The Einstein Couple, Denmark, 2013.

6. Anti-war poster. Image without words. Jukka Veistola, Finland, 1969.

7. Citroën C-Zero: 100% electric. Euro RSCG, Austria, 2011.

8. City by Cycle: for US bike company PUBLIC. The Partners, UK, 2014.

9. For a talk reviewing contemporary poster design. Johnson Banks, UK, 2001.

10. From the Don't Text and Drive series for Fiat. Leo Burnett, Brazil, 2013.

11. Richard House fundraising five-a-side football tournament. The Partners, UK, 2009.

12. For the Rainforest Action Network. Studio8 / Matt Willey & Giles Revell, UK, 2007.

13. Japanese film festival. Tabi Aziri, Macedonia, 2010.

14. For a Channel 5 series on American diplomatic history. Chermayeff & Geismar, USA, 1977.

15. For a talk on liking/disliking. NB Studio, UK, 2010.

16.

17.

18.

19.

20.

21.

22.

23.

24.

25.

26.

27.

28.

29.

30.

16. 'Sycamore Trees' for Signature Theatre. Design Army, USA, 2010.

17. Promoting the Gavin Martin Print Lounge with a stack of book spines – inspiration for the creatively curious. The Chase, UK.

18. The exhibition title is Women Fashion Power. Four extra words capture

19. Museum of Emotions. The Partners, UK, 2000.

20. 'Rapha's lips'. Raphael Abreu / Coca-Cola Global Design, USA, 2015.

21. Tour of Britain, for Transport for London. Gary&Neil, UK, 2014.

22. British summer party. The Partners, UK, 2009.

23. 'Jesus Saves' for the Brazil World Cup. Art of Sport, USA, 2014.

24. French Open promo for SCV Super Sport. Dentsu, Y&R, Singapore, 2001.

25. Invitation to a social fundraising event in aid of cervical cancer. Cossette, Canada, 2012.

26. For an international competition in Poland. A design statement of awesome simplicity and power, as the circle comes full round. Shigeo Fukuda, Japan, 1976.

27. For the '123 Years of the Best of British Music' festival. Taxi Studio / Sam Hadley, UK, 2014.

28. Art at Imperial War Museum North. True North, UK, 2004.

29. From the Beautiful Death series: chronicling notable deaths in the HBO series 'Game of Thrones'. Robert Ball, UK, 2014.

30. From a poster set for the Design Council, to get schoolchildren thinking about design. Johnson

PACKAGING

One of the first ways in which brands differentiated themselves in the era of mass production – and it's still hard to beat Oily Bird or Jif Lemon. More recently, packaging copy has played a greater role – for better and worse – along with witty ways of incorporating the product into the pack design.

Right Range of light-bulb packaging for Woolworths. Up come the watts. Smith & Milton, UK, 1988.

Above Wart-remover pack for Boots. Lippa Pearce, UK, 1992.

Right Clearly signalled packaging for Prize, a liquid water-softener for washing woollens. Ken Cato Design Company, Australia, 1980.

Above London Honey Company. Hats off. Red Stone, UK, 2010.

Left NYC Spaghetti: a mould at the base of the pack creates the spaghetti formation at the top. Alex Creamer, UK, 2010.

Above Perfect name and packaging – designer unknown. Ronson Consumer Products Corporation, USA, 1963.

Below Packaging for Silver Cross pushchairs, celebrating what children can do with the boxes afterwards. Love Creative, UK, 2009.

Fruit juice packaging:
'Juice Skin'. Naoto
Fukasawa, Japan, 2004.

Above Logo for Hiram Walker's Red Hot Schnapps liquor. A drink that usually has a cold chaser. Tharp Did It, USA, 1993.

Right Budget stationery range for WHSmith, finding humour in each humble item. The Partners, UK, 1989.

Left Simple, happy packaging for dogfood Denes. Blackburn's, UK, 1994.

Above Made for music: earphones packaging for Panasonic. Scholz & Friends, Germany, 2010.

Below Bubble gum pack. Flat, stretchy strips typography. Herb Lubalin, USA, 1976.

Above Organic sound design. Design Studio 36.5, South Korea, 2013.

Above A little joke for large tissues. Michael Peters Limited, UK, 1990.

Above Vodka with a twist. David Jenkins, UK, 2008.

Left Packaging for Tsaritsa Vodka. For drinkers who like vodka straight from the ice box. Michael Peters Limited, UK, 1991.

Left Vodka bottle concept. StudioIn, Russia, 2009.

Right Logical packaging for Egg Nog. Alt Group, New Zealand, 2012.

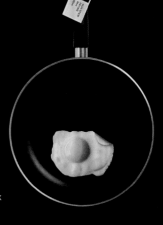

Above Homebase non-stick packaging, with easy-peel stickers. Turner Duckworth, UK / USA, 2005.

Left Pietro Gala pasta: good enough for the chef. Fresh Chicken Agency, Russia, 2012.

PIETRO GALA

radiatori

PIETRO GALA

conchiglie

Above Packaging for Jif lemon juice. Legend has it that the designer personally examined the entire stock of lemons in Harrods' food hall to obtain the perfect lemon shape. Edward Hack, UK, 1956.

Left A three-dimensional golden drip for a premium olive oil known locally as liquid gold. The Partners, UK, 2006.

Above The friendly face of Sanuki Udon noodles. Designer and year unknown.

WHAT ARE YOU WAITING FOR? ME TASTE HOM IN CASHEW NUTS TASTIC! LATER! THERE'S NUTS IN WE CANT DELIVER!

GUESS WHAT? I HOPE YOU'RE WE'RE NUTS! HUNGRY!

Nuts.com

FAMILY OWNED AND OPERATED BUSINESS SINCE 1929

WARNING: YUMMY GOODNESS INSIDE NUTS! NUUUUUUTSSSS

Nuts.com

OKAY, LET'S TALK NUTS. A FAMILY OPERATION SINCE 1929! NO, REALLY! TICKLE YOUR TASTE BUDS!

NUTS! NUTS! NUTS! NUTS! NOW SEE HERE, YA'LL

WE'RE ALL NUTS

Nuts.com

WARNING: dELICIOUS FRESH-PACKED GOODNESS INSIDE! DO YOU LIKE WONDERFUL THINGS? YA, WE THOUGHT SO!

I'M SEEING TONS OF NUTS!

Above Cheerfully nuts packaging for nuts. Michael Bierut / Pentagram, USA, 2012.

5 UTILITY KNIFE

しろくまのお米

Above Shirokuma rice (the name means 'polar bear'). Ryuta Ishikawa, Japan, 2014.

Left Dansk Design knife, the sharp blade safely hidden behind the trompe l'oeil packaging. Lou Dorfsman, USA, 1975.

Left No-nonsense packaging for Safeway sausages. Lewis Moberly, UK, 1991.

Right Bahlsen's Family biscuits, the product brought winningly to life. Lewis Moberly, UK, 1994.

Below Coca-Cola summer packaging: an iconic brand at its most confident. Turner Duckworth, UK/USA, 2010.

Left Boots dishwasher powder, as powerful as the proverbial storm. Robinson Lambie-Nairn, UK, 1991.

Right Label for a range of Californian wines for Marks & Spencer. The designers evoke the beach boy image of California with a label on a label. CDT Design, UK, 1988.

Below Talking packaging for an instantly recognizable brand. Williams Murray Hamm, UK, 2006.

Opposite Range of inks for Winsor & Newton. A solution that homes in on the colour name – and the urge to collect. Michael Peters & Partners, UK, 1977.

2D TO 3D

From Tibor Kalman to Alan Fletcher, designers have regularly travelled back and forth across the border between two-dimensional graphics and three-dimensional products. As access to manufacturing technologies becomes easier and cheaper, this is an increasingly rich area for designers to explore.

Above Whippy light fixture, inspired by spiral energy-saver bulbs. Alex Garnett and Nahoko Koyama, UK, 2006.

Above Olympic teaspoon set: long jump, javelin, archery and weightlifting. Nick Munro, UK, 2012.

Above Grasshopper stapler. Anthropologie Europe, 2014.

Left Crinkle cup: apparently throwaway, actually ceramic. Rob Brandt, The Netherlands, 1975.

Left Snow White's Revenge: laptop decal repurposing the familiar logo. Vinylville, USA, 2009.

Left Hot-water-bottle cover. Waldo Pancake, UK, 2013.

Is it hot in here or is it me.

Left Rainy Pot: indoor plant waterer with evenly distributed droplets to avoid over-watering. Jeong Seungbin / DailyLife Lab, South Korea, 2013.

Above M&Co Five O'Clock Clock: perfect for every office. Tibor & Maira Kalman, USA, 1984.

Right Focal ratio watch for photography studio The Glass Works. The Partners, UK, 2000.

Left Issey Miyake 'Twelve' watch, the angles of the case serving as hour markers. Naoto Fukasawa, Japan, 2005.

Above Display Book Shelf: artwork in which six feet of MDF bows under the weight of books satisfyingly selected for their height. Daniel Eatock, UK, 2009.

Right Tissue-box house. Keck & Lisa, The Netherlands, 2014.

Above Time is Money. Jamie Ellul / Supple Studio, UK, 2013.

Above Clock for Wimbledon tennis club. Hat-trick, UK, 2011.

Above Dropit Hooks: functional wall art. Asshoff & Brogård for Normann Copenhagen, Denmark, 2011.

Right Artist mug, exclusively created for Tate galleries. Designers Anonymous, UK, 2010.

Above Add some percussion to your dental hygiene with toothbrush maracas. Dominic Wilcox, UK, 2014.

Above 'Paint or Die, But Love Me': table made with steel and gloss paint. John Nouanesing, France, 2007.

Above Sky umbrella for MoMA. Tibor Kalman / Emanuela Frattini Magnusson, USA, 1992.

SIGNAGE & ENVIRONMENTAL

A witty intervention in the real world can feel like a wobble in the Matrix. Posters become benches, street lamps become coffee pots, and signs mysteriously shift and point somewhere else. In days gone by, an ambient advert might stir local word of mouth at best: now they are rapidly shared around the world.

Above Portable sign for a karate class that regularly switches venues. Extreme Group, Canada, 2010.

Above The Leaning Tower of Philadelphia: street art shared by millions online. Anonymous, USA, 2012.

Above IBM Smarter Cities outdoor campaign turning posters into socially useful objects. Ogilvy & Mather Paris, France, 2014.

Above Window display for Wakefield Fortune Travel. Giant postcards tell a big sales story with graphic impact. Pentagram, UK, 1982.

AMBLESIDE PARK
LAKE DISTRICT

BALA LAKE
SNOWDONIA

LECKFORD LODGES
HAMPSHIRE

Above Identities for John Lewis residential clubs. B&B Studio, UK, 2011.

Left & below Points: the world's most advanced directional sign – with rotating arms and updating text. Breakfast, USA, 2013.

Above Construction billboard on Fifth Avenue, New York. A life-size blueprint of the façades of the buildings being restored was painted on the billboard. Vignelli Associates, USA, 1987.

Above Street lamp given a caffeine boost. Cossette, Canada, 2009.

Above Flat billboard with a 3D effect turns a busy overpass into an ad for Mattel's Hot Wheels. Ogilvy & Mather, Colombia, 2011.

Right Sign for the Solow Building in New York. The number becomes a sculpture, made with 15,000 lbs of sheet steel. Chermayeff & Geismar, USA, 1981.

Right A drive-in parking spot turns any car into a Hot Wheels toy. Age Isobar, Brazil, 2013.

Left Reminder to beach-goers from Peter MacCallum Cancer Centre. CHE, Australia, 2010.

Above Sign for the Shipwright Yard scheme in London's Docklands. This has the air of having been hurled from the skies. Williams & Phoa, UK, 1985.

Right Restroom signs for The Photographers' Gallery in London. Skirts and stockings with a difference. The Partners, UK, 1992.

Right Clothes peg sculpture for the Festival 5 Saisons in Chaudfontaine Park, Belgium. Mehmet Ali Uysal, Turkey, 2010.

Right Double Yellow Line Bench, from theediblebusstop. org – a project to create green spaces in urban environments. Will Sandy, UK, 2012.

Above Concrete overpass in Wuppertal, Germany, transformed into a child's dream. Megx, Germany, 2011.

Left Pac-Man string-light installation, Geneva, Switzerland. Benedetto Bufalino / Benoit Deseille, France, 2012.

Above Repurposed trees advertise a local farmers' market. Owen Jones & Partners, USA, 2008.

Right & below Environmental graphics outside the Seibu building. The huge, seated man is on the building, and mounted on a wall in an adjoining park are animals and vehicles, so passers-by can see the man taking a series of rides. Shigeo Fukuda, Japan, 1979.

The Grand Tour: reproductions
of Old Masters displayed around
London. If people won't go to
the gallery, take the gallery
to the people. For the National
Gallery and Hewlett Packard.
The Partners, UK, 2008.

The Selfie That Never
Sleeps. Matt Blease /
Breed, UK, 2014.

WIT IN THE WORLD

WIT IN THE WORLD

In 2000, Chris Smith, the British Secretary of State for Culture, Media and Sport, secured a tax rebate that enabled the UK's museums and galleries to offer free admission to the public. His inspiration came from a poster he had seen three decades earlier.

He later explained: 'I remember, as a student, being very struck by a poster arguing against an attempt by Edward Heath's government to bring in museum charges. It said "We, the undersigned, deplore and oppose the Government's intention to introduce admissions charges to national museums and galleries" and carried the signatures of Van Gogh, Titian, Turner and other great artists. It made me realize a simple truth: that free admission is all about giving everyone, no matter what their means, the chance to see the greatest works of art, science and history that our nation has.'

The poster (opposite) is an effective riposte to anyone who argues that wit is an inward-looking designer game concerned only with its own cleverness. In small ways, and occasionally in big ways, wit has the power to change the world.

In this section we look at the influence of wit in business and in life. We begin with the creative sectors that are more obviously 'wit-friendly', and end with the big issues of politics and life and death, where wit may initially seem out of place. As the work shows, the opposite is the case: the serious-ness of the message makes the wit all the more effective.

In arts and culture, the challenge is to complement the natural creativity of the sector, not compete with it. Graphic wit adds to the richness of cultural life. A poster for a comedy festival can be as funny as any comedian. An identity for a theatre can be a stage for play and participation. An advertising award can be as clever as the work it celebrates.

Photography is one of those creative professions that lend themselves to witty ideas. Often aimed at designers and creative directors, the work shows an ability not just to understand concepts but also to choreograph them – to play one against another. That spirit of playfulness is equally appropriate in sport and leisure. Here, wit is like a ball that is thrown and caught. It implies a shared smile, and a mutual connection.

We turn next to the abstract worlds of digital and media – abstract in the sense that they are one step removed from the physical world, but as real as it gets given that we spend half our time experiencing life through a screen. Digital has created a new visual language for designers to explore, while the increasingly diverse media landscape has led to a greater focus on branding.

The heavyweight sectors of travel, industry and retail offer big opportunities for wit – on the side of planes, lorries and shopfronts. Retail is an especially fertile area, as brands respond to the rise in online shopping by creating ever more alluring physical environments. To walk into a store is to enter a temple to a particular commercial tribe. Customers leave as converts, carrying the portable billboard of the branded shopping bag.

Next we tackle some of the fundamental human needs: food and drink, health and education. It is there that wit shows its full range as a technique for thinking and communicating. It can be used to make certain brands fly off supermarket shelves, or to entice us into luxury purchases. But it can also carry socially useful messages about what to eat: is there any more persuasive ambassador for the 'eat more fish' campaign than the character on page 190?

Equally, is there a more compelling case for wit than the superhero casings for intravenous drips that have appeared in children's cancer wards in Brazil? Here, the wit is far from laugh-out-loud, but is powerfully life-affirming. A similar dynamic takes place when wit is applied to educational messages, where serious subject matter – including advice on how not to die – finds surprisingly joyful expression.

In not-for-profit and ecology, wit shows its power to re-engage people with ideas that can lose their impact through over-familiarity. When we are continually asked to give to charity and do our bit for the planet, an inevitable fatigue sets in. Wit is the wake-up call. It is a way of framing the familiar to make it new and urgent again.

From human needs and universal causes, we move to the white-collar worlds of law and finance – sectors where intelligence is the product and wit is a useful way to signal it. From finance, it is a short step to politics, where wit has the power to encapsulate a complex

message in a memorable and meme-able form. This can work for governments and political parties, but is equally effective as a tool of popular protest. A poster printed on banknotes is a beautifully sane expression of an economy gone mad.

We end with the small matters of life and death. As the American director Woody Allen said, 'I don't want to achieve immortality through my work. I want to achieve it through not dying.' For as long as that option is off the table, wit is the next best thing – a cheerfully defiant response to the difficulties of existence. The work in this section is both humorous and heartfelt. Like much of the work throughout this book, it testifies to the power of wit to outlive its creators – changing hearts, minds and even policy for decades to come.

This poster against museums charging eventually inspired a change in policy. Fittingly, it is now part of the V&A collection. Crosby Fletcher Forbes, UK, 1970.

ARTS & CULTURE

At its best, witty design can not only bring arts and culture to a wider audience, but also become a cultural experience in its own right. After all, the best way to brand a comedy festival is to make people laugh, the best way to advertise a gallery is to make people look, and the best way to market a museum is to make people think.

Below Identity for a mobile offshoot of the Dallas Museum of Art, playing on the US pronunciation of Van Gogh. Sibley / Peteet Design, USA, 1987.

Left Poster for the Winter Olympics in Sarajevo. A new use for the rings. Milton Glaser, USA, 1984.

Above A painterly neon sign for the Showroom at University of the Arts, London. Alphabetical, UK, 2014.

Above Logomark for The New Theatre in Sydney – a stage for twists and turns. Interbrand, Australia, 2012.

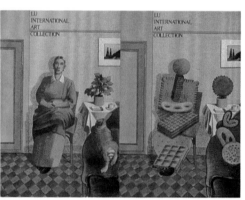

Left Poster for a biscuit company. Product as heroine. Milton Glaser, USA, 1989.

8TH SAN FRANCISCO INTERNATIONAL FILM FESTIVAL·OCTOBER 14TH TO 27TH 1964 CORONET THEATRE

Above Poster for the San Francisco international film festival. Saul Bass, USA, 1964.

Left Heavyweight packaging for the catalogues raisonnés of Andy Warhol. Julia Hasting / Phaidon, UK, 2002.

Left Confidently minimal identity for a London theatre. Rose, UK, 2010.

Right Book to accompany a retrospective of the sculpture of Claes Oldenburg. A softer approach to both the format and the way these things are titled. Chermayeff & Geismar, USA, 1970.

Opposite The Comedy Carpet: a granite and concrete installation in Blackpool, featuring catchphrases from comedians who have performed there. Gordon Young / Why Not Associates, UK, 2011.

OON, JAR. —
R, SPOON.

PLOUGHMAN'S LUNCH
THE OTHER DAY

WASN'T HALF MAD

GOT THE BEST WIFE IN ENGLAND.
THE OTHER ONE'S IN AFRICA.

HE'S A MAGIC WAND. THERE'S A WHITE TIP HERE
WHITE TIP THERE NOW THE REASON FOR THE WHITE TIPS
SEPARATE THE ENDS FROM THE CENTRE

HERE'S A POEM, A LITTLE POEM ENTITLED
"I CAN'T GET OVER A GIRL LIKE YOU...
SO GET UP AND MAKE THE TEA YOURSELF."

JUST LIKE THAT!

I ALWAYS SAY: "A FRIEND IN NEED IS A PEST... GET RID OF HIM."

I WAS HAVING A DRINK JUST BEFORE THE SHOW AND A MAN SAID TO ME
DO YOU ALWAYS DRINK WHISKEY NEAT?
I SAID, NO I DON'T, I SOMETIMES DON'T WEAR A TIE
AND LET MY SHIRT HANG OUT

MY WIFE HAD HER FACE LIFTED LAST WEEK. BUT IT'S NOT HIGH ENOUGH, I CAN STILL SEE IT.

MY WIFE SAID TO ME THIS MORNING, SHE SAID,
"YOU'LL DRIVE ME TO MY GRAVE.
I HAD THE CAR... TWO MINUTES.

I WAS IN MARGATE LAST SUMMER
A FRIEND OF MINE SAID, YOU WANT TO GO TO MA
IT'S GOOD FOR RHEUMATISM." SO I DID AND
AND WHILE I WAS THERE I TRIED TO GET INTO A H... HOUSE
IT WAS PACKED. SO I WENT TO THIS BIG BOAR... LADY
AND I KNOCKED ON THE DOOR AND THE... SAID,
PUT HER HEAD OUT OF THE WINDOW... SAID,
"WHAT D'YOU WANT?" I SAID, "I WANT TO STAY HERE."
SHE SAID, "WELL, STAY THERE." AND SHUT THE WINDOW.

WHILE I WAS THERE I BOUGHT ONE OF THESE FROGMAN OUTFITS. YOU'VE SEEN THEM, HAVEN'T
YOU? I DID. I BOUGHT THE WHOLE LOT... BIG FLIPPERS, BIG TANK ON THE BACK, GOGGLES, I BOUGHT
THE WHOLE LOT AND I HAD A PHOTOGRAPH TAKEN. LIKE THAT AND LIKE THAT. YOU NEVER KNOW
DO YOU? AND I WENT TO THE BAY AND I JUMPED IN. 'COS YOU'RE NOT SUPPOSED TO DIVE IN. IT'S
VERY DANGEROUS. NO IT IS. SO I JUMPED IN AND I WENT DOWN LIKE THAT. I MAY HAVE TURNED
A LITTLE BIT. NO, NO, I DIDN'T. I DIDN'T. NO. I THOUGHT I DID BUT I DIDN'T. AND I WENT DOWN
TO ABOUT 155 FEET AND IT WAS VERY QUIET. AND I'M GOING ALONG LIKE THAT. I'VE GOT THE
INSTRUCTIONS HERE. SEE... AND I GET RID OF 'EM. I'M SHOWING OFF A BIT. AND THE FEET ARE
GOING LIKE THAT. NO. NOT IN THE FRONT. IN THE BACK. AND I'M GOING ALONG LIKE THAT AND
ALL OF A SUDDEN I LOOK AHEAD AND I SEE A MAN WALKING TOWARDS ME IN A SPORTS JACKET
AND GREY FLANNELS. I THOUGHT, THAT'S UNUSUAL FOR A THURSDAY. SO I GO TOWARDS HIM
AND I DON'T CARE NOW. I REALLY GO TOWARDS HIM LIKE THAT AND I TAKE THIS PAD OUT
I WRITE ON IT, "WHAT ARE YOU DOING DOWN HERE WALKING ABOUT IN A SPORTS JACKET AND
GREY FLANNELS?" AND HE TAKES THIS PAD FROM ME AND WRITES ON THERE, "I'M DROWNING."

I HAD A FUNNY DREAM LAST
I DREAMT I WAS EATING A TEN-POUND
AND I WOKE UP THIS
AND THE PILLO

I'VE GOT A DOG. A NEW DOG. AN ALSATIAN.
... VELY DOG. HE'S A ONE-MAN
... HE TOOK A BIG

SHUT YOUR FACE!

SEE

Manchester
Comedy
Festival
16—
26
October
2008

manchestercomedyfestival.co.uk

 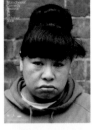

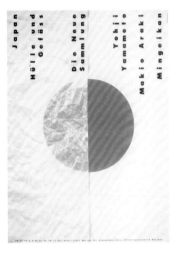

Above Mascot of the Brooklyn Children's Museum. For the first children's museum in the United States, Seymour Chwast designs a kind of polymath robot. The Pushpin Group, USA, 1977.

Left & above Manchester Comedy Festival: cheer up. MARK Studio, UK, 2008.

Below Thames & Hudson sixtieth anniversary identity: the dolphins making ripples. Neon Creative, UK, 2009.

Above Poster for an exhibition of Japanese packaging. Japan = sun, and packaging = wrapping, but the result adds poetry to the equation. Mendell & Oberer, Germany, 1993.

Below New York Festivals World's Best Advertising trophies, forming an abstract skyline the more you win, with a micro video projector on the base to display credits. Sagmeister & Walsh, USA, 2014.

Above Cover for the D&AD Annual. Yellow pencil to yellow ribbon. John Gorham, UK, 1995.

DESIGN MUSEUM

SOMEDAY THE OTHER MUSEUMS WILL BE SHOWING THIS STUFF

DESIGNS OF THE YEAR 2014

UNTIL 25 AUGUST DESIGNMUSEUM.ORG ⊖ TOWER HILL ⊖ LONDON BRIDGE

Media Partner dezeen

Left One line capturing the appeal of a contemporary design show. The Beautiful Meme, UK, 2014.

SLO

HUI
MITCH TAWHI THOMAS
15–23 MAR
Q THEATRE LOFT
silotheatre.co.nz

24 FEB — 17 MAR 12
TOP GIRLS

SLO
06 SEP — 29 SEP
Q—305 QUEEN STREET
PRIVATE LIVES
NOËL COWARD
silotheatre.co.nz

SLO
MIDSUMMER
DAVID GREIG & GORDON MCINTYRE
24 OCT–23 NOV
Q THEATRE LOFT
silotheatre.co.nz

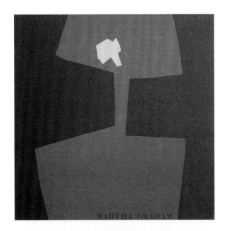

Left Programme cover for a performance by Martha Graham. The stark form of modern dance coincides with the crisp lines of seemingly abstract design. George Tscherny, USA, 1960.

Below Poster for Emu Wool, making elegant use of the needles. F.H.K. Henrion, UK, 1958.

Above British Film Institute 'lens flare' identity. Johnson Banks, UK, 2006.

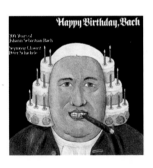

Left Cover of a self-promotional booklet celebrating the 300th anniversary of Johann Sebastian Bach. With the candles, a sort of visual offering. The Pushpin Group, USA, 1984.

Above Detail from a poster for New York City celebrating the 200th anniversary of George Washington's inauguration. Milton Glaser, USA, 1988.

Left Poster for the Los Angeles Bicentennial, bringing Matisse to the beach. Milton Glaser, USA, 1979.

LOS ANGELES BICENTENNIAL 1781 1981

Above The initials of the Victoria & Albert Museum become a single, elegant unit. Alan Fletcher / Pentagram, UK, 1990.

Right Poster for an exhibition of Picasso lithographs, drawings and sculptures. Summed up in one word. George Tscherny, USA, 1957.

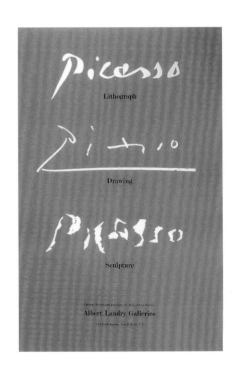

Left Everything looks different after a visit to the Tate Gallery. BDDP GGT / Paul Belford, UK, 1998.

Right Identity for Mama Shelter hotels. GBH, UK, 2013.

Right The Tate Gallery by Tube, for London Underground. David Booth / Fine White Line, UK, 1987.

A conker, noticed after a visit to the Tate. Minds open from 10am.
TateGallery

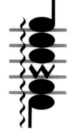

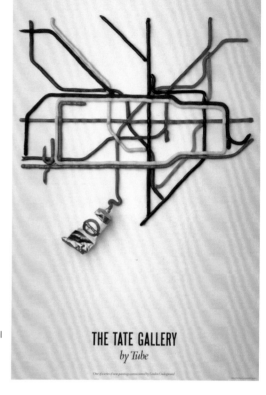

Above Logo for a series of doowop records. Musical notation offers everything the idea requires. Howard Brown, UK, 1987.

Right Drawing for *Radio Times*. Carl André's bricks installation in the National Gallery is given the critical once-over by a neighbour. Peter Brookes, UK, 1979.

DAMIEN HIRST FORGETS TO FEED HIS FISH.

Left & below Uneasy listening expressed through unnatural 'insectruments' for the London Sinfonietta. Harrison Agency, UK, 2014–15.

Above From the 'Alternate art histories' series. Christoph Niemann, Germany, 2009.

PHOTOGRAPHY

Photographers can be the authors of wit, or its subject. In the former case, photography reframes the world in a surprising way. In the latter, designers find inspiration in the tools and techniques of the photographer's trade.

John Edwards

Photographer

Telephone

01 681 8593

12 Aberdeen Road

Surrey CR0 1EQ

Left Concertina-fold business card for Peter Wood. The idea is revealed in the sequence of images, and echoed in the zig-zag shape of a folded card. Atelier Works, UK, 1995.

Right Letterhead for John Edwards. This photographer prefers simpler equipment, so the designer produces a versatile Box Brownie solution. The Partners, UK, 1986.

Above Original identity for the Paul Weiland Film Company, and a version amended by the client for a Christmas card. The 'seen-it-all' projectionist. John Gorham, UK, 1984.

Above A poster in a paper bag for an exhibition of black-and-white prints organized by AFAEP. The Partners, UK, 1989.

Above Eye-catching poster for photographer specializing in hosiery and lingerie. Kimpton Creative, UK, 2013.

Left A metallic tin-like cover for a book of photographs by Marcus Lyon documenting life in a Japanese fish market. The Partners, UK, 2001.

Above Broccoli Tree House: from a series of surreal food sculptures. Brock Davis, USA, 2011.

Above Light Breakfast. From the Faux Food photography series. David Sykes, UK, 2011.

Above Ninja knee – improvised artwork. Brock Davis, USA, 2013.

Above Street photographer discovers a strange creature. Matt Stuart, UK, 2006.

Right Logo for Joe Giannetti, possibly the only Italian photographer in Minneapolis. The designer takes one of the original symbols of photography and translates it. Sue Crolick, USA, 1985.

Ken Kirkwood AFAEP
Photographer
The Barns
Harborough Road
Stoke Albany
Near Market Harborough
Leicestershire LE16 8PY

Telephone 085 885 424

K   k

Above Business card for photographer Ken Kirkwood, with a hint of another photographic brand. The Partners, UK, 1986.

Left Stationery for Manfred Vogelsänger. Shoot away from the sun. John Gorham, UK, 1979.

Left Identity for sports photographer Steve Yarnell, for fans of the Subbuteo game. Broadbent Cheetham Veazey, UK, 1992.

Right Canon 500D DSLR handbag concept. Paradox Media, Singapore, 2011.

SPORT & LEISURE

Sport has produced some of the most powerful brands in the world, combining a tribal appeal with a motivating message. When that message is communicated with wit, it provides an extra workout for the mind – a pleasurable mental leap.

Above Royal Mail 'Football Heroes' stamps, forming a dream team photo. True North, UK, 2014.

Below Packaging for the Starck Naked range by PUMA and Philippe Starck. GBH, UK, 2007.

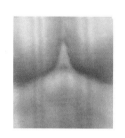

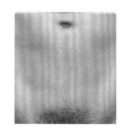

Left Persuasive ad for Gold's Gym. Lauren Hom / Jessie Gang, USA, 2014.

Above Bitten & Hisses: a sly way around tobacco advertising restrictions for Benson & Hedges. Jordan Grand Prix, Ireland, 1997.

Top Adidas Originals in-store display, doubling as a place to try on the product. True North, UK, 2008.

Above Motivational bench concept for Nike. Annie Chiu, Anna Echiverri, USA, 2008.

Right Spot the cyclist. Saguez & Partners, France, 2002.

Below Parking spaces at the Finnish Sports Federation. Bond, Finland, 2011.

Opposite Sport meets life: a family of icons expressing the PUMA state of mind. GBH, UK, 2009.

Left Footballs recycled into football boots. Sebastian Errazuriz, USA, 1993.

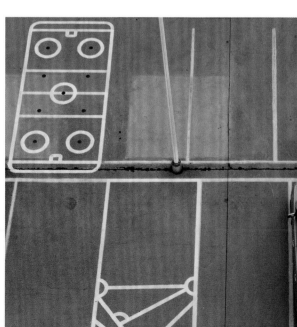

ACT YOUR AGE NOT YOUR SHOE SIZE
AHOY THERE
AIM FOR A BIRDIE
AIM FOR THE TOP
AIM HIGH
ALL HANDS ON DECK
ALWAYS BE YOURSELF
ALWAYS HAVE A VISION

BEAT THE SYSTEM
BE BRAVE
BE GENTLE WITH ME
BEG FOR IT
BE GREEDY SOMETIMES
BE KING FOR A DAY
BE MORE CHARMING
BE MORE GREEN

BLING IT UP
BOUNCE BACK
BREAK IN AN EMERGENCY
BRING A FRIEND
BRING IT ON
BRING OUT THE HEELS
BRING YOUR FRIENDS
BUST SOME MOVES

CLEAN UP YOUR DESKTOP
CLOSE THE WINDOW
COME BACK TO REALITY
COOK UP A STORM
CREATE A SCENE
CREATE OPENINGS
CUT IT OUT
CUT YOUR HAIR

DON'T BE ANGRY
DON'T BE A QUITTER
DON'T BE A SQUARE
DON'T BE A STRANGER
DON'T BE CHEEKY
DON'T BE LATE
DON'T BE MAD
DON'T BE SCARED

DON'T DRAG YOUR FEET
DON'T DRIBBLE
DON'T EAT RUBBISH
DON'T EVEN GO THERE
DON'T FEED THE ANIMALS
DON'T FORGET YOUR TOOTHBRUSH
DON'T GET CAUGHT
DON'T GET COLD FEET

DON'T LOOK BACK
DON'T PANIC
DON'T PLAY WITH FIRE
DON'T PUSH IT
DON'T RUB IT IN
DON'T RUN OUT OF STEAM
DON'T SHOOT THE MESSENGER
DON'T SNACK BETWEEN MEALS

DRINK RESPONSIBLY
DROP BY SOMETIME
EAT MORE FRUIT
EAT MORE GREENS
ENJOY THE RIDE
ENJOY YOUR TRIP
EXPECT THE UNEXPECTED
EXPECT THE WORST

FLIP OUT
FORGET ABOUT IT
FUEL YOURSELF
GET A BARGAIN
GET A DOG
GET A GOOD CUT
GET A GRIP
GET AHEAD

GET ONBOARD
GET ORGANISED
GET OUT MORE
GET OUT OF HERE!
GET OVER IT
GET OVER YOURSELF
GET SERIOUS
DESIGNED WITH LOVE

DIGITAL

The clean white page, the single search box, the story-telling logo: Google brought wit to the web. The digital arena offers designers an ever-changing set of references and tools – many ideas involving witty collisions of digital and analogue worlds.

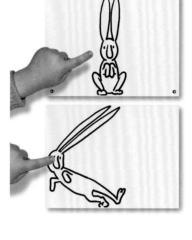

Right Petting Zoo: an interactive picture book for iPad and iPhone. Christoph Niemann / Fox & Sheep, Germany, 2013.

Above The witty 404 page: a must for any brand now. Lego, Denmark, 2015.

Right Logo for Hanaco, which designs electronic systems for home security. The key is the alarm. Joseph Rattan Design, USA, 1992.

Left Interactive doorbell concept. Announce your arrival with a personal tune. Li Jianye, China, 2008.

Right Baker Tweet: allowing London bakeries to alert customers as fresh products come out of the oven. Poke London, UK, 2009.

http://httpcolonforwardslashforwardslashwwwdotjenniferdanieldotcom.com

Left A literal web address for a designer, editor and illustrator at *The New York Times*. Jennifer Daniel, USA, 2007.

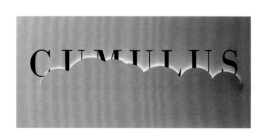

Left Identity for software company Cumulus, in the days before The Cloud. The Partners, UK, 1988.

Left Logo for Westinghouse. The designer transformed an earlier trademark to suggest a printed circuit, and later saw that it gained additional effectiveness in resembling a mask. Paul Rand, USA, 1960.

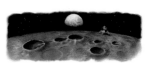

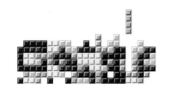
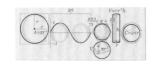

Google doodles: a never-
ending series of logo
variations to mark cultural
moments. Google, USA,
1998–present.

Above Spot the bull competition: real bull, real field, guess where he will be at 3pm. Poke London, UK, 2009.

Left Floppy-disk-inspired logo for software company Intex. May & Co., USA, 1989.

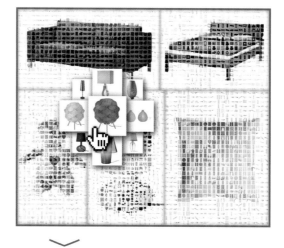

Above & left An entire working IKEA store in a 300 x 250-pixel web banner, for the space-conscious. Memac Ogilvy, Dubai, 2012.

Above Sonic Bloom installation at the Pacific Science Center: absorbing solar energy and releasing it as light and sound. Dan Corson, USA, 2013.

Left Geeks of Gotham, computer support company. The Partners, UK, 2011.

Below Trademark for telecom and electronics firm Plessey. An oscillograph yields the perfect solution. Norbert Dutton, UK, 1959.

Above Digital dandelion: installation combining a hairdryer and infrared technology. Sennep / Yoke, UK / Denmark, 2009.

Right Infinitely scrolling website to promote Orange's unlimited data offer. Poke London, UK, 2007.

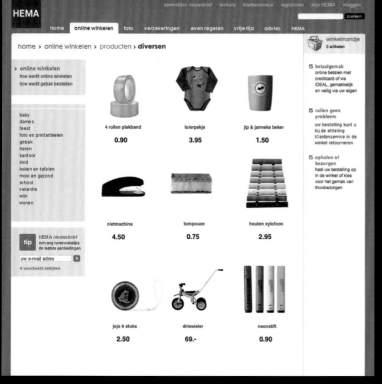

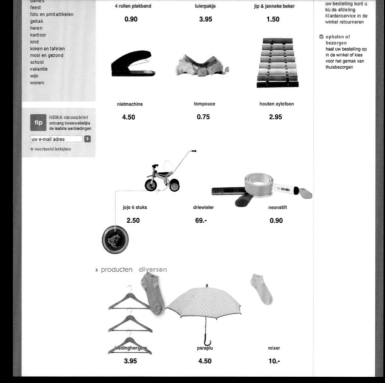

A beaker topples, setting
off a chaotic series of
events that dismantles
the entire page –
producten.hema.nl. Hema,
The Netherlands, 2007.

MEDIA

Media clients are bound up with creativity, enlightenment and entertainment. They are professional communicators, whose skill is to sweep people up instantly into conversation. Tabloid newspapers continue to put faith in the power of the pun, but there is room in the sector for subtler wit too.

Right Summer books promotion by *The New York Times*. Books for people on the beach. Louis Silverstein, USA, 1961.

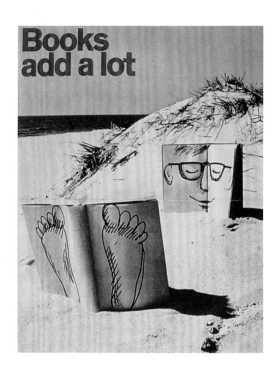

Above Symbol to accompany an article on wine-tasting in the *Sunday Express Magazine*. The famous *Express* crusader picks up a gentler implement. Malcolm Kennard Associates, UK, 1984.

Right Erotic type for cable TV series. Showtime / Abdallah Ahizoune, USA / France, 2011.

Left Logo for a magazine that was never published. Because filling in O's was a Herb Lubalin speciality, his assistant inserted the words 'and child' – from which the breakthrough solution emerged. Herb Lubalin and Tom Carnase, USA, 1965.

Left Identity for an independent production company – wise old digital tape spools. Alphabetical, UK, 2014.

Above Promotional item for Reuters. A clever, function-driven identity gains a little magic as it becomes an elegant game. Pentagram, UK, 1973.

Below Identity for a radio production company. The surfers on the airwaves. Smith & Milton, UK, 1985.

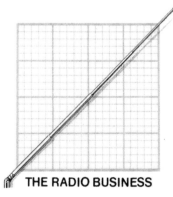

*blittzzpopzzuu…*Hi *there! cracklewhizzz…*and the all-**important** *corriander rrrttttzzzzgluur…*buenos dias **boys** popcrackleMabuhay…ooobleeppfffwu wwcrack…must have lunch*hhoooooo…*HELLO!
Tony Hertz

Left Logo for the Radio Business. One of those names that just asks for a two-in-one solution. Day Devito-French, UK, 1980.

Above Logo for a feminist publishing house. The identity continues the campaign. Donna Muir, UK, 1977.

THE RADIO OPERATORS
LIMITED, 40 GRAYS INN ROAD, LONDON WC1X 8LR. TELEPHONE: 01-405 0127
TELEX NUMBER: 8813271 GECOMS G

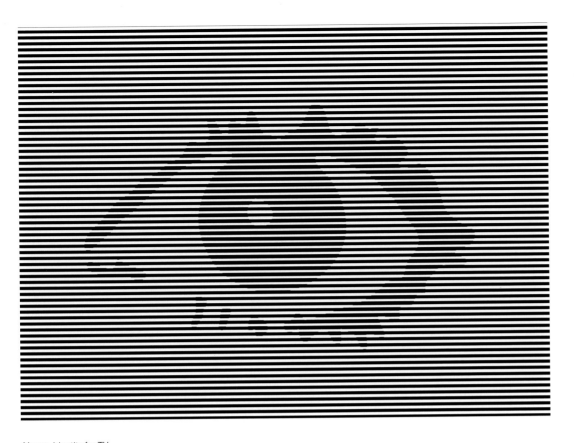

Above Logo and cover design for a small-budget graphic arts magazine in Germany. The same cover can run and run, with the issue number picked out in a second colour. Herb Lubalin, USA, date unknown.

Above Identity for TV series 'Big Brother,' the static image appearing to flicker, watching you watching it. Daniel Eatock, UK, 2001.

Right Logo for a film production company with two producers. Bob Gill, USA, 1970.

Above Cover and title page from a booklet for Xerox: a commentary on science and the media. R.O. Blechman, USA, 1965.

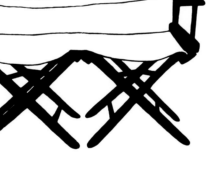

Right Identity for 4seven, extending the blockish identity of its parent brand Channel 4. Magpie Studio, UK, 2012.

Above An identity inspired by both parts of the name. The Partners, UK, 1988.

Right Comedy TV channel Dave found a suitably comedic name for its +1 sister channel. UKTV, UK, 2009.

Above Say it with flowers: winning entry for a newspaper cover wrap contest. The Partners, UK, 2010.

Diner: from a series in which the 3D form of the Channel 4 logo fleetingly comes into alignment. 4Creative, UK, 2005.

Textures and forms from childhood for Nickelodeon HD. ManvsMachine, UK, 2010.

Reality bending for 4seven. ManvsMachine / 4Creative, UK, 2012.

A previously conservative channel discovering a sense of mischief. Lambie-Nairn, UK, 2001.

Corporate colours meet childlike whimsy for Nick Germany. Dyrdee Media, Germany, 2009.

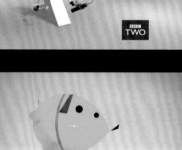

'Markets': from an endearingly playful series for The Business Channel. Lambie-Nairn, UK, 2007.

Smallest Shortest Film: lenticular stamp features a one-second, 30-frame film. Anton Corbijn / Kessels Kramer, The Netherlands, 2010.

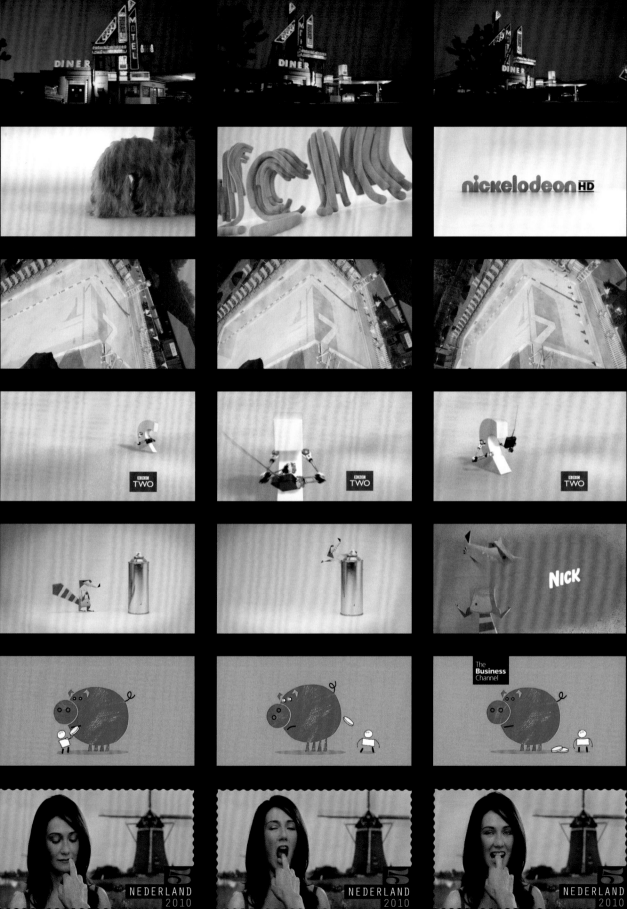

TRAVEL

The advert to book your holiday, the suitcase you pack, the train you take to the airport, the passport you show, the plane you board, the hotel where you stay – at all points, wit can make the journey as enjoyable as the destination.

Left Image from 'We're here to help' poster for London Underground. The roundel provides most of the solution. Tom Eckersley, UK, 1984.

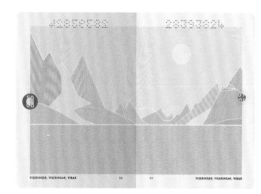

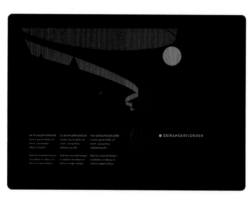

Above Norwegian passport design: under UV light, magical landscapes are lit by the northern lights. Neue, Norway, 2014.

Above Christmas card for British European Airways. Says the designer, 'You can get an aeroplane into anything you damn well like.' Abram Games, UK, 1959.

Below Poster for the twentieth anniversary of Alitalia Airlines. Candles fire the idea. Minale Tattersfield, UK, 1967.

Right Posters for the Jersey Tourist Board in the Channel Islands. The local committee asked for a girl on the beach, but got much more seductive sunshine and sand. Abram Games, UK, 1951, 1958 and 1963.

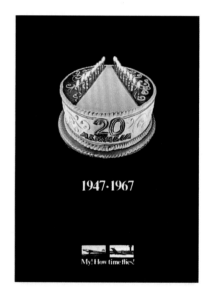

Left and below Brussels Airlines Airbus A320, cunningly disguised as Rackham the shark submarine from *The Adventures of Tintin*. Moulinsart, Belgium, 2015.

Below Lewis the Duck: part of an amenity kit for Virgin Atlantic passengers, including ear plugs, mints and a photo album. Turner Duckworth, UK, 2000.

Talking livery for
low-cost airline.
Kulula Airlines,
South Africa, 2010.

Above Identity for the inexpensive roadside motel chain Friendship Inns. Presumably they offer everything an insomniac could wish for. Designframe Incorporated, USA, 1985.

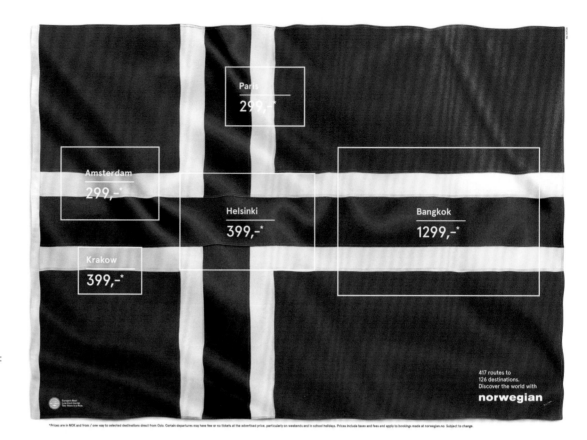

Right The flag of flags: elegantly advertising Norwegian Airlines destinations. M&C Saatchi Stockholm, Sweden, 2015.

Paris
299,-*

Amsterdam
299,-*

Helsinki
399,-*

Bangkok
1299,-*

Krakow
399,-*

417 routes to
126 destinations.
Discover the world with
norwegian

*Prices are in NOK and from / one way to selected destinations direct from Oslo. Certain departures may have few or no tickets at the advertised price, particularly on weekends and in school holidays. Prices include taxes and fees and apply to bookings made at norwegian.no. Subject to change.

NOW EVEN MORE DOGSHIT IN THE MAIN ENTRANCE
Hans Brinker Budget Hotel Amsterdam ☎ 31 20 6220687

NOW A DOOR IN EVERY ROOM!
Hans Brinker Budget Hotel Amsterdam ☎ 31 20 6220687

NOW EVEN LESS SERVICE
Hans Brinker Budget Hotel Amsterdam ☎ 31 20 6220687

Left Hans Brinker Budget Hotel – not the world's best hotel, but aiming to be the most liked. Kessels Kramer and Anthony Burrill, The Netherlands / UK, 1996.

Below Posters for the National Trust as part of a campaign to stop a bypass running through the grounds of Petworth House. Fighting the road using its own marks. David Gentleman, UK, 1977.

Left Trunki: ride-on suitcase turns every journey into an adventure. Rob Law, UK, 2006.

Above Flying logo for the Gatwick Express. The British Rail logo is adapted to launch a fast train service from Victoria station to the airport. Hedger Mitchell Stark, UK, 1984.

SAY NO!

INDUSTRY

Haulage, sewage, toilets, paper, paint, signage, lights, light bulbs – the stuff of life is useful raw material for wit, often more powerful for being unexpected. Long before the Hadfields fox first stalked around paint tins, firms with mundane products were using wit to add magic.

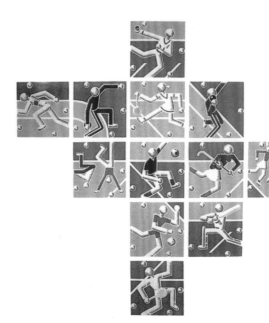

Left Enamel panels for the offices of sports surfaces manufacturer En-tout-cas. Balls double up as hands and feet, so the images link up in any configuration. The Partners, UK, 1986.

Below Logo for a reflective glass manufacturer, embodying its own name. Marketing Communications Group, USA, 1986.

ECLIPSE®

Above Made in Britain logo: an arrow made in the Union Jack. The Partners, UK, 2014.

Below Straight-talking rebrand for a company previously known as Envirotech. Elmwood, UK, 2005.

Left Small Christmas gift from a clothing company that had moved. A cartographical pin cushion, with a pin to mark the spot and add the Christmas message. Trickett & Webb, UK, 1980.

Below Detail from a 'What the Papers Say' poster for Thrislington Cubicles, after the company won a Design Council Award for its toilet cubicles and got marvellous press. The designers found an apt way to send round the cuttings. The Partners, UK, 1992.

**Garden Lighting
Company**

Above Identity for
the Garden Lighting
Company. The
Chase, UK, 2005.

Above Van livery for Benders.
Vehicles delivering the company's
paper cups and plates promote
Benders as makers of table-top
disposables for caterers.
The Partners, UK, 1993.

m^3

Left Logo for Cubic Metre
Furniture. The names of the
three founding partners all
began with M – and the rest
dropped into place. Minale
Tattersfield, UK, 1981.

Above & right The
Hadfields fox extended
its habitat to every
aspect of the company's
presentation, and made
the paint famous.
Wolff Olins, UK, 1966.

Left Milk Marque:
a proud identity for
the Milk Marketing
Board. Wolff Olins,
UK, 1993.

Above Restaurant guide to promote Connoisseur Papers. The scribble-on-a-napkin idea continues in the illustrations. Silk Pearce, UK, 1994.

Above Logo for the Pulp & Paper Information Centre of the British Paper and Board Federation. The tree-to-paper journey is symbolized in a leaf/leaf. Smith & Milton, UK, 1991.

Top & above Promotional items for Pirelli slippers. The point of sale shows a series of fetching dogs drawn by Bob Gill. The bus-side poster puts people at their ease. Fletcher Forbes Gill, UK, 1963 and 1962.

Above Identity for Bowater plc. The underlining device allowed any acquired company to signal its membership of the group without changing the name. The Partners, UK, 1988.

Left Poster for Agfa. Aligning what it's called with what it's for. Herbert Leupin, Switzerland, 1956.

Above Logo for Goodmans Loudspeakers. A woofer and tweeter help the message come through loud and clear. Associated Design Consultants, UK, 1992.

Above Direct mail for Stocksigns. Economy in communication, the product as the message. Tony Muranka & Ken Mullen, UK, 1992.

Left Haulage firm branding: driving trucks and solving problems. The Allotment, UK, 2013.

RETAIL

Retail space: that magical land where signs beckon you, windows entice you, branded spaces envelop you, desire overcomes you, and the sale is made. The design of the retail experience has become an art form where wit plays an influential role – occasionally with something as simple as a name.

Above Logo for Our Price record shops. CDT Design, UK, 1993.

Above Royal Mail 2008 Yearpack: reframing everyday life. The Chase, UK, 2008.

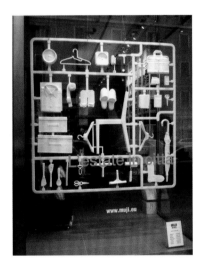

Left Kit out your home: Christmas window display. Muji, Europe, 2004.

Above Shopping bags for Barnes & Noble books, with tasters from the first page of classic books. Chermayeff & Geismar & Haviv, USA, 2015.

Above Window display for the launch of the limited edition Fiat 500 by Diesel. Two brands colliding. Dommo, Spain, 2009.

Above Christmas mailing for Harvey Nichols. Envisaging the presents actually on the tree. Foutts & Fowler for Leagas Delaney, UK, 1983.

Left & above Colourful Harrods promotion. When the store wanted to promote colour in fashion, the famous white lights on the store were replaced. The Partners, UK, 1989.

Right Ding dong, the witch is dead. Halloween window display for Harrods in London. Harrods, UK, 2009.

Left Carrier bag for the Early Learning Centre, appropriately done as a student project. Kate Emamooden, UK, 1990.

Below Miss Chiquita – an elegant way to sell bananas. Chiquita, USA, year unknown.

Right Curious carrier bags for houseware company Vinçon. Ena Cardenal de la Nuez, Spain, 2007.

Below Logo for Best. The idea of sequence implicit in the name is translated into a visual crescendo. Chermayeff & Geismar, USA, 1980.

BEST

Far left Hollywood Kiss window display for Isabel Marant, France, 2005.

Left Topman playfully appropriating the urban street code of trainers over telegraph wires. Topman/Arcadia, UK, Year unknown.

Left Logo for a toy store. The designer makes it childlike without adopting the cliché of childish letter forms. Bob Gill, USA, 1976.

Above Everton Football Club gets one up on local rivals with a cheekily named store in the Liverpool One shopping centre. Everton FC, UK, 2009.

Left & below Lego Store at Westfield, London: as fun as a Lego store should be. Fitch, UK, 2011.

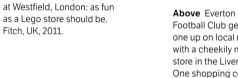

A projected image of a woman appears to blow the Hermès scarf. Serene wit for Maison Hermès Japan. Tokujin Yoshioka, Japan, 2009–10.

Left Apple Store window display for a hi-fi with unusually powerful sound. Apple, USA, 2006.

The new iPod Hi-Fi

Above Real models become living dolls in a playful shoot for *Vogue* Paris. Giampaolo Sgura, Italy, 2014.

Left Sorry, I Spent It On Myself: a budget gift range to allow shoppers to spend more on themselves at Harvey Nichols. adam&eveDDB, UK, 2014.

HARVEY NICHOLS
SORRY, I SPENT IT ON MYSELF
GIFT COLLECTION
REAL RUBBER DOOR STOP
£1.43

HARVEY NICHOLS
SORRY, I SPENT IT ON MYSELF
GIFT COLLECTION
MULTI·BRISTLED TOOTHBRUSH
95p

HARVEY NICHOLS
SORRY, I SPENT IT ON MYSELF
GIFT COLLECTION
METAL PLATED PAPER CLIPS
99p

Below Burberry store in Rome: importing a British sensibility, including an overhead effect of wind and rain. Virgile and Stone Associates, UK, 2002.

Below Giant Louis Vuitton trunks used as hoardings at the Paris store, 2004.

Clarks superlight

Above Heavyweight point of sale for Clarks Superlight shoes. Taxi Studio, UK, 2002.

Airfix identity for
Jamie Oliver food
retail concept – great
food in the making.
Williams Murray
Jamm, UK, 2008

FOOD & DRINK

In the only sector where it is justified to describe people as consumers, wit can be an effective garnish. From the daily branding battle on supermarket shelves to the more refined world of restaurants and gift-giving, a touch of humour can express confidence, creativity and good taste.

Left British Farm Standard quality mark, colloquially known as the Red Tractor. Assured Food Standards, UK, 2000.

Right Tiger Nuts packaging: the hidden face lies in wait then pounces. Design Bridge / Chris Weir / Chris Mitchell, UK, 2013.

Left Yes, they're Cheerios. Photograph for the cookbook *Eat Me* by Kenny Shopsin. Jason Fulford / Tamara Shopsin, USA, 2008.

Right Don't show the bread, show what goes with it. Williams Murray Hamm, UK, 2001.

Right Avian identity for Heston Blumenthal's Fat Duck restaurant. Design Laboratory, UK, 2008.

Above Curling poster for Kibon ice cream. Renata El Dib, Brazil, 2012.

Above Scotland meets China in these willow-pattern porcelain bottles to mark the launch of the Johnnie Walker House in Shanghai. Love, UK, 2012.

Left Festive mailer for Simply Sausages. Purpose, UK, 2006.

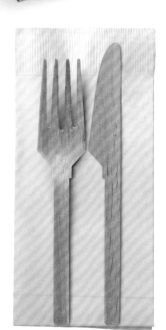

Left Identity for My Cuisine, a food-delivery business serving Canary Wharf, London. Radford Wallis, UK, 2006.

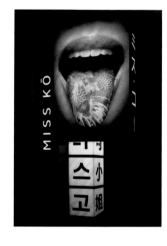

Above Miss Kō restaurant: an identity built around body art on a mysterious model. GBH, UK, 2013.

Above Quick-thinking identity for Rabbit restaurant. Steven Noble / Tasty Concepts, USA, 2013.

Above Tasty accessory: chocolate moustache on a stick. Diego Ramos / Ruiz+Company, Spain, 2011.

Right Gummy Bearskin Rug: from a series of surreal food sculptures. Brock Davis, USA, 2011.

The art of chocolate:
edible tubes containing
flavoured syrups.
Nendo, Japan, 2013.

HEALTH

The ambiguity of wit may not seem a natural fit for health messages. But wit can have a therapeutic value. Some ideas court controversy to promote an important message. Others show wit at its gentlest and most touching – bringing a smile to the darkest times.

Left & above Identity for the Eat More Fish campaign. A double-take idea, where the pig first puzzles, then persuades. Scholz & Friends, Germany, 1989.

Left A warning against a sedentary lifestyle. John Holcroft, UK, 2013.

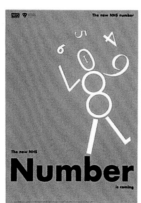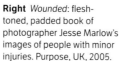

Left Posters for the National Health Service to introduce the new Patient Number. Changing the connotations of numbers. Atelier Works, UK, 1995.

Right Logo for a Paul Simon concert benefiting Aids research. Poignantly, the idea is a perfect example of fit. May & Co., USA, 1994.

Right *Wounded*: flesh-toned, padded book of photographer Jesse Marlow's images of people with minor injuries. Purpose, UK, 2005.

Left Superformula: casings for intravenous drip bags turn them into a source of superpowers for children with cancer. JWT Brazil / AC Camargo Cancer Center / Warner Bros, Brazil, 2013.

Above Packaging for digestion pills targeting heavy food in your stomach. BBDO, Germany, 2011.

Right Very limited-edition packaging for an erectile dysfunction remedy. Ogilvy & Mather, Czech Republic, 2012.

true or false?

Tam wants to have sex with Kirsty.
"Ma baws are full to burst Kirsty," he says. "And you know I'll use a condom."

Tam and Kirsty walk through the park. They see Anne-Marie sitting on the roundabout on her own. She's holding an empty bottle and she's covered in her own vomit.

Above Books for NHS trusts in Scotland, to encourage discussion of sexual health issues among children aged 12–16. NHS Glasgow and Partners / GRP, UK, 2007.

Above Letterhead for a doctor. Is it only British doctors who are renowned for an impenetrable script? Walker Izard, UK, 1992.

Above Elements from a signing system for the Westeinde hospital in The Hague. They say laughter is therapeutic. Studio Dumbar, The Netherlands, 1979.

BLOOMSBURY ISLINGTON
HEALTH AUTHORITY

Above Logo for the Bloomsbury & Islington Health Authority. An ampersand gets more than an extra twirl. Coley Porter Bell, UK, 1990.

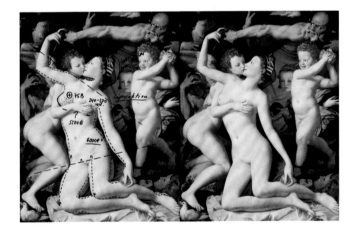

Above Renaissance paintings taken to a plastic surgeon then retouched – a sly comment on changing notions of beauty. Sarah Illenberger, Germany, 2005.

EDUCATION

Like a good teacher, wit can communicate complex information without making it feel like hard work. Wit can teach people how to enjoy a museum, think like a designer, or learn a new language. Usefully, it can also teach people how to stay alive.

Above A D&AD guide for design graduates, reinterpreting the classic Yellow Pages. Alphabetical, UK, 2012.

Above Natural History Museum children's learning guides, with covers that demand to be played with. Hat-trick, UK, 2006.

Left Poster for the School of Visual Arts in New York announcing full-time scholarships for free tuition: twelve plum opportunities. Milton Glaser, USA, 1974.

Left A distinctive voice for Quietroom, a writing and training organization. Baxter and Bailey, UK, 2014.

Left Signing and direct mail for Sunrise Preschools. New schools are marketed in their neighbourhoods with arresting signs, followed by a shovel mailer announcing ground-breaking, a saw reporting construction and a key indicating the doors are now open. Richardson or Richardson, USA, 1990.

fire

tree

person

mouth

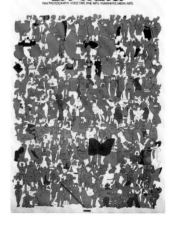

Right Logo for the alumni newsletter of the Cooper Union for the Advancement of Science and Art. Living up to the name above the door. Herb Lubalin, USA, 1972.

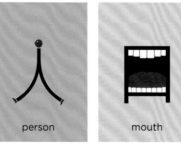

Above Chineasy: an ingenious system for learning Chinese by matching characters with simple illustrations. ShaoLan Hsueh / Noma Bar, UK, 2013.

Above Promotional poster for the School of Visual Arts in New York. Milton Glaser, USA, 1968.

STAY OFF THE TRACKS

Above Dumb Ways to Die: public safety campaign for Metro Trains complete with catchy song and endearingly doomed characters. McCann Erickson Melbourne, Australia, 2012.

City & Guilds

Left Logo for UK examining body City and Guilds. The institution already had a lion symbol, now put to a new use. The Partners, UK, 1995.

Right Logo for the Grady Gators Middle School. The unusual name of a junior high school opens the way for a playful identity. Pennebaker Design, USA, 1994.

Left Image from the cover of the D&AD Student Awards booklet. Students yearn for the short, fat, giant pencils that D&AD gives as awards. John Gorham, UK, 1995.

Right Enrolment poster for La Guardia College. Where students will no doubt learn even more about ambiguity. Milton Glaser, USA, 1984.

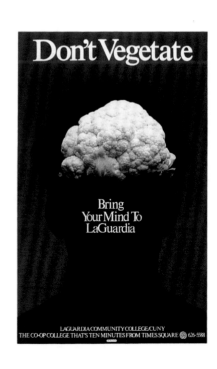

Don't Vegetate

Bring
Your Mind To
LaGuardia

LAGUARDIA COMMUNITY COLLEGE/CUNY
THE CO-OP COLLEGE THAT'S TEN MINUTES FROM TIMES SQUARE 626-5588

NOT-FOR-PROFIT

In this sector more than most, wit is distinct from laugh-out-loud humour. The messages may be serious and sometimes bleak, but the means of communicating them need not be. Charities use wit to engage people, elicit an emotional response and begin a relationship.

Above Postcard designed for the International Year of the Disabled. 'Nobody is perfect.' Klaus Staeck, Germany, 1981.

Above Poster for the United Nations Freedom from Hunger campaign. The designer finds a similarity and executes a haunting transformation. Abram Games, UK, 1960.

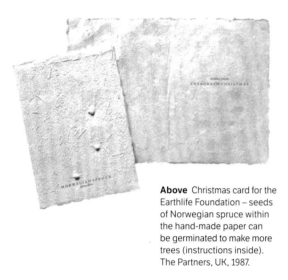

Above Christmas card for the Earthlife Foundation – seeds of Norwegian spruce within the hand-made paper can be germinated to make more trees (instructions inside). The Partners, UK, 1987.

ALCOÓLICOS ANÔNIMOS
CINQUENTA ANOS

Above Logo for the fiftieth anniversary of Alcoholics Anonymous. An upside-down reversal yields the right shape, and a comment on the subject. MPM Propaganda, Brazil, 1986.

Above Logo for Health Unlimited, a small charity running health programmes for communities isolated by conflict and its aftermath. Bringing health to people. The Partners, UK, 1992.

Below The Big Knit: the public knit the hats, Innocent smoothie bottles wear them, 25p from each sale goes to Age UK. Innocent Drinks, UK, 2003.

Above Symbol for Ocean Aid, campaigning for international ocean awareness and clean-up. Giving fish a helping hand. Michael Macintyre, USA, 1993.

Opposite Another side to the story: Depaul Nightstop posters challenging preconceptions about homelessness. Publicis London, UK, 2015.

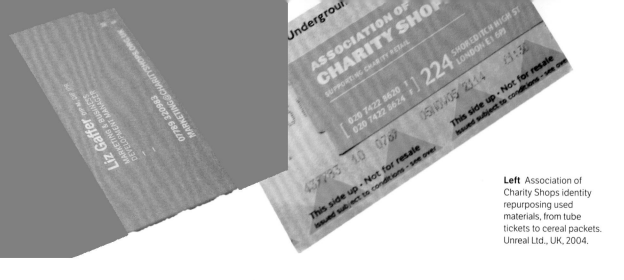

Left Association of Charity Shops identity repurposing used materials, from tube tickets to cereal packets. Unreal Ltd., UK, 2004.

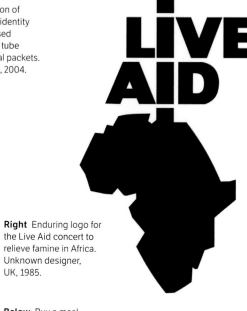

Right Enduring logo for the Live Aid concert to relieve famine in Africa. Unknown designer, UK, 1985.

Below Buy a meal branded One Feeds Two to give a child living in poverty a free school meal. The Clearing, UK, 2014.

Above Poster for Recipeace, an initiative to promote world peace through a shared understanding of food. Leo Burnett, USA, 2012.

Left Ambigrams reveal the hidden reality of depression for Samaritans of Singapore. Publicis Singapore, 2013.

Left Still here: celebrating cancer survivors for Cancer Research UK. OgilvyOne, UK, 2006.

Below Logo for a friendship walk sponsored by the Mental Health Association of Colorado. Ema Design, USA, 1990.

The jarring reality of children living on the streets: a campaign for the Consortium for Street Children. The Partners, UK, 2013.

ECOLOGY

When the issue at stake is the future of the planet, it can be hard to keep a sense of humour. But one of the challenges of environmental campaigning is keeping the message fresh and urgent. Wit has the capacity to make the familiar seem new again. Witty design can communicate the problem and be part of the solution.

Right Bear hand for Greenpeace. Mauro Gatti, Italy, 2013.

Above Birch biodegradable paper straws. Kikkerland, The Netherlands, 2004.

Above Polar ice: ice cubes with a message. Atsuhiro Hayashi, Japan, 2011.

Left Modified paper-towel dispenser makes a point for WWF. Saatchi & Saatchi Copenhagen, Denmark, 2007.

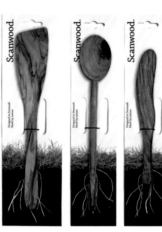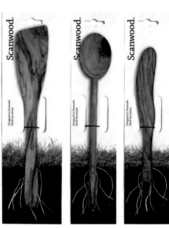

Right Scanwood kitchen utensils: product of nature. Goodmorning Technology, Denmark, 2011.

Above Dead leaf: the holes representing deforestation in South America. Christopher Scott, UK / Ecuador, 2008.

Left Clay honey pot that can be reused as a flowerpot: a thank-you to the bees. The Partners, UK, 2007.

Left Tree of Life poster: animals and habitat inter-dependent. DDB Group Singapore, 2015.

Above Visualizing the environmental impact of exhaust emissions for WWF. Ogilvy & Mather Beijing, China, 2007.

LAW

In a field where precise meaning is crucial, you might expect some wariness of puns and hidden meanings. But lawyers are also used to seeing two sides of a story. Some of these ideas project intelligence to potential clients, others find humour in stressful times.

Left Christmas card for solicitors Lewis Silkin. The designers rework the Christmas message for the legal mind. The Partners, UK, 1986.

Above Fashion meets law. Michael Bierut / Pentagram, USA, 2010.

Above Privacy International prospectus: the cover doubles as a perforated envelope to keep the contents private until opened. Paul Belford / Martin Brown / Joe Carter, UK, 2013.

Above Cover for *The Lawyer* magazine. In an issue that questions police honesty, an American designer works out what an English cop looks like when he lies. Bob Gill, USA, 1966.

Above *Inversions* magazine for law firm Robin Simon, playing on its inverted 'N' identity. Webb & Webb, UK, 2008.

Below Cover for *The Spectator* magazine. Observation permits an uncanny substitution. Peter Brookes, UK, 1988.

Left Booklet for Adlaw International, which advises on the impact of local laws on international advertising. Showing not saying: a sixteen-page booklet has most of its content torn out. Trickett & Webb, UK, 1994.

Left Brand poster for law firm Berwin Leighton Paisner. Curious / Noma Bar, UK, 2010.

Right
Typographic wit for Austrian law firm Wolf Theiss. The Partners, UK, 2008.

Divorce attorney tissue
box: one side each.
Mathilde Corbeil,
Canada, 2010.

FINANCE

Wit can reveal an unexpectedly human face to a financial organization, but is a technique to be used with caution in troubled times. It can also be a journalistic tool for conveying financial and political issues with an immediacy that transcends language. Wit is a universal currency.

Right Identity for the venture capital organization Investors in Industry, or 3i. The logo was designed to take many forms –watercolour and neon as well as black and white. Michael Wolff and Wolff Olins, UK, 1983.

Above Poster for the Post Office Savings Bank. From a 'pull together' period in British life. F H K Henrion, UK, 1944.

Left Investor aspiration meeting reality. Richard Turley / *Bloomberg Businessweek*, USA, 2013.

Above Identity for an investment advice service, the clue in the name. Mytton Williams, UK, 2014.

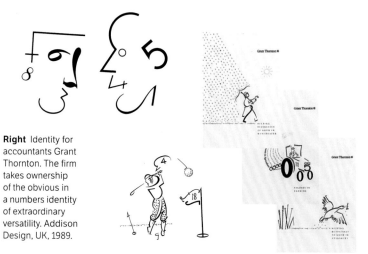

Right Identity for accountants Grant Thornton. The firm takes ownership of the obvious in a numbers identity of extraordinary versatility. Addison Design, UK, 1989.

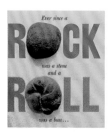

Far left Cover for an insurance company booklet. Herb Lubalin, USA, 1956.

Left Cover of a house magazine announcing a change of name from Ernst & Ernst to Ernst & Whinney. George Tscherny, USA, 1979.

Above *Reflections & Beyond*: a personal collection of 'verbal histories' by staff of Asian Development Bank who came from around the world to work in Manila. Webb & Webb, UK, 2010.

Left Print campaign making creative use of Deloitte's full stop. The Partners, UK, 2009.

Right Feline identity and promotional item for Russian credit bank Poidyom. NB Studio, UK, 2010.

Opposite *Bloomberg Businessweek* cover in the wake of Obama's troubled healthcare.gov launch. Josh Tyrangiel / Richard Turley, USA, 2013.

Bloomberg Businessweek

Crashed
One year—and one
epic fail—into his second
term, Barack Obama
needs a reboot p14

POLITICS

They say comedy should punch up, not down. The same is true of wit. Verbal and visual play can be an effective form of political protest, distilling complex messages to a single image, and turning the iconography of power against itself. You don't have to agree with it to admire it.

Right LGBT magazine sarcastically and pointedly names Vladimir Putin person of the year. David Gray / Advocate, USA, 2013–14.

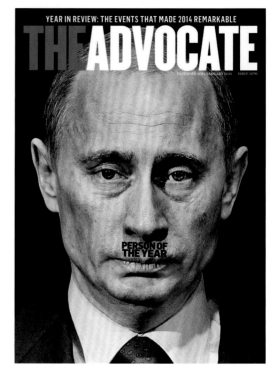

Above Mock currency protesting against surreally high inflation in Rio de Janeiro. Andrea Cals, Patricia Kalil and others, Brazil, 2014.

Above Image from the book *A Special Relationship* provoked by the American bombing of Libya from UK bases. A designer known for his quiet, civilized approach turns to cruder visual language. David Gentleman, UK, 1987.

Above Detail from anti-racism poster. Attacking by showing the crude and ugly. Victore Design Works, USA, 1994.

Left Liquidated logo street art. Zevs / Toke Lykkeberg, France, 2006.

Above The Autocomplete Truth: uncomfortable truths in Google predictive searches. Memac Ogilvy & Mather Dubai, UAE, 2014.

Right Maggiemite: advert for a *Guardian* newspaper special supplement following Margaret Thatcher's death. BBH London, UK, 2013.

Left The rubber glove rebellion: protest branding for cleaners hit by austerity in Greece. Unknown designer, Greece, 2014.

One woman, a nation divided
See Posy Simmonds' take on Thatcher's life tomorrow with the Guardian

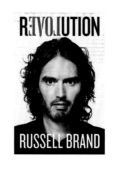

Above Revolving type with a revolutionary message. Shepard Fairey / Dean Chalkley / Penguin Random House, UK, 2014.

Above Poster commissioned by Amnesty International Israel. Yossi Lemel, Israel, 1995.

Poster for newspaper *The Zimbabwean*, printed on real currency, protesting against the country's economic collapse. TBWA\Hunt\Lascaris, South Africa, 2010.

LIFE & DEATH

Even, or perhaps especially, when set against the big issues of life and death, wit has an affirmative and consoling effect. These ideas range from the blackly humorous to the beautifully elegiac. At root, wit is about the human instinct to play, create, be remembered and be understood.

Right Safe sex poster for the Terrence Higgins Trust, coinciding with the Barcelona Olympics. Simons Palmer Denton Clemmow & Johnson, UK, 1992.

Below Darwin Chair: a free-swinging structure with 200 tearable sheets telling the story of evolution. Sagmeister & Walsh, USA, 2010.

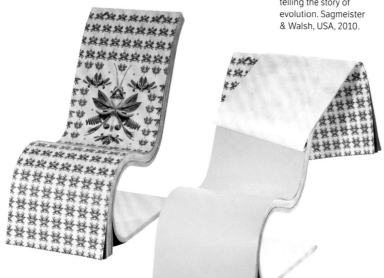

Be a good sport

The Terrence Higgins Trust

For more information about safer sex call our helpline on 071-242 1010.
Charity Reg. No. 288527

Left Issue of Push Pin Graphic in response to civil rights activism in the south of the USA. Popular images of Dixie are juxtaposed with newspaper photographs of activists shot, murdered and assassinated, and a bullet hole is die-cut through every page. The Pushpin Group, USA, 1969.

Above Poster for Corning Friends of the Earth to celebrate the twentieth anniversary of Earth Day. Symmetry and simplicity. Harp & Company, USA, 1990.

Right Gravestone: sculpture in granite and gold leaf. David Shrigley, UK, 2008.

Far right Gravestone for comedic actor Jack Lemmon, USA, 2001.

Gravestone dancefloor.
From an anniversary set
of fifty D&AD Annual covers.
Coy! Communications,
UK, 2012.

In Memoriam

18°N/72°W
Haiti
12/01/2010
16:53
Earthquake 7.0 RS

Killed 217,366
Wounded 300,572
Missing 383
Displaced 411,505

Above Merchandise for St Kea church in Cornwall, playing on the unique selling propositions of Christianity. ArthurSteenHorneAdamson, UK, 2003.

Below El Santo: reading chair transforming the sitter into a saint. Sebastian Errazuriz, USA, 2002.

Left Detail from 'Don't you care' anti-smoking posters, advertising No Smoking venues in Moscow. BBDO, Russia, 2013.

Left Poster to commemorate the fiftieth anniversary of the outbreak of the Second World War. Alan Fletcher sees the double meaning in 1.9.39. Pentagram, UK, 1989.

Above Memorial poster following the earthquake that devastated Haiti. Harry Pearce / Pentagram, UK, 2010.

Right Kikkerland Day of the Dead corkscrew. Stephanie Suarez, Mexico, 2012.

Right From a series of posters inspired by punctuation: the apostrophe eliminates letters. Stefan Sagmeister / Matthias Ernstberger, USA, 2005.

Left Boat Coffin: wood, metal fittings, cotton, stainless steel and a dark sense of humour. Sebastian Errazuriz, USA, 2009.

Left Evian 'Baby Inside': the promise of eternal youth. BETC, France, 2010.

Opposite Blood Swept Lands and Seas of Red: 888,246 ceramic poppies progressively fill the Tower of London's moat to mark the First World War centenary. Paul Cummins and Tom Piper, UK, 2014.

HOW I GOT THE IDEA

HOW I GOT THE IDEA

One of the most famous shots in all cinema is in *Lawrence of Arabia*, when Omar Sharif's character enters the film – as a disturbance in the air on the horizon, a speck, a trembling cloud of dust that slowly solidifies, gradually takes shape and endlessly approaches until it becomes the blackly menacing Ali ibn el Hussein. It is the long arrival.

We mention this lingering traverse of the border between absence and presence because it is the complete opposite of the swift zap that marks the arrival of an idea. One moment it isn't there, and the next it is – with nothing in between. In the memory, this is the missing instant. 'You can never', said Henry Wolf, 'get the split second when it happened.'

The moment may be elusive, but we have asked designers to talk about the process that precedes it. In this section they explain what works for them. Some include a health warning. Saul Bass talks of placing a 'rational overlay' over what is an irrational process. Ivan Chermayeff talks of logical answers arrived at through a route that is not logical. Many talk about the playful, mischievous and magical.

In his book *The Act of Creation*, Arthur Koestler attempts to put a theoretical structure around these mysterious events. He emphasizes the importance of the unconscious as 'a breeding ground for novelties', with a specific role in 'bringing forms of ideation into play which otherwise manifest themselves only in dreaming states'. The unconscious aids creativity by keeping the problem constantly on the agenda while the conscious attention is otherwise occupied; without this constant pressure, a favourable chance constellation might pass unnoticed.

For Koestler the 'most fertile region seems to be the marshy shore, the borderland between sleep and full awakening, where the matrices of disciplined thought are already operating, but have not yet sufficiently hardened to obstruct the dreamlike fluidity of the imagination'. This half-sleepy state was known to the American inventor Thomas Edison, the man responsible for more patents than anyone else. He would try to induce it by sitting in front of a big roaring fire, holding in his hand a large ball bearing borrowed from a friend's factory. As he nodded off, the ball would fall and awaken him, so he could remember and capture any idea he was having at the time.

Designers may not go quite that far, but Phil Carter talks of ideas coming to him as he is about to fall asleep, while Mary Lewis is at her best when she is 'tired and perhaps a bit cross'. Milton Glaser believes that readiness is all: 'You need to put your mind in a state where it is willing to accept, if you will, God's grace.' It is not unusual for awe to figure in the conversation when designers talk about being inspired by, in the service of, led by and in thrall to ideas.

Some invoke higher powers; others talk of blind luck. A fruitful area for ideas is accident, error and chance – when a mistake, unintended effect or fortuitous event provokes the brain to make a startling link. But can you get into this area deliberately? Alan Fletcher talks of 'just scratching around to see if something comes out of it, like automatic writing'.

It is remarkable how many designers work with words – as a starting point, as something to play against, or as the main carrier of the wit (as in John Gorham's *New Doctor* cover comparing NHS surgeries with private practice, which juxtaposed 'cough' and 'cough up'). Michael Johnson talks about the verbal process that precedes the design thinking. Dean Poole finds inspiration in the words themselves, as graphic and physical objects.

In all our conversations with designers, we have been struck by the common themes in what is essentially an activity of the individual mind. Without common themes, there would be nothing to be learnt, since each insight would have truth only for the designer concerned. Without differences, the conversations would be repetitive, with everything relevant said in the first one or two. As it is, it is the differences that give these accounts their bite and character.

Alan Fletcher talks of cerebral acrobatics; Abram Games takes it step by step. Jim Sutherland talks about joy; Mary Lewis talks about anger. Sarah Illenberger sees explosions in a flower shop; Noma Bar had his first idea in a bomb shelter. John Gorham remembers every detail of every design; Seymour Chwast has such a poor memory that he once repeated a solution exactly, and for the same client.

Being based on personal conversations, these accounts often have a startling honesty and intimacy. Some are recent contributions; others are retained from the first edition of this book, featuring designers whose reputations – already legendary then – have only grown over time. Several are no longer with us, but remain vividly present in their work and thinking. In what follows you can overhear, as it were, designers from across the generations talking about the secret of secrets – how to get ideas.

Arnold Schwartzman
on an idea that instantly
came to mind

When I was design director for the 1984 Olympic Games in Los Angeles, I commissioned a series of posters, each depicting an Olympic sport. I made out a list of what I thought would be important events, and nobody wanted track cycling. So I decided to do it myself.

Given the choice, I probably would have picked weightlifting, because I was a champion weightlifter in my youth. Consequently I might have done something more sophisticated. But I knew nothing about cycling, so this was a very simple idea.

At that time I was using the Olympic rings every day, for one graphic purpose or another. I was so locked into them that the wheels idea almost instantly came to mind.

I located three Olympic contenders and arranged to photograph them at the newly completed velodrome. I showed my sketch of the result I wanted to achieve before they started circling the track in formation.

It wasn't the usual bright Los Angeles day, and I was disappointed with the light at first, until I realized that the normal

hard 'Hockney-esque' shadows would have created a myriad of rings, confusing the design.

I needed to photograph the cyclists on the part of the track that has a high wall, so I was restricted to shooting them only once per circuit. The cyclists had to complete more than a hundred laps before I felt confident that I'd got the shot.

Nowadays I suppose you could do it on a computer.

The poster was popular among cyclists, and people often had it and liked it, and then suddenly it dawned on them what it was: 'Oh my God, it's the Olympic rings.'

NOMA BAR

Graphic artist, UK

I think of ideas as already existing, waiting to be found. Just try not to step on them while you are looking.

Some are about capturing a moment. 'Night Train to London' came while I was travelling late at night and a drunk guy was slumped against the window, McDonald's carton at his side, ketchup on his tie. But as the train came to a stop, there was this strong white light from behind him. I saw the silhouette and a transformation took place. It was as though he was protected by the moon – an embryo in the womb. I sketch those moments like a photographer.

Other ideas come from serendipity. I remember meeting with the *GQ* art director a few years ago to discuss a portrait of Michael Jackson at a time when the news was full of stories about mothers who left their children in his care. I was washing my hands in the bathroom when I glanced at the nappy-changing icon and saw Michael Jackson's face around it: the solution revealed itself.

Growing up in Israel, I was surrounded by humour. I come from a reality where there were always two sides in my life – a constant duality. When I discovered wit and designers like Paul Rand and Milton Glaser, I saw the connection with my own past – a tradition of Jewish and Eastern European humour where puns and close observation were important.

When I was six years old, there was a man who owned a tractor repair garage in my small town. When he retired, he took all the spare parts and turned them into works of art. Suddenly, the whole town was full of his sculptures. One appeared in the middle of my school, and I would gaze up at it every day. At some point, someone put a flag at the top, turning it into a functional object again. I was amazed at how things could move from one state to the next, how the ready-made could find a new life.

As I grew up, wit became a way to deal with the world. It helped me through school and my service in the army, where I always had my sketchbook and would draw caricatures of my commanders. I like the idea of the pencil as a weapon. It was during the first Gulf War, sitting in a shelter in Israel, that I came up with my portrait of Saddam Hussein that adapts the radiation symbol. I sent it to *The Guardian* when I arrived in the UK and everything started from there.

With an editorial portrait, I read the copy first to work out the story. From there, I start to sketch. I never trace photos. I look to see what is motivating the face. I sit in front of a mirror and try to mimic the expressions. It's amazing that we all have two eyes, a nose and a mouth, and yet no one looks like anyone else. Only much later will I move to the screen. I'm comfortable with the screen, but aware of its weakness. I've learned to control the machine, not be controlled by it.

It's wonderful that people ask you to do things you have never tried before. Chineasy (p.192) began as a small project with no sense of where it might end up, but I was attracted by the passion of the founder. Now it has turned into a phenomenon.

The series of *Wallpaper** covers (p.52) was an opportunity to work in three dimensions. All the images are created with room sets, with extra jokes that reveal themselves the more closely you look. I am exploring other new opportunities now – from champagne packaging to building a tree house in Japan.

My advice to students is to stay a student. Stay curious. Don't be comfortable. If you can move to another country, do it – it's a new lease of life. It was because I came to the UK and didn't know the language that I developed this non-verbal approach. Visual pantomime, as I call it.

I am attracted by artists who wake up every morning and do the same thing, but every day it's different. A lifelong exploration.

Design and branding culture changes every day: there is a continual search for difference and novelty. Paper cutting is in, then it's out. But the people behind it carry on cutting paper all their lives. I want to be on the side of those with a longer journey. This is what interests me.

A quietly controversial portrait of Michael Jackson. Noma Bar, UK, 2004.

Night Train to London
– a late-night moment
of illumination. Noma
Bar, UK, 2007.

SAUL BASS

(1920–1996)
Designer and film-maker, USA

In my work I frequently wrestle with how to achieve wit or humour. I observe the conditions under which it occurs. I note its characteristics. I know when it works. But I can't define how and why it happens. I once made a film with my wife, Elaine (my frequent collaborator), on the subject of creativity. It didn't attempt to explain what the creative process is, except to note that it looks peculiar, is frequently contradictory, takes surprising turns and occurs under strange circumstances. That's also a fair description of what making humour looks like.

One of the general characteristics of both is unexpectedness. When the audience expects the material to go one way, it goes another. It zigs. You zag. It's also unpredictable. Will it or will it not work? It's a quixotic endeavour. In a process like film-making, which forces you into a constant re-encounter with a presumably witty moment (in writing, in performance, in shooting, editing, mixing, etc.), it's easy to begin asking yourself 'is it really funny?'

The nature of the process, to one degree or another, involves failure. You have a go at it. It doesn't work. You keep pushing. It gets better. But it's not good. It gets worse. You go at it again. Then you desperately stab at it, believing 'this ain't gonna work.' And it does. That is the nature of the process.

I don't believe those neat stories about how one arrives at ideas. What happens, in my view, is that we mask the process with a rational overlay. I'm not only referring to corporate work, which must of course be highly rationalized in order to provide a basis for understanding with the client, for whom the design discipline is mysterious and unclear. I'm referring to the basic nature of process.

Because of our uneasiness with what we do, and the uncertainty of the result, we develop a sort of intellectual conceit about it. This is our Linus blanket. As the work proceeds, if something interesting or valuable emerges, we develop a hypothesis about why it occurred. Then in retrospect we transfer the post-hypothesis to a pre-hypothesis, so that it becomes an explanation of how we were thinking and what we did that led to the result. When designers talk about or present their work, the explanation is almost always a clear line of development in which wavering, false direction, dead-ends and intuition are never discussed.

When I began to work as a designer I had a very determinist point of view. I really believed I could develop a rational process for producing good work, including humour. When I did a piece of good work which occurred outside that

rational process, I distrusted it. I felt it was an accident – that in my flailing around I merely got lucky and hit on something that worked.

Finally it dawned on me, as I moved along in my career and developed a sufficient track record, that maybe these were not accidents. Maybe they sprang from some wellspring within me. I began to work in intuitive modes. I entered hypothetical worlds and lived freely within them. I became comfortable with premises that were irrational. I frequently set up some sort of absurdist condition that forced me into considering relationships and ideas and experiences that would not be conjured up within the restrictions of the familiar world. I would also set up some reductive, provocative condition that frequently involved metaphor or ambiguity or both. I could then use that juxtaposition to startle, stimulate or seduce the viewer into examining the work and giving it a few moments of their time.

About students – they're not privy to the process in the work they admire. They see its final form – a wonderful golden sphere. What they may not understand is that the sphere is made of little bits and pieces carefully fitted together, plastered over, sanded, painted, lacquered and then given the gold coating. It looks like it sprang full blown out of somebody's

head, when in fact it was probably the result of a tedious, tortuous, uncertain process.

Wit is an important tool in communicating with people, particularly about things they would not accept, believe or tolerate if presented in straightforward terms. People will smile and respond empathetically to situations that embody beliefs which contradict their own. Making people laugh is a way of opening them up to alternatives. And everybody enjoys that wonderful feeling of saying something that causes people to laugh. People who can't make humour remember jokes.

Poster for Otto Preminger's film *Bunny Lake is Missing*. Torn paper adds emotion to the idea. Saul Bass, USA, 1965.

Starring James Stewart/Lee Remick/Ben Gazzara/Arthur O'Connell/Eve Arden/Kathryn Grant and
Joseph N. Welch as Judge Weaver/With George C. Scott/Orson Bean/Murray Hamilton/Brooks West.
Screenplay by Wendell Mayes/Photography by Sam Leavitt/Production designed by Boris Leven
Music by Duke Ellington/Produced and Directed by Otto Preminger/A Columbia release

MICHAEL BIERUT

Pentagram, USA

I could take you to the exact spot in a store in Parma, Ohio, where I got the idea for my first poster. It was for the school play, and I must have been fourteen or fifteen. The moment was electric, seeing the design whole in my head. It was agony spending three hours sorting soda-pop bottles before I could go home and put something on paper. If I am fortunate, once or twice a year I have that sensation now.

With me, getting an idea can happen two ways. The first is really hard work. It is as though there are two big sets of gears that you have to align: if you are lucky there are two teeth that connect nicely. Suppose the problem is to make a connection between horticulture and quantum mechanics, you assume there is some place where visually you can find a correspondence. It is a laborious mental process working through all the possibilities in both categories in your mind. You just keep trying to make the teeth fit, until they finally engage.

Other times, with no conscious thought at all, the solution seems to drop from a shelf and land on your desk. It comes as a gift, from some other place, and has none of the hammer marks and bruises of an idea which has been forced into its spot.

One job that had absolutely no premeditation to it was the invitation I did for two events at the International Design Center in New York. I had initially been commissioned to do two separate announcements – and both were juicy subjects, avant-garde furniture and design for outer space. I was well into the design when I got a call from the client saying budgets had been cut and could I combine the two in a single invitation. I told her the idea was absurd, but she insisted.

After I hung up the phone I sat fuming, looking at all the work that would have to be scrapped. I wanted to demonstrate how stupid her idea was, how inherently unsuited to juxtaposition the two subjects were. I literally picked up a pencil and did a drawing, thinking: 'Well, what do they expect? Something ghastly like this?' Then I realized that what I had drawn would work (see p. 29).

By happy coincidence this was the mid-1980s, when Sottsass was big. It was possible to draw an end table with fins and funny legs on balls that looked like a plausible Memphis piece. Given the tenor of the moment, it was dead-on accurate. Five years before, people would have wondered what it was supposed to be. If I had this kind of idea even once a year, I would

be the most famous graphic designer in the world.

I thought that the poster for America's most progressive design competition, the One Hundred Show, would be the ultimate easy problem to solve: no restrictions whatsoever, an audience of other designers, nothing but commonality. How could I help but be brilliant? But people crash and burn on jobs like this.

I was frozen by it. I put it off repeatedly, even when I was pestered to make decisions about colours and size. Then the organization pleaded with me to produce at least my statement as chairman to go on the back. I looked through the last five years of competitions, made what I thought was a fairly even-handed inventory of recurring conceits and motifs (most of which I had been guilty of myself), wrote out a statement on 'What is good design?', and went back to worrying about the front.

It was the organization's idea to adopt a typographic solution for the front using my statement. The type needed to be neutral of any design affiliation, and I realized at the eleventh hour that I had to abdicate personal responsibility for how it looked by having my young

daughter write it. I gave her a piece of paper and dictated it letter by letter. The minute I saw the result, I saw something else. Making it appear to be a kindergartener's essay gave it an aching truth.

When I first started as a designer, it seemed that wit was the only way to pursue a project. I believed that the activity of juxtaposing forms and resolving white space was meaningful only in the service of an idea. Since then the approach has fallen on hard times, even though it provokes a more active response from the audience.

If you show people a completed picture it doesn't engage them as much as when they connect the last few dots, and have the moment of discovery. My favourite kind of graphics is where the design works on three different levels. It looks cool even if you make no attempt to decode the idea. It means one funny thing if you get most of it. But it means an extra-special funny thing if you get the last hidden part of it. When I see work like that, it stuns me.

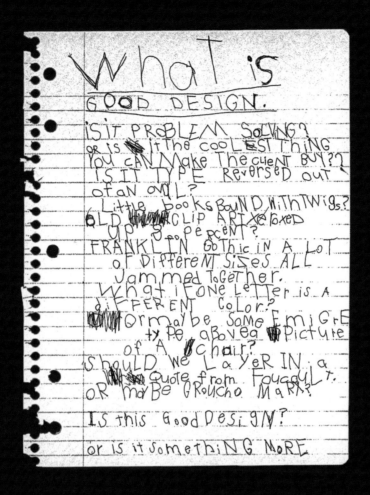

CALL FOR ENTRIES
THE FIFTEENTH ANNUAL AMERICAN CENTER FOR DESIGN
ONE HUNDRED SHOW

ALEXANDER ISLEY, JILLY SIMONS, ERIK SPIEKERMANN, JUDGES
MICHAEL BIERUT, CHAIR

ENTRY DEADLINE: MAY 1, 1992

Call for Entries for the
One Hundred Show
of the American Center
for Design. Pentagram,
USA, 1992.

R.O. BLECHMAN

Illustrator, designer and film-maker, USA

Ideas come easily to me. I suppose that's due to the nature of my mind, described by somebody as 'juxtapositional'. The connections between one thought and another tend to be neither logical nor sequential, but skewed. I make crazy jumps – unexpected, non-sequential ones – tossing visual or verbal banana peels along the way. And isn't that what makes for both creativity and humour?

Having been in the graphics business for well over half a century has allowed me to refine my visual style so that I don't have to worry too much about rendering my ideas. And I'm able to draw upon a treasury of accumulated visual metaphors. Old age has some benefits.

My one problem, and this is an ongoing concern, is that I tend to abandon self-generated projects. When deadlines don't exist, when I don't have either purchase orders or contracts in hand, I find that fatigue, laziness, or self-doubt kicks in. I tend to drop what I had bravely and boldly begun.

In 1976 Olivetti commissioned me to illustrate Voltaire's *Candide* as a special gift edition for clients and friends. So far, so good. With a contract and deadline in place, I finished my work in several months. (initially I was unsure how to visualize the book, but fortunately came across an exhibition of Edward Gorey's

watercolours which suggested a visual approach). Once I completed the assignment it occurred to me: why not film the book? Why not do an animated version? In 1996, having already produced two one-hour films for PBS, I undertook to animate *Candide*, although I had no financial backers (not the best idea).

After filming twenty minutes of *Candide*, I abandoned the project a year later. Why? Because the story turned out to be Voltaire's *Candide*, not mine. I had followed the original too closely. (Rule: when adapting something, or even when illustrating something – an article, an ad, whatever – make it your own. Then, and only then, will it be authentic, will it sing with your voice, nobody else's.)

As it happened, I recut the film after having abandoned it, moving away from Voltaire's scenario to my own – and the film sang. But by then a combination of fatigue and confidence conspired against continuing the project, although I could have – should have – looked for financing based on my twenty minutes of film.

Regrets. Regrets. Who doesn't harbour them?

Fortunately with the poster for Museum Mile, the project came to me with a deadline and a budget. My only problem was coming up with an approach. That was simple as it turned out. Museum Mile was

a project by the many museums along New York's Fifth Avenue to open themselves to the public, admission-free. Fifth Avenue was closed to traffic, and pedestrians could walk from museum to museum. A pedestrian street suggested a pedestrian figure, and the different museums suggested a different visual metaphor for each museum – each to be visualized according to its specialty (whatever the 'specialty' could be for a place like The Metropolitan Museum of Art?).

The Yivo Institute for Jewish Research was a natural. I painted a *tallis*, the religious scarf for observant Jews. The International Center for Photography? A snap (no pun intended). A section of an actual photograph. And so it went. Some of the actual metaphors were somewhat arbitrary, such as the back of the pedestrian's jacket for the Guggenheim Museum – a cubist shape which I hoped suggested the gallery contents.

I chose to mix my mediums to give an exciting visual look to the whole. It went well, but not easily. After finishing the art I took to my bed the next day. Fortunately for me, none of the museums asked for changes. That might have put me in bed for a week.

My ideas, when they come, usually come at odd moments. When I'm taking a walk – like Beethoven, who thought up his melodies during

daily constitutionals. Or Montaigne, who thought best when riding his horse (but unhappily for him, far from plume or ink). Or me, in bed at night (never without a pen and pad by my bedside). Ideas tend to come and crystallize during off hours, off moments, when – to work with Freud's vocabulary – the ego is dropped and the subconscious kicks in.

When working on any job, I always try to please myself, to entertain myself, nobody else. I'm sometimes asked – especially when I'm working on a children's book – who's the audience? Why it's me, of course. Who else do I know better? And how different am I, essentially, from others? 'I contain multitudes,' Walt Whitman wrote, so I call upon one of those multitudinous Blechmans inside me. If I do a children's book, it's the child in me I call upon. If I do a political cartoon, it's the idealist adolescent in me I call upon. And whoever I call upon, I aim to please that audience of one – me – and never fail to reach others having first reached myself. Myself. That one-man focus group.

MUSEUM MILE 5TH AVE. NEW YORK

METROPOLITAN MUSEUM OF ART

GOETHE HOUSE

YIVO INSTITUTE FOR JEWISH RESEARCH

SOLOMON R. GUGGENHEIM MUSEUM

NATIONAL ACADEMY OF DESIGN

COOPER HEWITT MUSEUM

THE JEWISH MUSEUM

INTERNATIONAL CENTER OF PHOTOGRAPHY

MUSEUM OF THE CITY OF NEW YORK

EL MUSEO DEL BARRIO

AZIZ CAMI

Founder, The Partners, UK

In the early days I worked in isolation, and would get very grumpy when ideas didn't come as quickly as they should. The identity for CJS Plants (a company that provides plants for offices) was a tough job. There was a richness in the subject matter, but I could use nothing from the name of the company. Playing between two aspects of a subject often creates wit – almost like flints striking each other, which creates the third element, the spark. I had the plant aspect, but not the other piece of flint to spark against. The first solutions I tried seemed rather aimless and empty, and certainly not memorable, which is what is needed in an identity project.

It was the quality of the plants and plantings CJS installed that gave me the beginnings of an idea – green fingers (or green thumbs). I remember sitting down at a table, copying a hand from a book, colouring it with fleshy pink tones, and putting green tips on the fingers. It looked absolutely horrid. Yet it seemed such a promising idea, because it told you what Charlie Short did and also how he did it. It took a lot of headbashing to realize that perhaps you don't actually show the green fingers, but the result of green fingers, which is fingerprints.

The idea developed on the letterhead. The obvious idea is to put fingerprints on the front. But if these were really Charlie's

fingerprints, he'd be holding the letter, so it would be a thumbprint on the front and fingerprints on the back. There's wit on wit there. Sometimes people perceive wit as happening in a flash, as a one-hit event, but you can build on an idea. I think the best part of the whole identity was having fingerprints round the handles of the doors of his vans.

It not only worked in the sense that it was pleasing and charming, it actually helped his business. The bank manager he asked for a loan remarked that anybody who had such an interesting and intelligent letterhead was worth investing in. Someone saw his van in the City and shoved a business card under the windscreen wiper saying 'please ring me' – which led to an important contract.

What is great about wit is that it triggers questions in people's minds. They start imagining – what would a person be like who has a van like this? What kind of work would he do? And these are questions they want to resolve. Curiosity must be satisfied. I don't believe any of these thoughts were in my mind when I did the job, but that was the effect of it.

As it was lonely thinking of ideas on my own, I gravitated towards working more sociably in a team. The ideas in my team have always been more collaborative than individual efforts. Our poster for

an exhibition of flower photography was one of a series of jobs for the Association of Photographers where we'd been playing with the structure of the poster. We also did a print in a paper bag for the black-and-white print exhibition (p.164) and silkscreened lettering on to a black plastic sack for The Throw Away Show of photographs from disposable cameras (p.138).

The flowers poster came from one designer's idea for a poster wrapped to form a cone imitating the shape of a bunch of flowers. You look inside to see the type – a witty way of interpreting the structure of a poster and using it to carry an idea about flowers. I thought of printing both sides of the sheet: giant flowers on one side, type in a repeat pattern to mimic flower tissue on the other. Each designer can elevate the level of wit in a job, or engage with an aspect of an idea that isn't quite right and move it on.

The magic is in the combination of thoughts. It is when you bring ideas together that interesting things happen. That said, I have never felt comfortable in a think tank. I prefer to work on my own initially and then share ideas when they are half-formed. You can cover a lot of ground more quickly by yourself than you can in a team.

I've never felt it helpful to go off for a walk or found it easy to work in another environment. There is

something about the discipline of sitting at my desk, with all my things around me, that somehow kicks me into mode. I still find it amazing that I get any work done, considering the ambient noise level. I think the reason is I am basically lazy. I only get ideas when I have to. To set myself going, start the adrenalin flowing and focus my mind, I will even fix a meeting a few days ahead. I commit myself to presenting a solution before I have even begun to think of ideas.

Poster for the Association of Photographers exhibition of flower photography. A flat sheet becomes a bunch of flowers. The Partners, UK, 1994.

PHIL CARTER

Carter Wong, UK

When I was at the Royal College of Art, the teaching was all about ideas and lateral thinking. Then I went to Minale Tattersfield for three years, and the studio was like an extension of college. But I don't think anybody ever gave me any practical pointers about how to get ideas.

It's never easy. I remember doing a job years ago for what was then London Underground – a booklet about their employees' charter. I was finding it really difficult to combine the two parts of the message – London Underground and people. Sometimes I make lists, so I wrote down what it is that makes people different, noted the various ways of showing them, and also listed what London Underground represented. I was thinking of possible ways to link the two and looking at the tube map, and suddenly it occurred to me – certain tube stations have people's names in them, like St James's Park and Stanmore.

You know when you've cracked the idea. I get that shiver on my back. I can't wait for other people in the studio to see it, but don't

want to say 'look at this'. First you have to make sure it can work. I thought there must be more than two names. That's when it got really exciting: I immediately found ten. The bonus is that the names fit because they cross all walks of life – Victoria and Marylebone as well as Alperton and Warren Street.

I love the thrill of ideas, other people's as well as my own. I remember seeing an ad for a campaign to save the tiger. The poster was done as one of those lost cat notices you see in your neighbourhood. The headline was 'Lost Cat' and underneath was a picture of a tiger, and people had gone round pinning them on trees – a lovely idea.

The Howies wardrobes came from something I saw when I was cycling into work. I noticed young bikers and skateboarders using a broken-down wardrobe as a ramp. So it made sense to use old wardrobes as point-of-sale installations in the handful of retail outlets that Howies had in London at the time.

We asked fourteen artists and illustrators to decorate the

wardrobes, each one expressing a Howies point of view – ours drew attention to the diminishing sparrow population in London.

The whole thing is an example of how inspiration can strike at any time: the breakthrough doesn't necessarily happen at work. Ideas sometimes come to me when I'm just about to fall asleep.

The right environment also helps. I love it when we are busy with a lot of projects and the studio is buzzing. That is when I feel I can really achieve something. Other people are doing good work and it drives you on. We had that feeling at college. I hate it when things go quiet, or people are on holiday, and there's a really dead atmosphere. I think you need the buzz.

The idea for the Cypressa olives packaging came to me just after I'd judged the D&AD graphics category. I'd spent all day looking at creative work and I came away on a high. Marcello Minale gave me a lift and we went for a drink. It was while we were in the pub, I was just doodling away listening to him, that it came to me. I saw

the olives and thought of the 'o' in the word. I almost wanted to tell Marcello. I remember that moment so well. You can't wait. I was scribbling all weekend before being able to work on it properly.

This is one of the luckiest professions in the world. I cycle in every morning past these people in their cars going to work, and many of them have a nine-to-five job they'd rather not be doing. I can actually come in and draw. My kids can't believe it.

Cypressa olive range for Katsouris Brothers. Still in use decades later. Carter Wong, UK, 1987.

Howies wardrobes: point of
sale with a point of view. (L–R)
Marion Deuchars, Graham
Carter, Paul Blow, Brian Cairns,
Ian Wright, Richard Beards,
Phil Carter & Nicky Skinner
& Nicola Taylor, Billie Jean,
Aldous Eveleigh, Roderick
Mills, Jeff Fisher, Eduardo

IVAN CHERMAYEFF

Chermayeff & Geismar & Haviv, USA

Humour in graphics is a rare commodity. There are few commercial opportunities for wit to emerge, and this kind of solution requires a lot of talent and salesmanship. It is not easy to be witty in print, without a soundtrack and with no movement. And wit is essentially fragile, in that bad wit is less productive than no wit at all. In a design office like ours, working each year on a great many projects, witty jobs are relatively few and far between. But there is no doubt that wit communicates better, because it commands more attention, and is more memorable. What the designer does is to get people to participate in the event of finding a new way of thinking about the subject.

Mobil has given us many opportunities to produce witty solutions. In commissioning posters for its Masterpiece Theatre productions, the company has shown itself open to risk, being supportive rather than cowardly. The design work has never been approved by committee: it has always been a smart and bright individual who has made the decisions. Our firm has not designed all the posters, but I suppose we have done more than anybody else. We have been a consultant to Mobil for so long that normally we don't even present two alternatives.

I do the work personally. One of the privileges of being a principal in the office is that you need not give away the best jobs. One of my favourites is the poster for the play about Churchill, 'The Wilderness Years'. What with the hat, the cigar and the title, it doesn't take more than a fraction of a second to figure out that the subject is Churchill, though the man himself does not appear. When I started work on the poster, the 'wilderness years' hardly conjured up an image of Churchill being buried in a cloud of cigar smoke. I started with some very straightforward images, and tried to make other connections.

When I think of Churchill I think of brandy, cigars, the Homburg hat, the boiler suit, the summer hat, the funny pictures and the easel. It becomes a matter of finding something you can play against, that connects Churchill with the idea of being lost in the wilderness, out in the middle of nowhere, out of office and out of touch. I suppose I must have moved eventually to the idea of obscurity and of being obscured. The final connection is to the cigar, of being obscured by smoke.

I cannot remember the exact sequence of thinking. The image has to mean Churchill, obscured but not altogether concealed, and that added a layer of difficulty. You go through possibilities, latch on to something, push it around, then 'ha' – cigar and smoke. The solution is logical in the end, but you do not arrive at it through logic.

I do half my work in taxis, not in the office. As I go from one place to another thinking about things, I may suddenly have an idea and will put it down on paper. Sometimes the idea is OK, but it may evolve into other forms. My ideas may come quickly, or not at all. I have no compunction about driving around and being late if necessary. The ideas that are quick, even instantaneous, are the best.

I sometimes have a great idea while the problem is still being described by the client. I have learned that the worst thing you can do is to put that idea forward immediately, because then it has no value.

My notion of wit is essentially positive: I see it as the ability to make lively and friendly connections. It is hard to make tough wit, about a subject like the Third Reich for example. Normally a witty solution becomes relevant because of the aura of the subject matter – which lends itself to a playful attitude, an openness to other ideas. That kind of playfulness is an essential part of my personality, independent of my life as a designer. It is also expressed in my collages, which are nothing to do with commercial problem-solving but are also about making connections. The delight of wit arises from unusual and unexpected observations.

Winston Churchill: The Wilderness Years

He lost favor, brooded, fought and waited.
The time before his finest hour.

Starring Robert Hardy as *Winston*
Sian Phillips as *Clementine*

Mobil Masterpiece Theatre
Beginning January 16
Sundays at 9 pm Channel 13 PBS

SEYMOUR CHWAST

Pushpin Group, USA

Wit is the way I solve problems. It is a way of thinking that allows me to come up with graphic ideas. Although the wit is there, the work is not necessarily funny. Design is play, and designers use a whole gamut of techniques that could be considered playful. Some are funny: some have serious intent.

I discovered how powerful and serious wit can be when I was in the Czech Republic judging a poster biennale during the Yugoslav Wars of the early 1990s. Two Sarajevo designers were showing about thirty posters, hand-drawn, all based on puns and American clichés like Coca-Cola and Andy Warhol's soup cans. They were presenting the war as totally absurd while living through it at the same time. Their intention was to make people aware of what was happening, but their technique was light and funny.

In my work there is always some sort of graphic play, in that there is an idea which is surprising. Wit usually involves the juxtaposition of elements that do not belong together. I frequently take two points that have to be addressed and combine them in one image. The result may be crazy or surreal, but it makes sense because the subject has both those sides to it. The way I go about it is to fool around with the two elements until the combination makes the most sense. It has to work as an idea as well as being graphically valid. If I find I have to try too hard, or stretch too much, I forget it and try something else.

I guess people do different things when they get stuck. I just forget about it, go to sleep that night, and when I wake up I usually get a perfect idea. I have to be in bed, coming out of sleep, half awake, and then things come together. It is curious that after I have worked on a job all day long and failed to come up with a solution, the next morning it pops into my head.

I am sure it is because my mind is clear of all the other junk it has to go through during the day. Early in the morning my brain solves graphic problems. Not that these are always good solutions. Sometimes when I start to work on the idea in the studio, it is really awful. I think it makes sense until I try to put it down on paper.

Funnily enough, some of the ideas that might be thought of as my best work I considered just ordinary when they first came into my mind. Only later did it become obvious that the solution would be terrific. As soon as I tried it, it came to life.

There is no way to predict other people's reactions, of course. There have been times when I have done a lousy job and people love it. On the other hand an idea I consider exceptional very often never sees the light of day. I can rarely say how I arrived at a particular idea, because I have little memory for past jobs. I once did a little drawing for a new financial magazine to go with a story about investing in stocks or bonds. The idea was about people gambling with your money, so I drew a hand throwing a pair of dice. It ran. A year later I was asked to do another drawing for the same magazine, and the drawing I did came out exactly the same. I had completely forgotten about the first one, and it really amazed me that not only the idea but also the drawing were identical. I must be in a rut.

In graphic design in the States there seem to be fewer people who draw. The computer has encouraged designers to go for graphic tricks using existing material, and any wit in a design tends to be based on collage. But drawing is more personal and expressive.

I do a lot of illustration, but I prefer assignments that involve both illustration and design. I most enjoy working on posters, because they are such complete assignments. The mere fact that museums have poster collections also makes me think of the job in a different way. A poster is a big statement: there has to be an idea and a point of view. I do not start with humour: I am not a cartoonist. I start with a graphic idea.

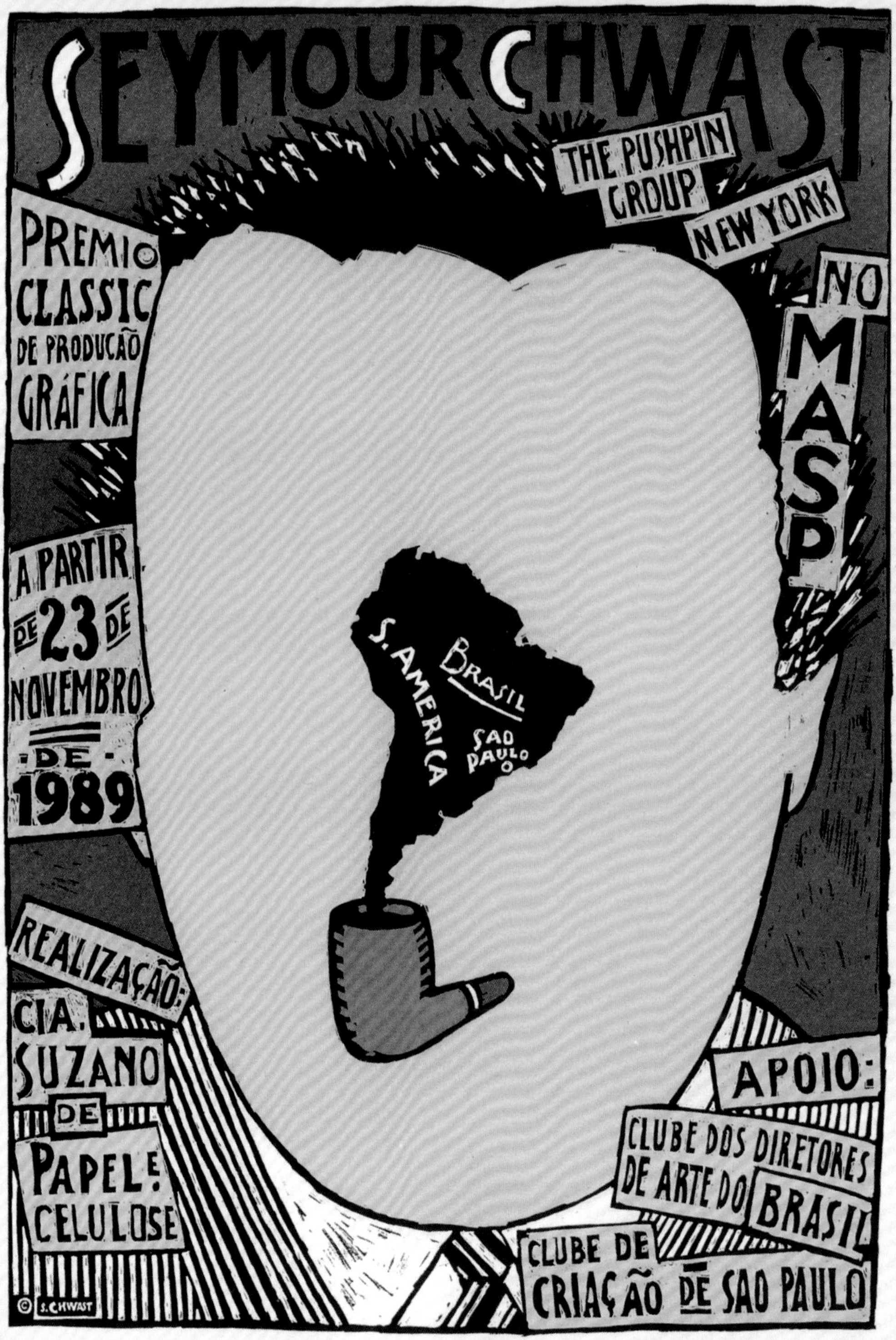

Impresso em Capa-Texto Classic 180 g/m², da Cia. Suzano

ALAN FLETCHER

(1931–2006)
Pentagram founder, UK

I was taught the disciplines of the Swiss school: it was the ethic of the anonymous typographer. The other influence was American design, the wisecrack if you like. I guess I'm a product of both of those, and I'm more interested in wit than in humour. Humour is entertaining, but wit makes you look at something in a different way. Buster Keaton said that a comedian does funny things; a good comedian does things funny. The second is more subtle.

Work should express the kind of person you are, and I do not have a linear mind. I like to put odd things together. I see wit as cerebral acrobatics. You stand thoughts on their head. You have little pictures in your mind and juggle them around. An idea may come in microseconds, or a few minutes, or months. I have no rules or regulations about how I think. Sometimes I sort through my mental archive, up pops a card and that's it. Other times I go to bed without an idea in my head, and I wake up to find it's all there – and I've written the caption too.

I don't encourage myself to think in an elliptical way. My problem is the reverse. I have to control it, otherwise I could be amusing myself all day, and nobody else would understand what I meant. If an idea is not coming as quickly as it should, my mind takes off somewhere else. I'm probably thinking about another job. So I'll go over to this other job and start that, and the same happens. I actually have to discipline myself.

The worst thing that anybody can say to me is 'Do whatever you like.' Then I have to set up my own boundaries, and fence myself in. The Designers Saturday poster was a job where I had to set my own challenges. I thought 'what are the three most boring colours?' – the primary colours; 'what are the three most boring shapes?' – the triangle, circle and square; and 'what else is boring?' – grey. I thought I'd turn the ingredients into a party, which is what Designers Saturday is.

I remembered that Kandinsky wrote about certain colours relating to certain shapes. Red is for squares, and so on. I actually did a little exercise in the studio and got people to colour in the triangle, circle and square. Only two designers did it the way Kandinsky recommended. He had done a similar survey in Weimar and got a 90% score, which proved his theory was right. I found two

out of thirty. That is one of the private jokes in my jobs. I often feed these in for my own entertainment, an extra 5%, my little treasure.

I can't use a computer, and the further the work gets from the hand and the head, the more difficult I find it. A lot of my solutions are influenced by my wish to shed the number of people I'm dependent on. If I think of an idea that probably should be done photographically, I tend to try and think of something else. I often hand-write the words: why should I look through all these type books and pay some guy to set it? It says what it says.

Ideas have to be massaged into reality. What you think of in your head isn't the same as on a piece of paper. Sometimes it's better on paper, often it's better in your head. I'm very dogged, and will exercise an unbelievable degree of patience to try and get to where I'm trying to go. I'll do a job six or seven times. But it has to look like I did it in three minutes.

Being a perfectionist means I feel quite ill if a job goes out that I'm not happy with. On occasion I've asked the client to send back the artwork on some pretext or other, and I do

it again. The reason might be just that I picked the wrong yellow. I can't just say 'oh, that'll do', whether the job is for a palace or a garage – it's against my nature.

Some designers don't like to check their work with others. I'll ask anybody. I value all sorts of comments. I may think my idea is better, other times I change my mind. I'm interested in getting the idea right, not in being the one who thought of it. If someone has a better idea and is willing to give it to me, I'll take it.

It's a tough business. When you present your work, you are revealing yourself. I think designers like undressing in front of total strangers two or three times a day. Some, of course, merely have commercial tricks up their sleeve that they put on the table, but that's not design, that's greengrocery.

Designers Saturday
London 9·X·82

Alan Fletcher

SHIGEO FUKUDA

(1932–2009)
Sculptor, graphic artist and designer, Japan

Designs differ from pictures in that they have an object. Thinking about the object allows the idea to materialize naturally. I do not put the ideas I have straight on to paper. Rather I toy with them, and create them visually on the table in my studio.

I do not employ assistants, but do all the design work by myself. That means I am always thinking about the next job and about ideas for designs. I have no lack of ideas, but I try to think of ideas which suit me.

When I start to work on a job, first I wash my hands with soap. Then I sharpen ten or more pencils with a cutter-knife. This is a sort of ceremony aimed at putting the ideas I have into shape. I do not use a computer. My ideas appeal to the visual sense and I use the computer within my own brain. Then I develop my ideas with pencil on paper.

I have no lack of ideas because I think of everything in day-to-day life and culture in visual terms. I am very fond of my work.

Design is a creation to satisfy yourself, your client and everyone who sees it. You cannot convince your client unless you have confidence in your own sense and your own ideas.

I enjoy my daily work and creation. I think I shall continue doing so as long as there are people who depend on me. I do not think it is a matter of genius, but more of continuing something you like after your own manner. I have liked making things ever since I was a child and I still do. Age does not come into the question.

I hope my happy days will continue. I have known the pleasure of creating things ever since my childhood, and it has always been dearer to me than eating or sleeping. I like thinking of things that no one else has thought of.

Japanese designers these days use computers. I want to go on thinking of what creation is without computers. I believe there is a whole world out there that needs to be thought about. I am glad to be here in this interesting age.

Newspaper illustrations. The umbrella stands for the weather not between the weather. Shigeo Fukuda, Japan, 1978.

ABRAM GAMES

(1914–1996)
Graphic designer, UK

The most valuable accessory in my studio is a large wastepaper basket. Getting ideas is easy: deciding on the right idea and developing it is the difficult thing. It can involve hundreds of sketches. I carry scraps of paper and work on train journeys, refining ideas as I go. Back at the studio, if a particular idea seems right I will work on it. Or next morning I will throw it out and start all over again. I am not lazy, but ruthless with myself in striving for a satisfactory graphic form. I believe in being an arch-critic, not selling myself an idea.

I never work large, because my interest has always been in poster design, and posters seen at a distance are small. If ideas do not work when they are an inch high, they are never going to work. I stimulate my mind by drawing. I will concentrate on a design for hours, not conscious of time at all.

For me it is a step-by-step approach. The starting point for my army poster 'Use spades not ships' was our wartime predicament. U-boats were sinking our merchant ships and destroying supply lines, so we had to grow food here. The poster had to encourage men to dig around their barracks wherever there was spare ground.

The issue was the need to bypass ships by growing food here. What do you do when you grow food? You use seeds. But you can't illustrate a seed, it is too puny. Is a bulb any good? No, it does not represent the variety of food. What would be true for all food? Preparation of the ground. You use tools. Which tools? A fork and spade. Is a fork any good? Could be. Is a spade any good? You draw lots of spades.

The other half of the message is ships. How can you bring them in? The first image that comes to mind is a ship with a funnel, sideways on. How can you integrate that? You keep on drawing the spade, a square spade, and it has nothing in common with a ship. But this is an upright poster not a landscape poster, so you draw the ship front view. 'Ah, I think so.' You can get a reflection of a spade shape. The two things begin to link together.

So far, though, it is just a symbol, not a poster. You need to show the productive results, you need earth. Eventually you put in the ploughed soil and the waves, so that everything is juxtaposed, on one side the sea, on the other the land. It takes a long time to get to it, but I am a very determined man. I will make it work if I know it is right.

A poster with a measure of intrigue engages the mind of the spectator, and he or she looks again. You have to take the spectator along with you so he or she follows your line of thought. The best way I can describe what happens is to say that as the designer you wind the spring, and it is released in the mind of the viewer.

If I get stuck on a job I go out for a walk, give myself a whisky and soda, or go to bed early. There have been some serious periods in my life when I have been badly stuck for weeks, and it is usually the result of being overtired. Sometimes I am in bed at half past eight. This block comes often. In fact the longer you are at it, the more often you experience it.

I have also seen it in young students. I remember a case with a student designing a book jacket for *The Travels of Marco Polo*. He was not getting anywhere. I talked it through with him. Who was Marco Polo? A great explorer and traveller. What does travel suggest? How would you analyse it? Well, you go to places. OK, what happens then? You go to other places and discover new territories. And after that? Well, you go again.

If you go to one place, which direction might you take – north, south, east or west? Let's say north. And when you get there, which way have you got to go to get back? I suppose you go to the south. What was his name? Marco Polo. Look (I'm drawing now), go north, go south, go north again, go south again, what's that? That's an M. What's M? M for Marco. That's it. You can do the same for Polo. That's your book cover.

I told him to go away and build on the idea. This was only the skeleton and he needed to make a design – to think in terms of shapes, forms, thicknesses of line and so on. I told him, 'Open your mind. Work on that basis. But when you've done all that, tear it up because it's my idea not yours.'

A. GAMES
USE SPADES NOT SHIPS
GROW YOUR OWN FOOD
AND SUPPLY YOUR OWN COOKHOUSE

MILTON GLASER

Milton Glaser, Inc., USA
Founder of Pushpin Group

Pushpin came out of a design tradition that was formalistic and post-Bauhaus, which thought about edges, shapes and scale, and was concerned with purity and reductiveness. At Pushpin we were interested in narration and storytelling, and approached design from an illustrator's point of view. When you begin telling stories, the opportunity for wit and humour becomes more obvious than when you are arranging red squares on a box.

Humour has a fundamental characteristic that relates it to design or communication. A unifying idea in both humour and design is the disruption of expectation. The issue in design is to make people pay attention, which is difficult. So what you often do is set the stage and then disrupt it.

The only way of establishing a first entry point is to understand what your audience knows. You basically use clichés to establish the context. Although clichés are your most powerful instrument, they need to be detoxified. You cannot use clichés unless you disrupt them.

I do not know how I get ideas. I think it is possible to describe everything except what is central. An act of insight or a creative act is not very definable. The process is not rational. It exists beneath the surface of your understanding. If it were quantifiable, it would not be creative or surprising.

The brilliance is in discovering concealed relationships. The process is similar to dreaming: you find an underground river. By definition, this activity is not susceptible to the will. In all descriptions that I have ever read, what happens is you put yourself in a state of readiness. One book said it is like a hunting dog getting set for the bird to fall. The bird hasn't fallen yet, the bird hasn't been shot yet, but the dog is ready.

This is very different from willing something. You cannot insist on getting an idea by two o'clock. You need to put your mind in a state where it is willing to accept, if you will, God's grace. These ideas happen when you release your mind from its wilful demand for something to happen.

In my life's experience, whenever I have needed an idea, it has happened. Robert Graves wrote about the idea of genius (in the Roman sense) as being your companion in life. It is at your side. Your genius is like a fairy godmother. Everyone has one. However, you have to respect it and encourage it, and not drive it away. In other words, you appreciate it for what it has given you, you are modest in front of it and you do not take it for granted.

Everyone has a different sort of mechanism for being able to trigger ideas. Hemingway worked standing up. Schiller had apples in his drawer because the smell of apples inspired him. We all have different wiring.

I have always started with words. That is part of the narrative imperative that Pushpin was interested in early on. How you get people to pay attention is always the central theme, and narration is an attempt to penetrate the immunity of an audience.

Today it is difficult to pierce people's consciousness because people are cynical and disbelieving about everything. The sense of irony is the most prevalent form of communication. In the poster I did for the School of Visual Arts in New York in 1994, I tried to create a believable document that explained why and how it was engaging your interest.

The idea is antithetical to the concept of the poster as a hermetic system. It is also antithetical to the historical idea of how you communicate. It is complex, and you are meant to be simple. It is unsure, and you are meant to be sure. It offers an alternative solution to what is presented. The issue is, does it still do what it is supposed to do: attract people to look at it, raise questions in their mind and lead them to believe that the school has some intellectual currency?

I think it is a characteristic of our time in all the arts that you understand a narration by what is left out as much as by what is included. It is the act of completion you make as a viewer or reader that engages you. Works are invitations to enter rather than the complete systems characteristic of other times. Instead of being a receiver of knowledge, you participate in its structuring. Then when you reach the conclusion it sticks in your memory.

Wit is a powerful persuader because it illuminates something that you agree with, but were never fully able to comprehend. It is a gift of insight.

Words

In words as fashions the same rule will hold,
Alike fantastic if too new or old.
Be not the first by whom the new are tried,
Nor yet the last to lay the old aside.

Alexander Pope

Image

Thoughts

This poem is impossible. Silas usually has a better touch with his choice of quotations. This one generates no imagery at all. Maybe the words can make the image without anything else happening. What's the heart of this poem? Don't be trendy if you want to be serious. (Isn't doing the poster this way trendy in itself?) I guess one could reduce the idea further by suggesting that the new emerges behind and through the old, like this:

Not bad, but more didactic than visual. Maybe what wants to be said is that the old and the new are locked in a dialectical embrace–a kind of dance where each defines the other.

Am I being simple-minded? Is it the kind of simple that looks obvious or the kind that looks profound? There is a significant difference. This could be embarrassing. Actually, I realize fear of embarrassment drives me as much as any other ambition.

Do you think this sort of thing could really attract a student to the school?

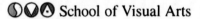

School of Visual Arts

A COLLEGE OF THE ARTS

B.F.A. Programs in Advertising, Animation, Art Education,
Art Therapy, Cartooning, Computer Art, Film and Video, Fine Arts,
Graphic Design, Illustration, Interior Design, Photography.
M.F.A. Programs in Computer Art, Fine Arts, Illustration, Photography
and Continuing Education Programs.

209 E. 23 ST., N.Y.C., 10010-3994 1-800-366-7820 FAX: 212-725-3587

JOHN GORHAM

(1937–2001)
Graphic designer, UK

I have learned over years of experience that you cannot consciously come up with a witty idea to solve a graphic design problem. It is a subconscious process. You have to rely on your brain to work for you while you are doing something else.

If you are consciously trying to think of an idea, all sorts of possibilities come to mind. But they are clichés. The conscious part of the brain can think only in terms of what it knows, what it has learnt, what it has seen. So if you think of a good idea, you know damn well you must have seen it somewhere. It is almost certain to be another designer's solution. It is the subconscious that comes up with the unexpected.

When I start a job I always use the same approach. I immediately get a bit of paper and start scribbling. I put down anything associated with the subject. This is just a nervous reaction really. I feel I must be doing something, but know it won't actually be any good to me. Usually the solution comes out of the blue, without my knowing it is going to happen. That really fascinates me. What is going on in the brain?

The *New Doctor* magazine cover is a good example of how an idea happens. I designed it for John McConnell in the early 1970s.

The main subject of the issue was finance, with one article on private practice and another on the NHS. I was very keen to do a good job for John, but days were disappearing and I still had no answer. I started to panic, because usually ideas had happened by then in my previous work. You start thinking negatively, and scare yourself.

At Waterloo station I was still worrying away at the problem, then decided to forget it and read the *Evening Standard* on the train home. I looked at 'Londoner's Diary' then turned to the next page and started reading something totally different. When I was about three lines into it my brain said: 'Hang on a minute. Go back to what you have just read. There is something there.' I turned back and found the phrase 'cough up'. I instantly knew that this was going to be the lever to open up Aladdin's cave.

I was so thrilled, my heart pumped. I thought I might be kidding myself, and couldn't wait to prove the idea on paper, to make sure it fitted together in the way my brain was telling me. The cover I did showed two doors of two surgeries – NHS and private – both doors slightly ajar, with speech balloons coming out, the first saying 'Cough', the second 'Cough up'.

I have noticed that the answer often comes from something accidental. Another good example is the poster I did with Howard Brown for the Jack Gold film *Red Monarch*, a black comedy about Stalin. As we were chatting after the private screening in Soho, Howard suggested it might be quite interesting to put a red nose on Stalin. I liked that, because the guy was a clown. But he was a tyrant as well, so I knew a red nose wasn't enough.

We were walking back along Old Compton Street when I suddenly knew what it ought to be. A tomato. Somebody has thrown a tomato at the image of a tyrant, and it ends up hitting his nose. That gets over the two opposing elements, the political and the comic, and brings them together.

I don't think this tomato idea would ever have happened to me if I hadn't bought a book of Michael English's pop paintings a few weeks earlier. One image fascinated me – a tomato splattered on a wall with pips and juice dripping down. That image was somewhere in my mind, and when I was thinking about this problem, my mind picked it up.

What is lovely about solving jobs this way is that a graphic idea will formulate its own way of putting down an image. Ideas seldom repeat themselves in terms of technique. The technique comes from the idea, so it is fresh. Another plus for this kind of thinking is that you get such fun out of it. You entertain yourself. I have had many thrilling moments of sheer elation.

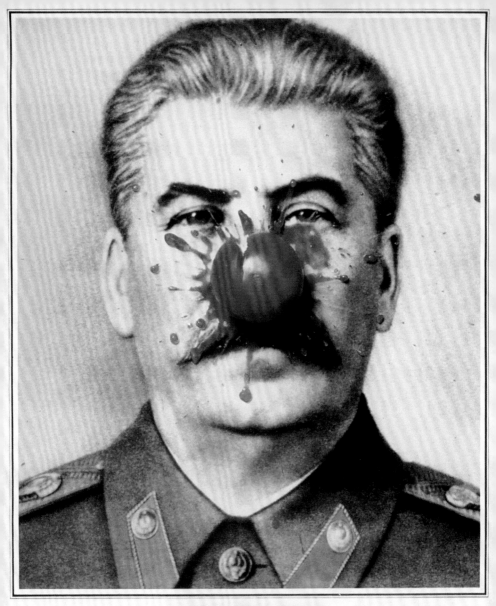

AN ENIGMA PRODUCTION
FOR GOLDCREST

★

COLIN BLAKELY

★

DAVID SUCHET

SPECIAL APPEARANCE BY
CARROLL BAKER

ЯED
MONARCH

EXECUTIVE PRODUCER
DAVID PUTTNAM

★

SCREENPLAY BY
CHARLES WOOD
BASED ON THE STORIES OF YURI KROTKOV

PRODUCED BY
GRAHAM BENSON

★

DIRECTED BY
JACK GOLD

SARAH ILLENBERGER

Visual storyteller, Germany

There is something biological about wit – it has a physical impact. When an idea comes to you and makes you smile, you feel that release of endorphins. I'm sure there's something addictive about it.

From a young age, I was surrounded by creative people. My playground was the work-shop above my mother's jewellery shop and the food store for my father's restaurant. I would spend hours playing with objects – painting them, combining them, experimenting.

I realized only recently that these elements were coming out in my work. The beetroot cut like a ruby – that is my childhood in a single image. The idea is part of a series that began as I was wandering around a food market and started to wonder how foods could become different things. It turned into a whole summer of play and exploration.

I was fortunate to have great contrasts in my childhood. My parents had a house on a little Greek island, where we would spend a few months a year. There wasn't much entertainment, but it makes you resourceful. I remember collecting shells from the beach and sticking them to some metal cigarette boxes, making little collages. I sold them in the harbour and made some pocket money.

I would define myself as a visual storyteller or a three-dimensional illustrator. When I started out, three-dimensional illustration wasn't such a recognized field – there was illustration and photography, but this got lost in between. It was a struggle to make people understand what I did.

Fortunately, I found a position at *Neon* magazine. It had a broad editorial mix – social, political, emotional, psychological – and I had the freedom to interpret those stories visually.

The vegetable infographics (p.133) came from a chance moment. My colleague had these coloured pencils on her desk and a book happened to hit up against them, leaving the bases aligned and the tips at different levels.

I noticed the resemblance to a bar chart and took the idea to my editor. It turned into a whole issue dedicated to a social survey of habits and attitudes. I hadn't seen that approach to data visualization before.

Working with journalists brings you closer to social issues. For example, I once worked on a series of plastic surgery portraits that came from reading about changing concepts of beauty in Western society (p.191). I thought it would be interesting to take some Renaissance portraits to a cosmetic surgeon and ask them what they would change – a tuck here, some liposuction there. The next step was to take the images to a photo retoucher and ask him to follow those instructions.

The work has a social and political dimension, but it is gentle and not explicit.

It is similar with the Flowerworks series. At the time, I was particularly interested in nature and had spent a while collecting leaves and shooting various installations – but it just wasn't working. Then I went to a flower shop, purely to get something for myself, and it hit me. The whole shop looked like a giant fireworks display.

My only aim with that project was to make something beautiful and playful, but people have taken different things from the images. One person told me how much they dislike fireworks – the noise, the warlike imagery and the wasted expense. For them, replacing the fireworks with flowers had a pacifist message. This is the interesting thing about wit – it is completed in the mind of the viewer.

I work independently now, in my studio in Berlin. I think studio architecture plays an important role in the creative process – I need space to move, play and experiment. It's so important to play. Don't wait to have the perfect idea before you start. Even if you spend time playing with something and it doesn't work out, that time is never wasted.

You also need to be hard on yourself – don't be too easily satisfied. Keep pushing yourself to go deeper into a subject. The search for an idea can be a form of physical torment, as though you are squeezing your brain. But I love that moment when the idea comes. It is the most magical part of the design process. After all the hard work, you get the spark – the moment of ignition.

Beet rubies, from the Tutti Frutti series. Sarah Illenberger, Germany, 2011.

Flowerworks – quiet
explosions of colour.
Sarah Illenberger,
Germany, 2014.

MICHAEL JOHNSON

Johnson Banks, UK

'When Michael Johnson stops doing funny work and starts doing graphic design, we'll see what he's made of.' I remember a journalist writing something to that effect about me many years ago. It seemed harsh at the time, but he had a point.

I started out immersed in ideas. Throughout the 1980s, that was how you gathered attention and awards. Ideas work with judges: that nice moment of recognition. And awards mattered back then. Before the Internet, getting into the D&AD Annual was one of the few ways to make an impression beyond your immediate circle.

By the turn of the 1990s, you could feel a sea change coming. There was a wave of people like Why Not Associates and Tomato pushing a looser, deconstructed, more anarchic kind of self-expression. And I remember feeling caught in the middle of that.

Of course, wit still had its place. Our identity for Shelter (p.103) is a classic logo with a twist. A type gag. It's no accident that the idea came up on the first afternoon of the project. You do that initial sweep for the typographic twist, because you don't want to miss the next FedEx (p.5). Usually you have to accept that there's nothing there and move on – there's nothing worse than straining for the witty twist. But occasionally you find

something and stick with it. With Shelter, we pinned the logo on the wall and spent the next twenty-nine days trying to beat it.

More often, the idea comes slowly, or by accident. Our fruit and veg stamps (p.33) had a long gestation. Almost a decade earlier, we'd pitched an idea for some customizable children's stamps, where you had a head on the main stamp and some other stickers that you could put above and below – hats and beards and so on. It went nowhere, straight into the client's bottom drawer.

Years later, for a different project, it came out again. One of the team was mulling this 'Mr Potato Head' idea and meanwhile I remembered a Japanese book I had, called *Vegetable Faces*. The original sketches we did looked nothing like the finished article. But through collaboration, conversation, trial and error, years of waiting, you eventually get to the idea.

That's a pure design project, but most of our work has a bigger scope now. In the early days of Johnson Banks, we worked with partners who helped with the strategy that formed the design brief. I sometimes found the results frustrating – there would be a serious disconnect between the early writing stage and the design stage. So we started to do it ourselves. I tell design students

about our process now and they are often mystified. We may spend months establishing the verbal framework for a brand: a narrative that shapes everything that will follow.

An identity like Shelter might still happen today, but we are more likely to create something like Cystic Fibrosis. During the research stage, we repeatedly came up against this problem of how to communicate what Cystic Fibrosis actually is: it's a perpetually misunderstood condition that is hard to make tangible for a general audience.

That led to a 'talking' identity, where the 'is' of 'Fibrosis' introduces a series of statements about the condition and the charity. It's identity doing the job of an advertising campaign. Is it witty? Not really, but it's doing more than you would expect a logo to do.

The same could be said of the Science Museum – an identity that sets up a wider visual language. The logotype is based loosely on codes and digital typefaces, but it is an idea that can be interpreted and decoded in several ways – which is important when it needs to be used for years to come.

That's where we are now: doing strategic work that sets a long-term direction for a brand. Design is in

the boardroom, where it always needed to be. But it means taking an interest in the whole process, not just doing the design bit. And why would you want it any other way? Research is fun. Writing is fun. Thinking up brand names is fun. Setting strategic directions is fun. And design is fun. Sometimes it's even funny.

Talking identity turns every application into a chance to communicate something more. Johnson Banks, UK, 2013.

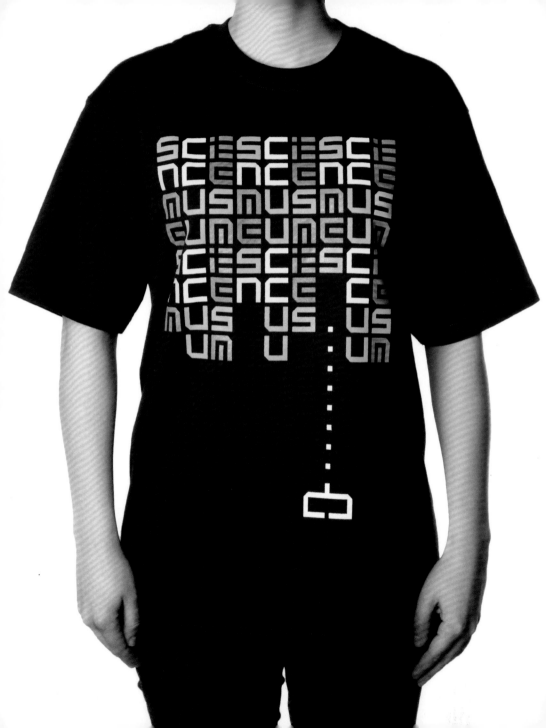

MARY LEWIS

Lewis Moberly, UK

I'm clear about my role as a designer. Artists write their own brief, but my imagination stirs when I'm given one. I love a problem, and I love the way that design can make the complex simple. This is what makes people smile. I'm wary of the laugh, it tires – but the smile returns, and is continually rewarding.

Lewis Moberly's early work was defined by design for high-street retailers. The Boots hosiery packaging (p.64) was inspired by a practical thought. Women want to see the product, therefore a window was mandatory. They also imagine it on their legs, so the window becomes the leg and the focus of the design. The black, gloved hand and classic court shoe create a visual dynamic and add a touch of glamour.

This is the kind of design I relish: concise and edited. Turning the problem – the must-have large window – into the solution.

I believe everything must earn its space: no free riders, communication is all. If it doesn't do a job, then it's an indulgence. Which is not to say that creating beauty can't be the job in hand.

In that case, it's permissible and must be out of the top drawer.

When we designed packaging for Boots rubber gloves (p.58), our idea was born of pragmatism. What are they? Light, medium and heavy. We avoided the clichés of dishwashing and drains – people can work out what to do with gloves. Instead, we let the hands do the talking. Each pack projects the title with the glove – and in doing so, expresses the 'weight' of each.

Boots laundry products followed. When you're washing clothes, the first thing you check is what the care label says. So why not make the label and its familiar icons the design idea?

When I'm designing a pack, it becomes a person. I dress it, talk to it and provoke it to get a relationship going. I introduce it to other people, get possessive about it, learn to defend it and speak up for it. It's a process of understanding the product and its purpose in life.

The way we work at Lewis Moberly has evolved, but some things remain central. We encourage ownership. All creatives craft and nurture their ideas, so they are allowed to be possessive. We are competitive with each other, to keep us on our toes. But we look to life, not design. Out there is where the ideas come from, not from studying our discipline inwardly and retrospectively. Being interested in people, not 'consumers', is important. An understanding of hopes, fears and dreams is the springboard for great ideas.

Ideas come randomly and through observation. They can't be forced. We need playtime and homework.

I'm an early-bird designer and a late-night one. I'm best in my own space, usually when I'm tired and perhaps a bit cross. Design is a release – the pleasure comes with the solution. I love the filing cabinet we designers have in our heads. We go through life accumulating visual information. It gets stored and processed and takes us by surprise when it surfaces, often years later, as an idea.

The German brand Bahlsen asked us to redesign their identity and portfolio of biscuits. The Bahlsen Family began life with the biscuits spread randomly across the studio

desk. Each one struck us as an individual, like members of a family. By arranging them in a particular way they became little characters, linking hands along the shelf.

Our work for Waitrose Cooks' Ingredients is copy-led and typographically styled. It sets a tone of voice to engage the foodie and make them smile. The calls to action – 'Just add a handful' or 'A generous helping' – make cooking feel effortless and pleasurable. The idea creates a collectable range that has been extended into exotic ingredients, recipe kits and home-baking products. Each subset has its own personality. The fresh herbs packaging tells a story about each herb: helpful usage tips, myths and legends. Tabloid-style typography commands attention.

The idea can support, drive, change, engage, disrupt and connect. All these and more, but it must never impose or distract. It has to just be right.

THE BEAUTIFUL
BAY LEAF

Waitrose COOKS' INGREDIENTS

SAVOURY OR SWEET
COMFORTING IN CUSTARDS, SUBTLE IN STEWS
INFUSE YOUR OILS AND PEP UP YOUR PIES
THE ESSENTIAL BOUQUET GARNI
OR 'BACCALAUREATE'
GARLANDS OF BAY TO HONOUR THE SCHOLAR

COOL COOL
MINT

Waitrose COOKS' INGREDIENTS

NOT JUST FOR JELLY!
INFUSE YOUR TEA, DRESS UP YOUR DRINKS
PAIR UP WITH PEAS OR SUMMER SORBET

ROMANTIC
ROSEMARY

Waitrose COOKS' INGREDIENTS

SYMBOL OF LOVE
GOOD LUCK AND FRIENDSHIP
BE LAVISH ON LAMB
AND CRUSH FOR AROMA

MAJESTIC
BASIL

Waitrose COOKS' INGREDIENTS

'KING OF THE HERBS'
ONCE REGARDED SACRED TO THE GODS
FRAGRANT BASIL STILL REIGNS SUPREME

TANTALISING
TARRAGON

Waitrose COOKS' INGREDIENTS

'FINE HERBS'
FAVOURED IN FRANCE
FAMOUS FOR TARTARE
MUSTARD AND VINEGAR

BORAGE
HERB OF
THE WEEK

Waitrose COOKS' INGREDIENTS

SOMETHING SEASONAL OR SIMPLY SPECIAL

JOHN McCONNELL

McConnell Studio, UK
Former Pentagram partner

I have always liked clichés. At art school I was accused of being too interested in them. Lecturers would say 'that's a terrible cliché', as though it was a disgusting habit. I now regret that I allowed that criticism to be painful.

When I looked up the word in a dictionary I found 'a cliché is a bankrupt idea.' The reason it is bankrupt is because it is overused: but being used regularly means that it is commonly and instantly understood. Therefore the game you play is simply to reinvest in the cliché, to put some money back in its bank, by using it in a way that is unexpected.

I get bored easily and like to get to a solution as quickly as possible. I ask myself, what is the point of the information I am communicating? Suppose the job is the cover for Rudolf Arnheim's book *Film as Art*. I need to communicate that it is about film and about art. What is the cliché for film? It is a piece of film. So I put that down as the first thing that comes into my mind. But no one is going to look at it twice. So what do I do to it to make it more relevant to the subject? The trick is to do something that furthers the point you want to make. So I cut the frame in half and offset it, to convey the idea of art affecting film.

I find it is an immense relief to have put down that first image, however dumb it is. I feel I have done the job in a way, and can relax. Then I revisit it in a cooler and more clinical frame of mind. I can manipulate it, turn it upside down, change the colour, or whatever. I have all these techniques at my fingertips that I can use to turn the image into something more relevant.

I tend to have several jobs running at any one time, and flip from one to another. When I was doing book jackets for Faber, I would do six simultaneously, putting the six briefs on my table in a row. It stopped me wasting time worrying about just one. One problem helps me with another. While I'm doing this, I'm really thinking about that. In fact it is all oblique. The best ideas come from just off vision.

With more complicated jobs, the real pleasure is taking a massively complex problem and thinking it through to an incredibly simple solution. I think about the job constantly, and all the time it is there in the back of my mind. I find that conversations about an entirely different subject can plant a seed. It is staggering how the insight to a solution comes from an unexpected connection.

When I come to work on the solution in the studio, the moment I arrive at the pad and pick up my pen, I feel tired. I know I have to raise the energy to do the job, but I already feel worn out. So I grab at something, anything, to get that mark down, and suddenly realize I have picked up something a friend mentioned in conversation a week ago. I have heard myself saying to my staff: 'I was thinking about this job last night.' But of course I wasn't: I thought the idea up at that moment. A lot of the most pleasurable ideas have been formed in that instant.

The trick is to get something down as quickly and cleanly as possible, without complication. For young designers the difficulty of achieving a good clear solution is that their feelings are mixed up. The main feeling is that they want this job to be brilliant. It is a real error to want the job you are working on to change the face of graphic design. If you start out carrying that baggage, you are dead in the water.

In the end the only question is – are the solutions you arrive at intelligent? I don't mean intellectual, where the solution is coded in a way that permits access to only a few. That is merely to demonstrate 'I'm so clever, you can't get anywhere near.' I see that as an exclusion game, and there is too much of it going on. Exclusion in the communication business seems to me a pretty unintelligent concept.

Wit and intelligence are pretty close. You start with mundane clichés but you hop sideways or jump into another path. It takes you into a new pasture you have never seen before. You work on more than one axis, and enjoy coupling them. Wit is not plodding, it is about speed. It comes from not burying yourself too deeply in rubbish, but keeping yourself out of the dross and enjoying moving around in the sunlight.

THE LANGUAGE OF MODERN MUSIC
DONALD MITCHELL

ff

MINALE TATTERSFIELD

Marcello Minale (1938–2000) & Brian Tattersfield, UK

We are an absolute mirror image in how we work. Our relationship is not a personal friendship, and we have never visited each other's houses, but from the design point of view we are exactly the same. If one of us genuinely likes an idea, so does the other.

For us the question is not so much how to get ideas, but how to play the game. If you play the game with certain rules, then you get certain results. All our ideas are based on joining two elements in one idea: we find the common denominator. Once the rules are established, the game is quite easy.

Ideas come without effort because they are instinctive. We believe that thinking is not the right way to get an idea. In tennis, if you think about answering the shot, you've missed the ball. If you think very hard about a problem you produce the wrong idea – you never find the pearl, which is untouchable. The beauty of an ideas approach is that there are no doubts about when the job is done. You solve it – finish. We have no second thoughts or worries that it could be done another way.

For example, we did a poster to promote a ball given by the Hangover Society, which is for amateur golfers. How can you link golf and a hangover? You may go through the usual hangover cures – aspirin, icepack and so on – and dismiss them very fast. But when you think of a glass of scotch, you know you are on to something. In the poster, the glass is on the floor, and on its side because the person is drunk. With a golf ball alongside, it becomes the glass hopeless golfers use when they practise their putting in the office. Even now, we don't think we could improve on it.

We have always been renowned for executing jobs with no technique or flair. That is because we tend to translate an idea in a dull way, because it is the most direct way. We designed a poster for the Italian Institute for Foreign Trade to promote an exhibition of Italian knitwear. The image was simply a long grey sock. If the sock had been too good-looking, people would have been distracted by the execution.

Brian Webb said that our type of job doesn't hit you straight away, but taps you on the shoulder after two hours. For us that is the sign of a good solution. If the idea is too immediate, it gives the game away in one go. We prefer that people don't understand the idea at first. Then, after it hits them, they really like it.

When we work on a small poster, there is little client resistance to a clever idea because the investment is so minimal. But it is much more difficult to solve a big job with an idea – and the jobs are getting bigger. In the first ten years of our activity we could solve jobs with ideas, in the second ten years we did so less often and in the last ten years even less.

But we always try to sneak wit in somewhere. In designing a massive mural for the new Hammersmith Underground station, we used an idea to surmount a physical constraint. The problem was that the coloured tiles to be used were only available in the standard rectangular shape, not as square half tiles. So the use of colour would be affected by the tessellation. Therefore we depicted not Hammersmith Bridge, but its reflection – using the way each row of tiles was offset to create the watery shimmer. The idea expresses the restriction.

Most ideas you create, but some you discover. We were asked to design the identity for the Royal Armouries Museum, the museum in Leeds, housing exhibits from the Tower of London. Among a thousand pieces of armoury we discovered this helmet, a gift to Henry VIII from a German king, and we immediately put two ideas together – the name of the museum and its subject. The helmet is an example of armoury, and it links with the name of the museum through the initials. It is the perfect solution: it squares the circle.

The ram's horn helmet is extremely memorable, and these days you don't run a museum unless you have a strong image you can use in merchandise. The success of the identity is that kids wear a T-shirt with this face. We are not inventing anything here: there is no difference in function between this and the Mickey Mouse symbol.

The armouries museum was a £40 million job, and the humour ran through all the signing, where we used other found images, mostly from the Plantagenet period. The essence of a great idea is that you can extend it. A classic example is the Minale Tattersfield scribble. We have done a thousand variations, and each one is a surprise. When you have the perfect idea, you can go on *ad infinitum*.

ROYAL ARMOURIES MUSEUM

Identity for the Royal
Armouries Museum.
A sixteenth-century
helmet fortuitously links
what the museum is
called with what it holds.
Minale Tattersfield,
UK, 1995.

CHRISTOPH NIEMANN

Illustrator and artist, Germany

Ideas don't fall from the sky. When I think of the most successful creative people I know, none of them would be where they are if they had to rely on a 'eureka' moment.

The two-part cover I created for *Zeit* magazine (pp.31, 32) is about this subject – the difficulty of the creative process. The end result may look like an 'a-ha' moment, but the process to get there is difficult and unglamorous. You start with something complex, then strip everything away until the answer reveals itself.

I have always been interested in drawing, but I studied graphic design, because at the time in Germany you couldn't study illustration as a separate discipline. This was useful, because in graphic design you're taught to think about a problem and how to solve it, before thinking about the appropriate style. My approach to illustration is still ideas-driven rather than style-driven. It's never about doing a watercolour because I feel like doing a watercolour. The style is in the service of the concept.

The challenge is to keep your vanity in check. You have to decide whether you want to make the idea work or show off your craft skills. Often the best answer is to hold back, but it's the toughest decision to make – to take away a beautiful decorative element, because the idea is stronger without it.

The Menu series is a good example. The drawings are basic and the captions are mundane, but the idea comes alive in the mind of the reader. It's like a comedian on stage. Do you want someone who laughs at their own jokes, or someone who keeps a straight face while you break down laughing?

Audience response is an interesting area now. When I began doing editorial work, you could only make assumptions about what the reader thought – you might get one or two letters, but nothing more. Now the feedback on social media is instantaneous. My greatest discovery was to realize how visually intelligent people are. I always suspected it but never really knew. Even with subtle references I thought I was doing for my own amusement, people that totally get it.

Technology has always been an influence on illustration. The Petting Zoo app (p.168) came from an ambition to do something with touchscreens, but stylistically it is inspired by some of the earliest keyframe animations done a century ago by Windsor McCay. I had to teach myself code to the point where I could explain to professional coders how I wanted it to work. It was an exhausting process, but rewarding.

Some of my work has a more political dimension, like the Xenophobia poster I produced for a conference in South Africa. I enjoy political work, but am aware of its limitations. In the history of design, has a poster ever saved a life? Is a dictator likely to look at a witty twist on a nuclear bomb and halt his weapons programmes? There is no designer witty enough to make that happen. But political art can motivate people who share your view. It can provide an image to rally around. That is a powerful thing too.

My Sunday Sketches (p.30) are an example of a side project that has become central to what I do. They began as a personal creative exercise and I have to remind myself that is still the main purpose. It's great to get positive feedback on Instagram, but it's also a trap. You have to be careful not to equate likes and retweets with quality. The point is not to come up with the most likeable idea but the most unusual. If thousands of people are liking it, maybe it's not so unusual.

Sometimes things have to fail: that is part of the process.

It's vital to keep experimenting. When I look at the backbone of what I do now, five years ago it was some weird, experimental thing I was doing on a spare evening. Flip that thought around and you realize you will be stuck in five years' time if you aren't continuing to experiment now.

It's not always easy. You have deadlines, you have a family. It's a tough decision to say I'm just going to sit here and play for a while. But it's the most important thing you can do.

Xenophobia: a topical piece commissioned by Design Indaba in South Africa. Christoph Niemann, Germany, 2015.

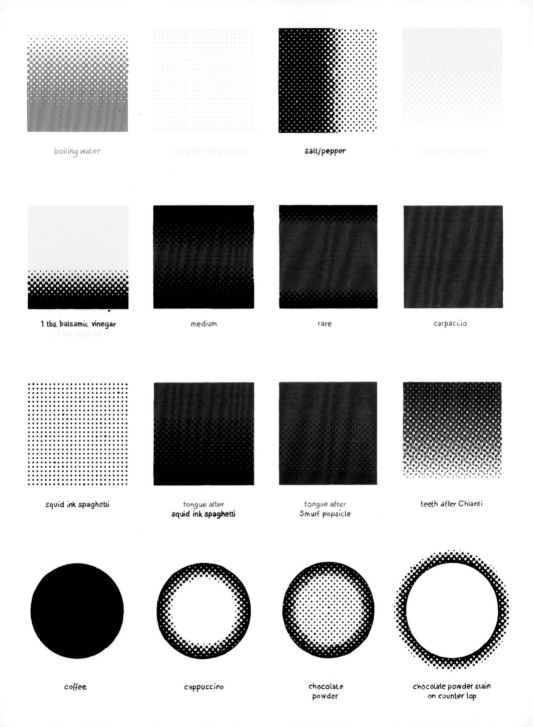

boiling water

spaghetti (top view)

salt/pepper

shaved parmesan

1 tbs. balsamic vinegar
3 tbs. olive oil

medium

rare

carpaccio

squid ink spaghetti

tongue after
squid ink spaghetti

tongue after
Smurf popsicle

teeth after Chianti

coffee

cappuccino

chocolate
powder

chocolate powder stain
on counter top

DEAN POOLE

Alt Group, New Zealand

Ideas come from under a rock at the back of my head. The idea is already there, but I have to uncover it.

I compare the creative process to wandering round a series of rooms. You put everything you know about one subject in a particular room. Over a period of time, those experiences accumulate. You might have a room full of everything you know about gravity. Then you get a project about paint. What does gravity do to paint? Or you may have a room full of cartoons. How do cartoons work with paint? You're exploring these rooms, playing with the brief in each one.

I like to get back to that childlike state of not knowing. Take wine bottles. Forget everything you think you know about them and go back to the beginning. Why are they 750ml? Because that's the lung capacity of a French glassblower. That's how it became the prototype of a wine bottle. Soon that develops into a stereotype for a particular region like Bordeaux – a branded object. Later it becomes the archetype – a symbol in your head that stands for wine in general. Prototype, stereotype, archetype – trace it back and you get somewhere interesting.

The Lean Year wine bottle (p.111) came from thinking about wine as an idea – a vertical product with a horizontal effect. What happens if you apply the effect to the bottle itself? The title only came later, at the end of a tough year.

The key question is never what the idea is, but what the idea has to do. With Auckland Art Gallery, we had this amazing collection of visual art in one place, but nobody wanted to come. So what do you need the idea to do? It has to make art a habit, part of people's daily lives. A logo isn't going to do that. You need more points of contact. You need to get people thinking about what art is or can be. So we set up this algorithm – a rule system where the phrase must always begin with an A, followed by two words that have an R and T stacked consecutively. The result is a game in which people can participate. The rules create the game.

We only ever present one idea. The challenge is getting the client to the point where they want to accept it. I compare it to being in a dark room. At the start of the project, the client takes you in and shines a torch at the problem. You send them away, bump around the room for a couple of weeks and eventually find the idea in a corner somewhere. Now it's tempting to run outside waving the idea in the air, but that isn't going to work. You need to take the client back into the room, show them where you were, explain the journey you took, the alternatives you considered and rejected. By the time you get to the idea, it should feel inevitable.

Looking at design and branding now, there's a lot of what I call The Attack of the Friendlies. Brands that look relaxed and friendly, but aren't really. Every bank wants to be your friend. But why? If anything, a bank should be a group of burly guys in suits standing outside steel doors. If you were being witty, you might play with that. But it's all about being friendly now. Like parental entertainment. Keep the kids happy.

I trained as a sculptor and artist before I got into design. Most of our teaching was about finding frameworks for thinking, as well as developing the craft skills to achieve that thinking. I'm fascinated by objects – the different ways of looking at a bottle or a broom. Words are objects too. Think about the letter A. An H designed by an architect. I followed this thought and it turned into a book called *Twenty Six Characters*.

I enjoy these explorations – *This Over That* is another example. Take a simple structure of one word over another and see if you can tell an entire story with it. The limitation is liberating.

I have a strong idea about the type of design I want to make. I'm not saying I force it on clients, but I want to make work that has both wit and generosity. Generosity in the sense that it invites you in and makes you a participant. I don't like branding that creates distance and exclusivity. I like ideas that welcome you with open arms.

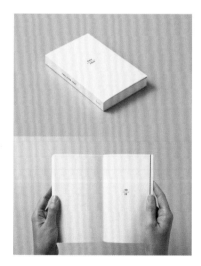

This Over That. A story told through a repeated device of one word appearing over another. From 'stay over night' to 'so over it'. Alt Group, New Zealand, 2011.

A CURIOUS VISIT

PAUL RAND

(1914–1996)
Graphic designer, USA

I have two goals. The first is that everything I do as a designer must have an idea: it cannot just look nice. The second is, it has to look nice. Without visual beauty, even a good idea will not pass. Graphic design requires both ingredients, but the first priority is the idea – and my train of thought happens to be funny.

I do not use humour consciously, I just go that way naturally. I accept that my nature is contrary. I do not know whether this is a useful quality in a designer, but it has worked for me. A well-known example is my identity for United Parcels Service: to take an escutcheon – a medieval symbol that inevitably seems pompous today – and then stick a package on top of it, that is funny.

Humour is important for serious problems because it makes people remember. Humour is also lovable, likeable and friendly. I get standing ovations when I speak to designers, because I make fun of my work and of our whole business. I hasten to say I do not debunk my work with clients.

I work alone and intuitively. I might think of an idea immediately, and I usually do. The working out is always the difficulty. What a graphic designer is doing is taking metaphysical problems and trying to reduce them to objects. That is one hell of a job, and there are many ways of doing it. The element of arbitrariness in our business is enormous. You decided to do it this way, but you could equally well have done it that way. But to do it straight is not interesting.

In the past I have written about humour in design, but my comments are speculation. I am not a psychologist or philosopher and am just trying to figure it out. Similarly, I am not an expert in explaining what I do. I can discuss what is right or wrong about proportions, letter forms or relationships of negative and positive spaces, but I would never try to explain wit. I just do things the way I do them, to see if I can solve the problem. It has never been any different.

When I sit down to think about a job, I do not try to direct my mind. In fact very often I don't think about the job at all, but while I'm eating, 'oh yes', an answer just comes. It is necessary to use ideas that are obvious, so that people understand them, but what is taxing about the process, and the main reason why it is difficult to consummate, is the need to lift the idea out of the ordinary, to make it unusual. The portrait I did of Stravinsky uses the visual language of writing music, which is made up of dots. But creating a portrait with dots is not ordinary.

If I have one good idea, I am happy. The big problem in our business is to have too many ideas, because then you have the problem of choosing. I tell my students, 'Don't make any sketches. Just think first, get an idea and then put it down.' The more sketches designers make, the more paths they are creating for themselves. They cannot then work intensively and in depth.

I believe that, in order to be interesting, a design has to be a little bit puzzling or even enigmatic. I know the value of abstraction, and by abstraction I mean how far you can go with an idea without destroying recognition. I usually check out my ideas with someone else. I ask my maid, my accountant or anybody who happens to be around. I want to see if they can understand it, if the message is clear. The degree of immediate recognition I need depends on two things – the function and the audience. For example, an abstract poster for the American Institute of Graphic Arts is not intended to be persuasive. Since I am not selling anything, it doesn't matter whether anybody can understand it.

People say I am a mischievous person, and that is probably because I feel there is something silly about our whole business. Being mischievous is a defence against the guilt induced by taking a lot of money for something that is both silly and enjoyable. When you solve a problem, it is a terrific feeling. When you are stuck, it is as though you are walking around in the rain.

Identity for United Parcels Service. The designer twists heraldry, as the humble parcel becomes a crest above an escutcheon. Paul Rand, USA, 1961.

Portrait of Stravinsky done
as a personal project.
Paul Rand, USA, 1950.

JIM SUTHERLAND

Studio Sutherl&, UK

If you put thought and joy into a project, the person at the other end gets some of that back. This is my main belief in design.

Wit is connected to both thought and joy. The problem with the word 'witty' is that it sounds flippant. People think you're not taking it seriously if you do something funny. But wit can have a serious purpose. The original sense is not just about humour – it's about thoughtfulness, intelligence, having your wits about you.

You can find joy in every project. It only seems inevitable afterwards. Wit is difficult to sell, because clients are wary of humour. Simplicity is tough too – people worry that it's too simple. You have to take them through the thinking. Don't just show the problem and the solution, but show what comes in between.

The Piccadilly Lights project (p.74) is about simplicity. There are so many ideas in that brief – different ways to explore light, the location or the nature of the client's business. In the end, we came back to the simplest idea – a light switch. When you have hundreds of ideas pinned to a wall, the simplest one keeps drawing you back.

Every studio needs a wall for posting up ideas. There's something about the physical process that aids the mental process. Before Studio Sutherland, I co-founded and spent thirteen years at Hat-trick Design. We often had forty live projects in a studio of nine people. The wall would contain all these ideas linked to different projects. Every morning you would come in, examine the work and spot new connections, within projects and between projects. Each project was better for having all the others around.

My other essential tool is a notebook. I need to scribble and sketch all the time. Just the act of drawing – often not drawing particularly well in my case – can spark off another idea or direction. In the briefing meeting, I'll scribble initial thoughts, looking for starting points. You need multiple starting points – some kind of structure to set you thinking. Then it's a case of exploring different routes and seeing where they interrelate. You never think in one channel – you think around the problem.

It is possible to labour too much for an idea. But ultimately I'd rather someone tried too hard than not enough. I don't buy into the distinction between ideas and style – the polarity is less defined than it used to be. Most people want an idea or thought in there, but in a beautiful, crafted way.

I like ideas that turn a problem into an opportunity – this is where the joy comes in. The Natural History Museum learning guides (p.192) are a series of educational booklets for children to write in and hand back to their teacher. The problem was, the children had nothing to keep for themselves. So we had this idea for detachable covers – and that in turn created the opportunity for die-cut covers that could be used as masks and toys. The problem creates the opportunity, which creates the moment of joy. It's hard to pick up that dinosaur cover and not want to put your fingers through the holes.

I have mentioned walls and notebooks, but another creative tool is curiosity. It helps to be interested in life. Go to museums, galleries and talks. Take pictures. Watch great films, listen to amazing music. Everything feeds into the work. If you see and listen to interesting things by interesting people, you will do more interesting work.

Years ago, I was with my wife [illustrator Rebecca Sutherland] at an exhibition that included a Victorian hold-to-the-light postcard. It got me thinking about how the same technique could work in a different context. Children like reading books with a torch under the bedcovers, so what if that torch revealed a new dimension to the story? That was the spark, but it was years before it turned into a book. I remember locking myself and the designer on the project in the studio toilet – the only dark place we could find – and shining a torch on the illustrations to check they were all working.

I've seen the illustrations in *Hide & Eek!* hundreds of times, but I still smile looking at them. Seeing the genie appear. Magic.

A self-aware self-promotional letterhead produced as a student. Jim Sutherland, UK, 1988.

Hide & Eek! A children's
book that reveals a hidden
dimension in torchlight.
Hat-trick / Knock Knock,
UK, 2013.

TRICKETT & WEBB

Lynn Trickett & Brian Webb, UK

When we decided to set up a design consultancy together, we recognized a common attitude. By our nature we tend to look for a witty solution in a job. For us the key word was 'ideas': it sounded a bit more like a basis for starting a company than 'wit'.

A lot of our ideas come from words. It never seems to happen that we have a flash of inspiration in visual terms. The ideas usually come out when we talk, one thought leading to another until something happens. We just keep trading ideas. Probably this habit is not so much playful as competitive: we suspect that we have always tried to score points off each other.

It may be that one of us has been talking to a client and come up with half an idea. The other then takes the looking-over-the-shoulder role, sees the drawing and usually suggests another way of doing it. Wit generally involves some kind of leap of thought. With two people working together, there is no need for one mind to change tack because the other mind is already on a different path. That is when the two-way process happens.

However, life would be an awful lot easier if we could really analyse what is happening, and set the process in motion whenever we wanted. The reality is that it is not easy at all. Each time we have to find a different entry point. It seems to help if the client gets involved too. Often the idea will be provoked in discussion as a result of the questions we ask. It is not just us sitting in the studio having magic ideas.

One client had difficulty describing exactly what his company did. It turned out that he supplied people to man exhibition stands and promotional events in England and Italy. He wanted to call the company Shazam, but we suggested choosing a name that underlined the Italian link. His own name was Carr so the company eventually became Carrozzato (which means coach built). It does not bear much relation to what he does, but it puts his name up front, sounds Italian and looks nice.

Our graphic ideas always have a logic behind them. It is often a conjunction of variables that brings a witty solution, and we find the variables within the situation. Clearly Carrozzato is a people business, and the other factor was the linking of England and Italy. We obviously looked at maps, and have always enjoyed metamorphosis, and consequently ended up with a Miss England and a Mr Italy.

Their relationship progresses as the identity unfolds. On the business card, when people are introducing each other, the interaction is formal. The letterhead is the next piece of communication, and the two are beginning to dance. The compliments slip comes later, and now they are really having a good time. By the time it gets to the parcel, Miss England is throwing Mr Italy across the room.

That is about as much as we can say about how we thought of the idea. We would find it difficult to retrace the steps in our thinking, which tended to be done in meetings with the client held quite late in the evening. You could say it was one of those things that described itself in the end.

On unpromising jobs we sometimes end up with a witty solution out of despair. Our first job for Boots was to package a series of assorted men's gifts. They were all cheap, like the three handkerchiefs and a golf-tee that kids give their dads or uncles. Boots wanted them to look like a range but each product was different, so we started looking for a method that would link them all together but give each one individuality. They became a library of books. The two advantages were that we could have fun, and customers would want to buy sets.

The justification for witty design is audience participation. An idea makes people think – it engages their imagination, gets their brain into gear, makes them respond and helps them remember.

Stationery range for Carrozzato. Identity as narrative. Trickett & Webb, UK, 1990.

INDEX &
CREDITS

INDEX

Page references in *italics* refer to images

CREDITS

Design groups or designers are credited alongside the images, where known, and additional credits are listed here.

Every effort has been made to contact the copyright holders of the images included in this book. If there are any inadvertent omissions these can be corrected in any future reprints.

5 Fedex van: photo Shutterstock.com.

10 Charles Barsotti illustration, *The New Yorker* Collection/The Cartoon Bank.

19 Nipper: by courtesy of HMV.

29 Table/rocket: designer and illustrator Michael Bierut.

30 Lewis Silkin newsletter: illustrator Malcolm English. Matilija Dam: © 2011 *Los Angeles Times*, reprinted with permission, photo by Mel Melcon.

33 Security Shopper: designer Michael McGinn. Innocent Targets: art director Ewoudt Boonstra; copywriter Zack MacDonald; photographer Robbie Augspurger; designer Anthony Burrill.

34 Books/palm tree: designer Woody Pirtle. Mint mouthwash: designer and typographer Sarah Shepherd.

35 Guinness pint: Jon Rogers, Phosphor Art.

36 Hand tools: designer David Lerch.

38 Bulldog clips cover: designer Mervyn Kurlansky.

39 Cuban Missile Crisis: art director Nicholas Blechman; designers Paul Sahre, Rachel Matts.

40 Star/daffodill: art director Nancy Williams; designer Lee Funnell. London & San Francisco: executive creative directors David Turner and Bruce Duckworth; creative director Paula Talford; designer Matt Lurcock; acount manager Kim Horner; illustrator Andrew Davidson; artworker James Norris. My other half wedding invite: creative director Stuart Youngs; designers Nathan Webb & Philip Skinner.

41 Main Street Grill: creative director Allen Wimett, art directors Pat Wittich and Allen Wimett; photographer Herb Cosby. September identity: creative director and designer Richard Scholey; typographer Andrew Harkcom; photographer Robert Walker.

42 Galt Toys: photographer Harriet Crowder. P with dovetail: designer Alan Fletcher. Coca-Cola: chief creative officer Graham Fink; creative director Francis Wee; art director Jonathan Mak Long; illustrators Jonathan Mak Long and Eno Jin.

44 Handy wipes: executive creative directors David Turner and Bruce Duckworth; designers Sam Lachlan and Christian Eager; photographer Andy Grimshaw; image retouching by Peter Ruane.

46 The Durutti Column: designers Dave Rowbotham & Anthony H Wilson.

47 Keep Britain Tidy: model by Mark Lawrence; photographer Pierre Rutschi.

48 Lego masters: senior creative director Kenny Blumenschein; junior art director Marco Sodano; business director Harshad Sreedharan; account manager Olivia Paul.

50 Money: designer John McConnell. Fedex truck: art directors Zoe Sys Vogelius, Thomas Ilum. Ballet classes: creative directors Favio Ucedo/Juan Oubiña; art directors Curro Chozas/Paula Oliosi. Classic album covers: Studio Dempsey; designers Mike Dempsey and Stephanie Jerey.

51 Dirty Old Man: designer Pierre Mendell; photographer Klaus Oberer.

52 Boots plasters: illustrator Terry Pottle. Coca-Cola tow truck: Turner Duckworth & Coca-Cola North America; designers Jonathan Warner & Rebecca Au Williams; creative directors David Turner & Bruce Duckworth.

53 Gavin Martin Colornet Limited proof bags: creative directors David Azurdia, Ben Christie, Jamie Ellul; designers Ben Christie, Tim Fellowes.

54 Breakfast club: designer Colin Forbes.

56 British Land: designer Mike Dempsey. D&AD New Blood campaign 2014: designer Craig Oldham; copywriter John Goddard.

58 R as column, bowl, tail: art directors Milton Glaser and Walter Bernard; illustrator Mirko Ilic. Watching Words Move: designers Robert Brownjohn, Ivan Chermayeff and Tom Geismar; photo credit Chermayeff, Geismar and Haviv. Great British Menu brand logo: Optomen Televison Limited.

60 Low-budget jobs: art director John Vitro; copywriter John Robertson; photographer Marshall Harrington.

62 Beer mats: illustrator Mick Brownfield.

64 Carter Wong: designers Alison Tomlin and Nick Downes. Milking cow: image for the book 'Odd Exports'. Ikea Skarpsill: image by SDL.

65 Kieler Woche: designer Pierre Mendell; photographer Hans Döring.

66 White shirts: designer Alan Fletcherl photographer Bob Brooks. The Vegetable Bar: creative directors David Azurdia, Ben Christie, Jamie Ellul; designer David Azurdia.

67 Nivea Night Cream product shot: creatives Peggy van Neer, Chanta Schreuder; photographer Paul Ruigrok.

71 Slow airport lounge: Grid Worldwide Branding and Design, Tonic Design and Comair/British Airways, Nathan Reddy, Paul Hinch, Shelley Atkinson, Jean du Plessis, Marette Koorts, Samantha Koenderman, Philippe van der Merwe, Greg Gamble.

72 The Economist Lightbulb: Paul Belford & Nigel Roberts. Poster for Black Sabbath's comeback album: McCann Copenhagen; art director Andreas Rasmussen; copywriter Janus Hansen; client: Universal Music Denmark. Coastal Erosion book: creative director Harriet Devoy; designer Stephen Royle; photographer Jason Orton.

74 Harry Obese: illustrator Michael Foreman. Pencil sculptures: Dalton Ghetti; photographer Sloan T. Howard.

75 Boss Print mailer: creative directors Gareth Howat/Jim Sutherland; designers Gareth Howat/Jim Sutherland; copywriter Scott Perry; photographer John Ross. Binoculars: photograph by © Kenneth Johansson/Corbis.

76 Smart Car: Shanghoon Westside Studio; client: Smart Canada.

77 Rubber duck: courtesy Studio Florentijn Hofman.

78 Paint pot on lamp post: Frederik Vercruysse/King George. Paper Dreams: photographer Moris Moreno. Big nude poster: art director Silas Rhodes.

80 Cricketer's Gin: principal designer Glen Tuttsel; illustrator Jooce Garrett. Success/failure: designer Michael Bierut. SITE Environmental Design, New York, concept by James Wines.

82 Champagne glass: designers Alan Fletcher and Tessa Boo Mitford; illustrator Alan Fletcher. Child gymnasts: photographer Phil Babbs.

83 Eurostar First Class Catering: creative directors Jason Gregory, Mark Bonner, Peter Hale; designers Mark Bonner, Russell Saunders. Wrong poster: Kevos Van Der Meiren.

84 Dallas Symphony Orchestra: designer Brian Boyd.

86 High school reunion: designer Brian Boyd.

88 Wool book: illustrator Francis Mosley. Art & Architecture: designers John Rushworth, Nick Finney, Vince Frost and John Powner. Sweet Thoughts: design director John Blackburn; designer/copywriter Belinda Duggan; illustrator Gray Jolliffe.

89 Stamps pack: art director Nancy Williams; designer Richard Scholey. IDl: partner David Hillman; designer Lucy Holmes; photographer Peter Wood. Arthur Andersen: designer Nicholas Thirkell; illustrator Bob Haberfield.

90 Marmite Ma'amite Limited Edition Packaging: design firm Hornall Anderson; creative director Alastair Whiteley; design director Matt Gandy; designers Jamie Wright, Clare Lett; production designers Adam Miller; account service manager Liz Arney. Baxter and Bailey moving card: design and art direction Matt Baxter, Dom Bailey and Emma Grencis; words: Emma Grencis and Reed Words.

92 RNLI Homewares: The Workshop; director Richard Palmer; copywriter Roger Horberry; designer Sam Witt. Puccino's: designer/copywriter Jim Smith.

93 1000 words: creative directors, designers, typographers Ben Casey, Peter Richardson; typographer Lionel Hatch; copywriters Nick Asbury, Ben Casey, Lionel Hatch, Joe Davies; client: Paul Thompson Photography.

94 WHSmith: illustrator Geoff Appleton. *How* magazine: designer Ivan Chermayeff.

95 Face to Face: designer Jean Robert. Icograda poster: designer Alan Fletcher. OzHarvest Annual Report: agency Frost*collective; executive creative director Vince Frost; design director Carlo Giannasca; designers Vince Frost, Adit Wardhana.

102 Lila Burkeman: designer Mervyn Kurlansky. Masseuse: designer John Bull. Alvin Ailey: designer Steff Geissbuhler. TM (Tony Muranka) logo: creative director Tony Muranka; typographer Colin Moody/Straightedge.

103 Spratts dog: courtesy of Dalgety Spillers Foods. Design pivot logo: art director and designer Brock Haldeman. Destination: creative director Arthur Eisenberg; designer/art director Philip Waugh. Freedom identity: creative director Ben Casey; designer Jens Wickelgren; client: Co-operative Travel.

104 Mr & Mrs Hair: designer Woody Pirtle. Double phone: illustrator Terry Pottle. ENO: designer Mike Dempsey. Hostage Films: designers Chris Jeffreys, Stuart Price; photographer Emma Sinclair. Layezee Beds: client Silent Night Group; creative director Peter Richardson; senior designer Oliver Maltby.

105 Lone Star: designer Rex Peteet. K walks: designer Tom Geismar. Fashion Center: designer Michael Bierut. Conception logo: creative director Ben Casey, designer Ivan Rowles. Hall & Rose: senior deisgner Rob Skelly; design directors Chris Jackson & Jon Stubley; creative services director Mark O'Donnell.

106 Gates: designer Alan Fletcher.Dinosauriers: designers Marianne Vos and André Toet.

108 Mini-workout business card: art director/designer Adam Pickard; writer Chris Hirsch; creative director Duncan Bruce; photographer Michael Banasiak.

109 Used Cards: creative chairman and copywriter Sajan Raj Kurup; art director Bryan Elijah.

110 Revolution: designer Georg Staehelin. Allan Jones letterhead: designer Paul Rodger. Stationery with holes: designers Martin Devlin and Brigid McMullen. Steve Li Acupuncturist: designers Jason Little, Erin Hoffman; creative director Jason Little. Paul Wenman Emergency Electrician: creative director Ben Case; designer, typographer Abi Stones; typographer Peter Richardson.

111 Recorded delivery: art director Phoa Kia Boon; designer Martin Cox.

112 W11 to WII: designers Philip Carter and Amanda Harrington. Rubber stamps: designer Dean Narahara; copywriter Bruce Henry Davis.

114 Cade moving card: designer Andy Cade. Tennis invitation: designer Keith Cullen.

115 Heart sweets: copywriter Simon Rodway; illustrator John Bradley. Bite identity: designers John Rushworth and Vince Frost.

116 Holly wing: designer Mike Dempsey. Reindeer: designer Mike Dempsey. Screwed up paper: designers Adam Thomas and Steve Lloyd.

117 Reindeer pull chair: designer Philip Carter; illustrator Allan Drummond. Snow chair: designer and illustrator Philip Carter. Judge flickbook: illustrator Geoff Appleton.

118 Connected Thinking: creative director Ranzie Anthony; designer Philip Skinner.

119 Fetch Dog Care: Williams Murray Hamm; creative director Garrick Hamm; designer Emma Turland; artworker Jason Budgen.

120 Cotton book: illustrator Mick Brownfield. Primer: designer Alan Fletcher.Mini-brochure in business-card-sized folder: designer Michael O'Shea, creative director Malcolm Stewart. Machell Builders business card: Lee Bradley, Andrew Droog.

121 Gizmo & mouse: photographer Nadav Kander.

122 Centrum 100: photographer John Edwards, also Magnum Photos. Central radio: art director Tony Muranka; copywriter Ken Mullen. Fountains brochure: copywriter Simon Rodway. Blackpool School of Arts Promotional Poster: creative director Peter Richardson; designer David Thompson.

125 Burton Group: principal designer David Stocks. 'Genuinely Basic': designer Thomas Schneider; creative director Burghard Drews; creative agency: antwerpes; brand: DocCheck AG; client: DocCheck. Manchester City report: photographer Tim Sinclair.

126 Waste agency: designers Steve Pattee and Kelly Stiles. Manchester Dogs' Home Annual Review 2001–2: creative director, designer, copywriter, typographer Harriet Devoy; senior designer, typographer Stephen Royle; photographer Mat Wright.

127 Calgary Society for Persons with Disabilities report: WAX partnership inc.; creative director Trent Burton; design director Monique Gamache; art director Hans Thiessen; designer Hans Thiessen; copywriters Trent Burton, Elise Russell; photographer Johann Wall; printer Blanchette Press.

128 Pirelli: principal designer Paul Wills. Christopher Doyle Identity Guidelines: creative director Christopher Doyle; copywriter Christopher Doyle; photographer Ian Haigh.

129 Out of the Box: Special Projects, Clara Gaggero & Adrian Westaway, 2010.

130 Chocolate Pie Chart: designers Mary Matson & Matt Even; photographers Mary Matson & Matt Even. The Most Honest Chocolate Tablet: studio Ruiz+Company; creative director David Ruiz; graphic designer Vicente Ruiz.

131 Fountain graph: photographer Brian Griffin. Grande Reportagen Magazine: FCB Lisbon;

executive creative directors Luís Silva Dias/Duarte Melo; copywriter Icaro Doria; art director João Roque; account director Andrea Valenti.

132 Super Cheap Auto Annual Report: Frost*collective; executive creative director Vince Frost; design directors Vince Frost, Ray Parslow; account director Beverley Hall.

134 Almost Extinct Calendar: creative director Oliver Maltby; senior designer Chris Challinor; designers Rebecca Low, Dulcie Cowling, Adam Cartwright. Land Rover Calendar: TBWA Istanbul; executive creative director İlkay Gürpınar; creative group head Zeynep Karakaşoğlu; art director/ designer Zeynep Orbay; copywriter Emre Gökdemir.

136 Face Ronchetti: illustrator Arthur Robins. Puchi-Puchi calendar: art director Akio Okumura; designer Takeshi Kusumoto; illustrator Takato Okemoto.

137 Napoli: designer John McConnell. Between the wars: designer Ivan Chermayeff. Digital subway ads for Apolosophy: advertising agency Åkestam Holst; client: Apotek Hjärtat, Fredrik Kullberg; creative directors: Andreas Ullenius, Åkestam Holst; art directors Lars Bæcklund, Åkestam Holst; copywriters Mariette Glodeck, Åkestam Holst; account director Sara Clewemar, Åkestam Holst; account managers Jennie Strinnhed, Åkestam Holst; digital producers Sofia Swedenborg, Åkestam Holst; planning Patrik Karlsson, Åkestam Holst; photographer Elisabeth Frang; production company Stopp Family.

138 The Italic Poster: photographer Michaela Klouda.

140 Japanese Film Festival: design Tabi Aziri; client: Albanian Theatre, Skopje. Nymphomaniac poster: art direction The Einstein Couple; graphics Tobias Røder, StudioMega; client: Lars Von Trier, Zentropa.

141 Women Fashion Power: The Beautiful Meme; writer Tom Sharp; designer Ben Haworth; client: Design Museum. Tour of Britain: creative director Grant Parker; art director Neil Ritchie; copywriter Gary Arnold; account handler Anna Lloyd; photographer Nick Meek. French Open: creative directors Patrick Low/Mark Fong; writer Mark Fong; photographer Hon (Shutter Bug); client: Singapore Cable Vision. Sycamore Trees: creative directors Pum Lefebure, Jake Lefebure; designer Lucas Badger. '123 years of best british music': creative partners Spencer Buck & Ryan Wills; associate creative director: Stuart Tallis; designer: Karl Wills; client: IAM. 'Jesus Saves': Solv, creative directors Rob Duncan, and John Paul Stallard.

142 NYC Spaghetti: designer Alex Creamer; 3D modeller Ben Thorpe; tutors Billy Harkcom, Andrew Bainbridge, Jon Harker.

143 Fruit juice packaging: Naoto Fukasawa Design; photographer Masayoshi Hichiwa.

144 Stationery items: cartoonist Larry. Denes petfood: designer John Blackburn; illustrator John Geary. Frosted vodka bottle: principal designer Glen Tuttsel.

145 Homebase non-stick packaging: executive creative directors David Turner and Bruce Duckworth; designers Christian Eager, Paula Talford, Mike Harris, Charlotte Barres; photographers David Lidbetter, Steve Baxter, Andy Grimshaw; retouching: Peter Ruane, Matt Kay, Josh Kitney.

146 Californian wine: designer Nicholas Thirkell. Dishwasher powder: illustrator George Hardie. Jaffa cake packaging: Williams Murray Hamm; creative director Garrick Hamm; designer Gareth Beeson; client: McVities. Coca-Cola summer: creative directors David Turner and Bruce Duckworth; design director Sarah Moffat.

147 Winsor & Newton: principal designer Madeleine Bennett.

148 Five O'Clock Clock: Tibor and Maira Kalman; photograph MoMA Design Store. Rainy pot: Jeong Seungbin/DailyLife Lab.

149 Tissue Box House: Umbra.com, designer Mauricio Affonso. Sky umbrella: Tibor Kalman and Emanuela Frattini Magnusson; photograph MoMA Design Store. Dropit hooks: Asshoff & Brogård for Normann Copenhagen. Toothbrush Maracas: photograph by PEC Studio.

150 Postcards: designer David Hillman; illustrator Bob Norrington. The Leaning Tower of Philadelphia: photographer Kate McGovern. Karate class sign: Extreme Group, Toronto, Canada; chief creative officer Shawn King; creative director Matt Syberg-Olsen; copywriter Matt Hubbard; art director Mike Schonberger.

151 Large number nine: designer Ivan Chermayeff; photographer Santi Visalli; courtesy of Universe Publishing. Shipwright Yard: art director Phoa Kia Boon; designer Nancy Williams. 'Take a break from the sun': executive creative director Jason Ross; copywriter Sharon Condy; art director Josh Murrell. Hot Wheels: Mattel, Inc. McDonald's Lamp Post: Cossette; creative directors Bryan Collins, Rob Sweetman; art director Eric Arnold; writer Michael Milardo; design Dyna Graphics Ltd.; account supervisor Kim Prosser; group account director: Nadine Cole; product: McDonald's Free Coffee Promotion, client: McDonald's.

152 Restroom signs: photographer Adrian Flowers. 'Double Yellow Line BenchTM' designed by Will Sandy © 2012 The Edible Bus Stop® 'www.TheEdibleBusStop.org. Clothes peg sculpture: Mehmet ALİ UYSAL, Skin 2, 2010, Image courtesy of Pi Artworks Istanbul/London and the artist. Giant carrot: Owen Jones & Partners LTD Portland & Hood River Oregon.

158 Go van Gogh: designer Rex Peteet. Claes Oldenburg book: designer Ivan Chermayeff.

159 Comedy carpet: Gordon Young/Why Not Associates; photographer Jonathan Farman.

160 Japanese packaging: designer Pierre Mendell; photographer Hans Döring. Other Museums: The Beautiful Meme; writer Tom Sharp; designer Ben Haworth; client: Design Museum. The Comedy Store: Agency Mark Studio; designer and art director Mark Lester; photographer Richard Moran.

162 Martha Graham: publisher Dunetz & Lovett. Bach: designer Seymour Chwast.

163 GBH Mama Shelter hotel identity: creative directors Jason Gregory, Mark Bonner, Peter Hale; designers Jason Gregory, Ross Goulden, Josh Nathanson. Tate by Tube: © TfL from the London Transport Museum collection. London Sinfonietta: Harrison Agency; creative director Chris Harrison; designer Scott Welti; retouching: Ben Darvill. Tate Gallery poster: TBWA; art director Paul Belford; copywriter Nigel Roberts.

164 Paul Weiland: illustrator Allan Manham. Neil MacKenzie Matthews promotional poster: Kimpton Creative; designers David Kimpton, Harry Grundy; photographer Neil MacKenzie Matthews.

165 Manfred Vogelsänger: photographer Manfred Vogelsänger. Sports photographer: designers Andy Cheetham, Simon Broadbent and Tony Veazey; photographer Robert Walker. Canon 500D DSLR handbag: Paradox Media Pte Ltd.; account manager Sebastian Lee; art director Lynn Ho. Light breakfast: photographer/art director: David Sykes; stylist: Jennie Webster; model maker: Ridley West.

166 Nike bench: Annie Chiu and Anna Echiverri. Finnish Sports Federation parking spaces: creative director Arttu Salovaara; designers Tuukka Koivisto, Aleksi Hautamäki; photographer Paavo Lehtonen. Bitten & Hisses: photograph by © Sutton Images/Corbis.

168 Hanaco: designer Alan Colvin. Lego 404 error page: © 2015, The LEGO Group.

170 Sonic Bloom: Dan Corson/Corson Studios LLC, landscape design Dan Corson/Corson Studios LLC; photographers Dan Corson and Frank Huster; client: Pacific Science Center; funded by Seattle City Light and Pacific Science Center.

173 River Films: illustrator Terry Pottle.

174–5 Nickelodeon identity: ManvsMachine™ Audio: Ian Chattam/ Rada @ Prime Focus. Nick Germany: lead agency Nick On Air & dyrdee Media GmbH & Co KG; client: Nick Germany/ MTV Networks Germany GmbH.

176 Norwegian passport: designers Benjamin Stenmarck, Lars Håvard Dahlstrøm; typographer Øystein Haugseth; illustrator Benjamin Stenmarck; project manager Gørill Kvamme.

178 Leaping sheep: Michael McGinn.

179 JPL/ NASA Exoplanet Travel Poster: creative director Dan Goods; project art director David Delgado; illustrator Joby Harris.

180 Serious**: Jonathan Sands & Kevin Blackburn, Elmwood.

181 Garden Lighting Company: creative director Ben Casey; designers Chris Challinor, Stuart Price; photographer Mat Wright.

182 Stocksigns: art director Tony Muranka; copywriter Ken Mullen.

183 Our Price: designer Iain Crockart. Harrod's Halloween window display: photograph by Neil Mockford/Getty Images.

184 Topman telegraph poles display: photograph by Joe Neary. Lego store: photographs by Amandine Alessandra/ The Interior Photographer. Hollywood window display: photographer Emilie Faïf.

185 Maison Hermès window display: courtesy of Hermès Japon.

186 Apple Store window display: photographer: Chris Tingom. Vogue living dolls: Barbie; hair: Laurent Philippon; makeup: Lloyd Simmons; model: Magdalena Frackowiak; post-production: Digital Area. Giant Louis Vuitton trunks: © Louis Vuitton Malletier / Marc Plantec. Burberry store Milan: designers Virgile & Stone; photographer Fabrizio Bergamo. Clarks Superlight: creative partners and designers: Spencer Buck & Ryan Wills.

187 Jamie Oliver Recipease: creative director Garrick Hamm; designer Fiona Curran; typographer Fiona Curran; illustrators Fiona Curran, Vanessa Wright; account manager Panna Patel.

188 Mr Chocolate: Ruiz+Company; creative director David Ruiz, graphic designer Jorge Alavedra, client: Chocolat Factory. Hovis baked beans packaging: Williams Murray Hamm; creative director Garrick Hamm; designer Stuart Devlin. Rabbit restaurant identity: Noble Illustrations, Inc. Donut seeds: photo illustration by Jason Fulford and Tamara Shopsin, from the cookbook, *Eat Me: The Food and Philosophy of Kenny Shopsin* by Kenny Shopsin and Carolynn Carreno (Knopf, 2008). Kibon ice cream poster: designer Renata El Dib; copywriter Aricio Fortes; photographer Rodrigo Ribeiro. Johnnie Walker packaging: executive creative director David Palmer; concept by Chris Myers; illustrator Chris Martin; production by Dani Wedderburn; client James Thompson, Diageo.

189 The Art of Chocolate: Nendo; photographer Ayao Yamazaki.

191 NHS Books: GRP; art director Mark Williams; writer Martin Cross; illustrations by Alan McGowan; typographer Mark Williams; client: Nicky Coia NHS Scotland.

193 City & Guilds: illustrator Fiona Robinson. Grady gators: designer Jeffery McKay. Dumb Ways to Die: © Metro Trains Melbourne, Dumb Ways to Die (TM). All Rights reserved.

194 Mona Lisa: © Edition Staeck. 50th AA Anniversary: designer Adeir Rampazzo.

195 Depaul Nightstop poster: executive creative director Andy Bird; copywriter Ben Smith; art director Dan Kennard, head of art and design Andy Breese; designer Dave Stansfield; business director Will Arnold-Baker; account manager Tom Froggett; planners Ant Harris, Louis De La Moriniere; head of operations Debbie Burke; executive agency producer Steve McFarlane; agency producer Greg Collier, Ed Page; photographer Mark Wesley; art buying Claire Lillis, Sarah Clifford.

198 Polar ice: designer Atsuhiro Hayashi; art director Masayuki Kurakata; manufacture monos. WWF paper towels: Saatchi & Saatchi Copenhagen/ art director: Cliff Kagawa Holm/art director: Silas Jansson. Tree of life poster: DDB Group Singapore; creative directors: Joji Jacob, Thomas Yang; art director/illustrator: Gary Lim, Aaron Koh; copywriter: Khairul Mondzi

202 3i logo watercolour: artist Phil Sutton. Poidyom cats by NB Studio: illustration by Jenny Bowers.

204 Racism: designer James Victore. Russell Brand Revolution: published by Century in the UK, a division of Penguin Random House; cover photography of Russell Brand by Dean Chalkley; title lettering by Shepard Fairey.

206 SOS: designers Douglas G Harp and Susan C Harp. Jack Lemmon gravestone: photograph by Barry King /WireImage/gettyimages. Terence Higgins Trust poster: image courtesy Wellcome Library, London. Darwin Chair: art direction Stefan Sagmeister; designers Joris Laarman, Paul Fung, Mark Pernice, Joe Shouldice; technique: Laminated Tyvak, Tyvak, Inkjet printing; photography by Johannes vam Assem for Droog.

208 Anti-smoking poster: Alexey Starodubov, Creative Group Head, BBDO Russia Group. Boat Coffin and El Santo: images by Ari Espay.

209 Tower of London ceramic poppies: photograph by © John Devine/Alamy.

219 Good design: designer Michael Bierut.

222 Olives: designer Philip Carter.

225 Wilderness Years: designer Ivan Chermayeff.

227 South America: designer Seymour Chwast.

233 Grow Your Own Food poster: Imperial War Museum, London.

237 Red Monarch: photographer Tony Evans.

Acknowledgements

To Rick, who quietly made sure an author could author at her best.

To Susan, who smiled when DS had doubts.

To people at The Partners who worked on the book: particularly Toni Marshall who conceived the design; Karen Morgan and Rhoda Maw who did so much to bring the book into being; Lyn Jarvie, Kate Emamooden, Liz Carrow, Gareth Howat, Rosa Löffel, Steve Hutson, Paul Shriever, Stephanie Cochrane and Martin Lawless; and Karin Höfling, Cornelia Reinhard and Caroline Mee.

To those who took part in the wit round tables, who made research seem like an evening off.

To friends, who took an interest, and put their own smiles into this book.

To the designers we interviewed, who spoke with such honesty.

To all the people who helped with advice and information.

And to all the designers who contributed: we appreciate not only their collaboration, but also the work which has given us such pleasure.

Beryl McAlhone & David Stuart

To Leone, Sam, Tom, Olly and Phoebe for putting up with GQ's absence, both physical and mental.

To Sue and Robin for smiling and not minding.

To Jim, Claire, Nat, my partners and friends in leading the business and all at The Partners for their suggestions, especially Dave R, Keith, Kevin, Leon, Mark, Miranda B, Miranda H, Rob, Sam H, Scott, Stuart and Tony. Along with technical help from Martin D and Pip plus additional help from Adam, Leah, Martin H, and Milly.

To the interviewees and everyone who contributed brilliant work.

To Jim Sutherland for being a fellow traveller and adviser in in the project.

To Victoria and Kim for their patience, tact and smiles.

To the many design companies and supporters who believed in the idea of an update and helped make it happen.

To the mentors – Aziz and David.

And to Jonathan Brodie, a young designer who volunteered to help in his spare time and became an old designer in the process. This book wouldn't have happened without him.

Greg Quinton & Nick Asbury

...licated with
...iration to

...aff:
...e of the wittiest of men and
a proper person besides who
died before his time in 1994.

Patrick Wilson:
client, friend and collaborator
for two decades – a Tasmanian
devil of energy who ran out
of steam way too soon.

And to those contributors who
are no longer with us but remain
vividly present in their work and
thinking, especially Saul Bass,
Alan Fletcher, Shigeo Fukuda,
Abram Games, John Gorham,
Marcello Minale and Paul Rand.

Phaidon Press Ltd
Regent's Wharf
All Saints Street
London N1 9PA

Phaidon Press Inc.
65 Bleecker Street
New York, NY 10012

www.phaidon.com

First published 1996
Reprinted in paperback 1998, 2001,
2002, 2003, 2004, 2005, 2006, 2007,
2008, 2009, 2010, 2011, 2013
© 1996, 2015 Phaidon Press Limited
Revised and expanded edition 2015
Reprinted 2016

ISBN 978 0 7148 6935 3

A CIP Catalogue record for
this book is available from the
British Library and the Library
of Congress.

Designed by The Partners

Printed in Hong Kong